Supplements to the Vetus Testamentum

VOLUME 118

The Interpretation of Wisdom Literature

Edited by

Leo G. Perdue

Animal Imagery in the Book of Proverbs

By

Tova L. Forti

BRILL

LEIDEN • BOSTON
2008

This book is printed on acid-free paper.

A C.I.P. record for this book is available from the Library of Congress.

ISSN 0083-5889
ISBN 978 90 04 16287 7

PRINTED IN THE NETHERLANDS

In loving memory of my parents, Shmuel and Sofia Rosenthal,
who imparted to me a love of wisdom

CONTENTS

PREFACE

This study is the result of a long journey of investigation in the realm of animal imagery, which grew from a master's thesis into a large chapter in my doctoral dissertation, submitted to the Hebrew University of Jerusalem in 2000.

From the beginning I was aware that any treatment of the figurative and symbolic function of animal imagery in biblical literature requires special attention to its contextual meaning and cultural evaluation. I chose to conduct a combined investigation that considers the zoological traits of the animal alongside its literary image in the Bible. The didactic framework of Proverbs and its impressive use of various literary patterns are essential points of reference in any analysis of the image and its rhetorical implications. Philological aspects of the relevant texts were not neglected in the search for the rhetorical implications of the image.

Animal imagery must be evaluated differently than images borrowed from other realms, such as flora and climate. Thus, in addition to observing the dynamics and interrelation between the image and the object to which it is compared, one has to be aware of the ancients' intimate familiarity with the behavior of animals and remember that animals were objects of both admiration and scorn, hence imitated or rejected.

This study has benefited from the proliferation of monographs on fauna in ancient Near Eastern literatures since 2002. These works encouraged me to sharpen my contextual approach and multi-level methodology and to make my work as up-to-date as possible.

Through this long process of research many persons illuminated my path, supporting and encouraging me with advice and deeds. Prof. Moshe Weinfeld was the first to open the door of the treasures of wisdom literature for me. His devoted guidance, together with that of Prof. Shmuel Aḥituv, enabled me to complete this study. I would like to express my special gratitude to Prof. Mordechai Cogan, who has provided me with much valuable advice and constructive criticism from my first steps as a student until now.

I would also like to thank my colleagues at the Department of Bible, Archaeology and Ancient Near Eastern studies of Ben-Gurion University of the Negev, and especially professors Zipora Talshir, Victor Hurowitz, and Meir Gruber, who as department chairs enabled me to devote time to research along with teaching.

I would never have been able to complete this study without the love and support of my parents-in-law, my sister Channa, my husband Eli, and my children Efrat, Michal, Tamar, and Nir.

I am most grateful for the financial support of the Memorial Foundation for Jewish Culture and grants from the Faculty of Humanities and Social Sciences at Ben-Gurion University.

I would particularly like to thank Mr. Lenn Schramm, who edited and revised my English.

ABBREVIATIONS AND SHORT REFERENCES

SERIALS, REFERENCE WORKS, PERIODICALS

AB	Anchor Bible
ABD	Anchor Bible Dictionary. Ed. D. N. Freedman. 6 vols. New York, 1992
ABL	*Assyrian and Babylonian Letters Belonging to the Kouyunjik Collections of the British Museum.* Ed. R. F. Harper. 14 vols. Chicago, 1892–1914
AcOr	*Acta Orientalia*
AEL	*Ancient Egyptian Literature.* M. Lichtheim. 3 vols. Berkeley, 1971–1980
AfOB	*Archiv für Orientforschung: Beiheft*
AHW	*Akkadisches Handwörterbuch.* W. von Soden. 3 vols. Wiesbaden, 1965–1981
AJSL	*American Journal of Semitic Languages and Literature*
AKA	E. A. W Budge and L. W King, *The Annals of the Kings of Assyria.* London British Museum, 1902
ANET	*Ancient Near Eastern Texts Relating to the Old Testament.* Ed. J. B. Pritchard. 3rd ed. Princeton, 1969
AnOr	Analecta orientalia
AOAT	Alter Orient und Altes Testament
ASAW	Abhandlungen der Sächsischen Akademie der Wissenschaften
BASOR	*Bulletin of the American Schools of Oriental Research*
BDB	F. Brown, S. R. Driver, and C. A. Briggs. *A Hebrew and English Lexicon of the Old Testament.* Oxford, 1907
BETL	Bibliotheca ephemeridum theologicarum lovaniensium
BHK	*Biblia Hebraica.* Ed. R. Kittel. Stuttgart, 1905–1906, 1973[16]
BHS	*Biblia Hebraica Stuttgartensia.* Ed. K. Elliger and W. Rudolph. Stuttgart. 1983
Bib	*Biblica*
BibOr	Biblica et orientalia
BWL	*Babylonian Wisdom Literature.* W. G. Lambert. Oxford, 1960
BZAW	Beihefte zur *Zeitschrift für die alttestamentliche Wissenschaft*
CAD	*The Assyrian Dictionary of the Oriental Institute of the University of Chicago.* 1956–
CAT	*The Cuneiform Alphabetic Texts from Ugarit, Ras Ibn Hani and Other Places.* Ed. M. Dietrich, O. Loretz, and J. Sanmartín. Münster: Ugarit-Verlag, 1995
CB	Coniectanea Biblica
CBC	Cambridge Bible Commentary
CBQ	*Catholic Biblical Quarterly*
CTA	*Corpus des tablettes en cunéiformes alphabétiques découvertes à Ras Shamra-Ugarit de 1929 à 1939.* Ed. A. Herdner. Mission de Ras Shamra 10. Paris, 1963

EA El-Amarna tablets. According to the edition of J. A. Knudtzon. *Die el-Amarna-Taflen*. Leipzig. 1908–1915. Reprint, Aalen, 1964. Continued in A. F. Rainey, *El-Amarna Tablets*, 359–379. 2nd rev. ed. Kevelaer, 1978
EM *Encyclopedia Miqraʾit* (Encyclopaedia Biblica). 9 vols. Jerusalem: Bialik Institute, 1950–1982
ErIsr *Eretz-Israel*
FAT Forschungen zum Alten Testament
GKC Gesenius' Hebrew Grammar. Ed. E. Kautzsch. Trans. E. Cowley. 2nd ed. Oxford, 1910
HALOT L. Koehler, W. Baumgartner, and J. J. Stamm, *The Hebrew and Aramaic Lexicon of the Old Testament*. Trans. and ed. under the supervision of M. E. J. Richardson. 4 vols. Leiden, 1994–1999
HAT Handbuch zum Alten Testament
HAWANE *A History of Animal World in the Ancient Near East*. Ed. B. J. Collins. Leiden, Boston, and Cologne, 2002
HdO Handbuch der Orientalistik
HS Holy Scriptures. New York, 1988
HTR *Harvard Theological Review*
HUCA *Hebrew Union College Annual*
ICC International Critical Commentary
JANESCU *Journal of the Ancient Near Eastern Society of Columbia University*
JBL *Journal of Biblical Literature*
JNES *Journal of Near Eastern Studies*
JQR *Jewish Quarterly Review*
JSOTSup Journal of the Study of the Old Testament: Supplement Series
JTS *Journal of Theological Studies*
KAI *Kanaanäische und aramäische Inschriften*. H. Donner and W. Röllig. 2nd ed. Wiesbaden, 1966–1969
KAT *Kommentar zum Alten Testament*
KBL L. Koehler and W. Baumgartner, Lexicon in Veteris Testament libros
LCL Loeb Classical Library
Leš *Lešonénu*
LUÅ Lunds universitets årsskrift
LXX Septuagint (ed. Rahlfs)
LXX^{A} Septuagint, Codex Alexandrinus
MSL *Materialien zum sumerischen Lexicon*. Ed. Benno Landsberger
MVAG Mitteilungen der Vorderasiatisch-ägyptischen Gesellschaft
NICOT New International Commentary on the Old Testament
OBO Orbis biblicus et orientalis
OIP Oriental Institute Publications, University of Chicago Press
Or *Orientalia*
OTL Old Testament Library
OtSt *Oudtestamentische Studiën*
PEQ *Palestine Exploration Quarterly*
PTMS Pittsburgh Theological Monograph Series
RA *Revue d'assyriologie et d'archéologie orientale*
RB *Revue biblique*
RS Ras Shamra
SAA State Archives of Assyria
SAIW *Studies in Ancient Israelite Wisdom*. Ed. J. L. Crenshaw. New York, 1976
SANT Studien zum Alten und Neuen Testament

SAOC	Studies in Ancient Oriental Civilizations
SBLDS	Society of Biblical Literature Dissertation Series
SBLSP	*Society of Biblical Literature Seminar Papers*
SBLWAW	Society of Biblical Literature Writings from the Ancient World
SED	*Semitic Etymological Dictionary*
SJT	*Scottish Journal of Theology*
STDJ	*Studies on the Texts of the Desert of Judah*
SubBi	*Subsidia biblica*
SVT	Supplements to *Vetus Testamentum*
TCL	Textes cunéiformes. Musée du Louvre
TGUOS	Transactions of the Glasgow University Oriental Society
TLZ	*Theologische Literaturzeitung*
UT	*Ugaritic Textbook.* C. H. Gordon. AnOr 38. Rome, 1965.
VT	*Vetus Testamentum*
WBC	Word Biblical Commentary
WMANT	Wissenschaftliche Monographien zum Alten und Neuen Testament
WOO	Wiener Offene Orientalistik
ZAW	*Zeitschrift für die alttestamentliche Wissenschaft*
ZTK	*Zeitschrift für Theologie und Kirche*

MISHNAH, TALMUD, AND OTHER RABBINIC WORKS

Abot R. Nat.	*Abot de Rabbi Nathan*	*Mek.*	*Mekilta*
b.	Babylonian Talmud	*Midr.*	*Midrash*
B. Bat.	*Baba Batra*	*Pirqe R. El.*	*Pirqe Rabbi Eliezer*
B. Qam.	*Baba Qamma*	*Qidd.*	*Qiddušin*
Ber.	*Berakot*	*Rab.*	*Rabbah* (+ biblical book)
ʿEd.	*ʿEduyyot*	*Šabb.*	*Šabbat*
Giṭ.	*Giṭṭin*	*Sanh.*	*Sanhedrin*
Ḥul.	*Ḥullin*	*Taʿan.*	*Taʿanit*
Ketub.	*Ketubbot*	Tg. Neb.	Targum of the Prophets
m.	*Mishnah*	*y.*	Jerusalem Talmud
Meg.	*Megillah*	*Yad.*	*Yadayim*

CHAPTER 1

INTRODUCTION

1.1 General Remarks

Observation of the environment inspires and enriches authors' literary expression of their daily experiences. The figurative descriptions that result form an integral part of the cultural legacy of authors and their audience.

Ancient wisdom literature spiced its rhetoric with analogies and images inspired by different spheres of life. Those which are related to natural phenomena (climate, flora, and fauna) reflect the impact of such phenomena on a person's emotional and intellectual perception of the world. These images propose a comparison, explicit or implicit, between two disparate objects and challenge us to find the similarities between them.[1] This work of discovery involves both cognitive and emotional processes.

The summary of Solomon's wisdom refers to an accumulation of observations to the point of comprehensive encyclopedic knowledge: "He spoke of trees; from the cedar that is in Lebanon to the hyssop that grows out of the wall; he spoke also of beasts and of birds, and of reptiles and of fish" (1 Kgs v 13).[2] Admiration of the wisdom discerned in nature and of the unconscious intelligence of beasts, who

[1] See J. Bronowski, *The Origins of Knowledge and Imagination* (New Haven and London, 1978), pp. 10–18; L. Alonso Schökel, *A Manual of Hebrew Poetics* (SubBi 11; Rome, 1988), pp. 95–107; Ch. E. Watanabe, *Animal Symbolism in Mesopotamia: A Contextual Approach* (WOO, vol. 1; Vienna, 2002), pp. 16–21.

[2] See Albrecht Alt, "Solomonic Wisdom," in J. L. Crenshaw (ed.), *Studies in Ancient Israelite Wisdom,* trans. D. A. Knight (New York, 1976), pp. 102–12 [originally published as "Die Weisheit Salomos," *TLZ* 76 (1951), pp. 139–44]. For a reconsideration of the Onomastica as a wisdom genre, see John Day, "Foreign Semitic Influence on the Wisdom of Israel and its Appropriation in the Book of Proverbs," in J. Day et al. (eds.), *Wisdom in Ancient Israel: Essays in honor of J. A. Emerton* (Cambridge, 1995), pp. 61–62.

share a mysterious and at times esoteric knowledge inaccessible to human beings, is a recurring leitmotif in the hymns of praises to the Creator that are prominent in wisdom traditions: "But ask the beasts, and they will teach you; The birds of the sky, they will tell you; Or speak to the earth, it will teach you; The fish of the sea, they will inform you" (Job xii 7–8). Another facet of this esteem for animals and their behavior is the recognition of their mysterious ability to orient themselves in their natural habitats: "Even the stork in the sky knows her seasons, And the turtledove, swift, and crane Keep the time of their coming" (Jer. viii 7a). Animals move in three different spaces—earth, sky and sea—where they seem to share with God an intimate secret of His creation (Prov. xxx 18–19; cf. Jer. viii 7).[3]

In the book of Proverbs, which is firmly grounded in the daily fabric of life in biblical times, a variety of models of human behavior are linked to the wisdom teacher's understanding of the order and balance of the natural world.[4]

1.2 Survey of Scholarly Approaches

Noteworthy among scholars who investigated animal imagery in ancient Near Eastern literature are the following: Schott's study (1926) of the language of imagery in the Assyrian royal inscriptions[5]; Heimpel's study (1968) on the imagery of animals in Sumerian literature, in which animals are treated as metaphors and similes, and categorized according to the trait emphasized,[6] and Marcus's investigation of stylistic changes in the *kīma* paradigm indicating the relation between simile and similitude of animal imagery in the Assyrian royal inscriptions.[7] Black's monograph (1996) focuses exclusively on images of winged creatures in Sumerian poetry. His study analyzes

[3] On Prov. xxx 18–20, see §4.2.3.

[4] See James L. Crenshaw, "The Sage in Proverbs," in J. G. Gammie and L. G. Perdue (eds.), *The Sage in Israel and Ancient Near East* (Winona Lake, IN, 1990), pp. 204–16.

[5] See A. Schott, *Die Vergleiche in den akkadischen Königsinschriften* (MVAG 30; Leipzig, 1926).

[6] W. Heimpel, *Tierbilder in der Sumerischen Literatur* (Studia Pohl 2; Rome, 1968).

[7] David Marcus, "Animal Similes in Assyrian Royal Inscriptions," *Or* 46 (1977), pp. 86–106.

the relation between the imagc, the imaginary, and the literary sample in expressing the diverse rhetorical function of the image.[8]

Rimbach's comprehensive study on *Animal Imagery in the Old Testament* (1972),[9] arranges the discussion according to zoological categories, placing special emphasis on conventional features of each animal in the Bible and its parallel perception in ancient Near Eastern literary sources. Rimbach investigated the rhetorical function of the image in light of various poetic types: synonymous, antithetical, and synthetic *parallelismus membrorum.* He did not, however, study the role of the image as a literary model, nor did he examine the conceptual 'locus' of the image within the theoretical framework of his book. For example, in discussing the literary image of the *nešer* 'eagle'/ 'vulture' in its many occurrences in biblical literature in comparison to its occurrences in Mesopotamian literary sources, Rimbach left out investigating the dynamic reciprocal relations between the literary image of the eagle and its setting within the rhetoric pattern of the admonition speech (Prov. xxiii 4, 5) or that of the Numerical Saying (Prov. xxx 18–20).[10]

A contextual approach to interpreting the symbolic role of animals in literary uses and iconography in Mesopotamia is offered by Watanabe in her study of *Animal Symbolism in Mesopotamia* (2002), where she mainly deals with the royal and divine attributes of the lion and the bull from a wide, cultural perspective of textual analysis, art history, and anthropology.[11]

Riede's anthology *Im Spiegel der Tier* (2002) presents a collection of ten essays concerning the relationship between man and animal in ancient Israel.[12] Riede provides philological and terminological clarifications on the animal's species, nomenclature, habitat, and behavioral aspects. His meticulous approach offers a discussion on idiomatic expressions linked with the animal kingdom as well as with wisdom terminology.

[8] See Jeremy Black, "The Imagery of Birds in Sumerian Poetry," in M. E. Vogelzang and H. L. J. Vanstiphout (eds.), *Mesopotamian Poetic Language: Sumerian and Akkadian,* vol. 2 (Cuneiform Monographs 6; Groningen, 1996), pp. 23–46.

[9] J. A. Rimbach, "Animal Imagery in the O.T: Some Aspects of Hebrew Poetics," (Ph.D. dissertation, Johns Hopkins University, 1972).

[10] Ibid., pp. 46ff.

[11] Watanabe, *Animal Symbolism in Mesopotamia.*

[12] P. Riede, *Im Spiegel der Tier* (OBO 187; Fribourg and Göttingen, 2002).

Strawn (2005) dedicates a comprehensive monograph entitled: *What Is Stronger than a Lion?* to leonine imagery and metaphors are examined in the Bible and the ancient Near East. His investigation describes naturalistic descriptions of the lion in the Bible, including its anatomic and physiologic traits, and the nature of its habitat. This kind of interpretation anticipates his discussion on positive and negative metaphorical usages "because of the light they cast on the user's sign-context."[13] Strawn adds three appendixes, offering etymological data relating to the lion's names, predicates, and syntactical relations.

The book with the broadest horizons in the field of fauna in the ancient world is *A History of the Animal World in the Ancient Near East* edited by Billie J. Collins (2002). The book opens with an exhaustive survey of native fauna in the southwestern corner of Asia. The zoogeographic data of domesticated and wild species and the distribution of animals in various climatic and ecological regions are accompanied by archaezoological studies. Chapters II-IV present artistic, literary, and cultic-religious aspects of fauna in ancient civilizations (Anatolia, Mesopotamia, Egypt, ancient Iran and Syro-Palestine) that reflect the significant impact of ancient human-animal interaction. Despite the title of the book, as its introduction emphasizes, "the volume is not so much a history of the animal world in the ancient Near East as a narrative of human relations with animals told from the human perspective."[14]

1.3 Methodology

The present study focuses on the zoological, literary, and conceptual aspects of animal images in Proverbs. Our investigation examines the syntactical and thematic setting of animal images within their literary pericopes and clarifies their conceptual linkage to the thematic framework. For each passage, I begin by identifying each animal and its zoological characteristics as they emerge from the literary context, and the specific human traits to which it is related. The discussion of the poetic image as both a stylistic device and a rhetorical vehicle involves a linguistic and stylistic investigation of the elements of the

[13] B. A. Strawn, *What is Stronger than a Lion?* (OBO 212; Göttingen, 2005), p. 46.
[14] B. J. Collins (ed.), *A History of the Animal World in the Ancient Near East* (HdO 64; Leiden, Boston, and Cologne, 2002), p. xix.

comparison. Finally, I consider the semantic implications of the analogy as a whole.[15]

We also consider a number of parallels from ancient Near Eastern literary texts, which employ typological imagery from the animal world.

1.3.1 *The Problem of Zoological Identification*

Anyone who investigates references to animals in ancient literary sources faces the problem of the zoological identification of the animal in question.[16] Philological comparisons with cognate languages do not always solve the problem, because some names have lost their original significance and do not necessarily apply to the same creatures in modern nomenclature as they did in ancient times.[17] Moreover, when ethnic groups migrate to different climates with different fauna they bring with them familiar and well-loved names from their countries of origin and may apply them to animals common in their new country (much as occurs in the migration of other culturally laden words).[18] Nor can the application of two other methods of identification—one based on onomatopoeia, the other on identifying the

[15] See Alonso Schökel, *A Manual of Hebrew Poetics*, pp. 105–107.

[16] Dor defines ten principles for identifying ancient names with modern extant animals. See M. Dor, *Animals in the Days of the Bible, the Mishnah and the Talmud* (Tel Aviv, 1997), pp. 10–11 [Hebrew]; Black ("The Imagery of Birds," pp. 25, 31) demonstrates the problem of identification through his table presenting the $buru_5$ ^{mušen} both as a small bird and as locust. Another example is the problematic identification of the sur-du ^{mušen} with *Falco* as a defined class of raptors, in contrast to the identification with hawk as a general name for predatory birds, excluding the falcon and eagle, based on the type of sacrifice of such birds as mentioned in the image. See also Edwin B. Firmage, "Zoology (Fauna)," in *ABD,* vol. 6, pp. 1144, 1151, and nn. 34–64.

[17] Tristram employed comparative philology, with Arabic as the referent language, to identify animal names in the Bible. See H. B. Tristram, *The Fauna and Flora of Palestine*: *The Survey of Western Palestine* (London, 1884); idem, *Natural History of the Bible*, (London, 1867). Bodenheimer criticizes the method of comparative philology and etymology across cognate Semitic languages; his example is the Hebrew word *ṣab* 'tortoise', whose Arabic cognate *ḍab* means a large lizard. See: F. S. Bodenheimer, *Animal Life in Biblical Lands* I (Jerusalem, 1950), pp. 19–23 [Hebrew]; David Talshir, "Haṣṣab, Haḥardon Vehaqarpadah," *Leš* 65 (2003), pp. 351–73.

[18] In addition to climatic shifts, anthropogenic environmental changes caused by the expansion of settlement or industrialization have influenced avian patterns of flight, residence, and breeding. For a recent observation of bird behavior in the Levant (Syria, Lebanon, Jordan and Israel), see Allen S. Gilbert, "The Native Fauna of the Ancient Near East," *HAWANE*, pp. 32–37 and Table 1.2, p. 62.

animal's characteristics as deduced from the etymology—lead to a clear-cut identification, because many such characteristics are shared by many different animals.[19]

For the vast majority of domestic and common wild mammalian species, the Hebrew names are often attested in Semitic cognates that signify the same animal. The identification of birds, fish, reptiles, and insects is not always certain, however.[20]

In this context we should note Landsberger's *Fauna of Ancient Mesopotamia* (1960–1962), which deals primarily with the identification of the animals named in parallel columns of Sumerian-Akkadian lexical lists of *ura* = *ḫubullu*. These ancient lists make it easier to identify the animals thanks to their division into several categories: domestic animals, wild animals, reptiles, fish, and fowl.[21] For biblical literature, we can draw on the comprehensive and pioneering studies by Tristram and Bodenheimer. Tristram based his research on the fauna and flora of Palestine (1867, 1884) on personal observation, which he then checked against relevant passages from biblical literature. He also compared the biblical names with those used in his day by the local Arab population.

Bodenheimer's study of fauna in the Bible lands (1950) draws on archaeological findings and ancient literary sources, including the Bible, New Testament, Hellenistic Jewish literature, rabbinic literature, Aramaic and sources, Arabic literature, and more, with placing special emphasis on religion, folklore, and popular beliefs.[22] Other important sources are the zoological studies by I. Aharoni (1923), G. R. Driver (1955), J. Feliks (1954), and M. Dor (1955).

[19] Onomatopoeic names include *tôr* 'turtledove' and *sîs* 'swift'. Identifications based on etymological criteria include *dᵉrôr* 'sparrow' (*Passer domesticus*), the bird of "freedom"; *yanšôp/yanšûp* 'owl' (*Asio otus*), derived from the noun *nešep* 'darkness' or verb *nšp* 'blow out, hiss'; *tinšemet* 'barn owl' (*Tyto alba*), from *nšm* 'breath' (also identified with the chameleon in Lev. xi 30: "among the creeping things that creep upon the earth"). See David Talshir, "The Nomenclature of the Fauna in the Samaritan Targum" (Ph.D. dissertation, Hebrew University of Jerusalem, 1981), p. 4 [Hebrew].

[20] See the list of biblical animal names and their Semitic cognates in Firmage, "Zoology," Appendix 1, pp. 1152–56; A. Militarev and L. Kogan, *SED,* Vol. II: *Animal Name*s (AOAT vol. 278/2; Münster, 2005).

[21] See B. Landsberger, *Die Fauna des alten Mesopotamien* (Leipzig, 1934), as well as his later study of Tablets 13, 14, and 18 of the *ura* = *ḫubullu* lists (*The Fauna of Ancient Mesopotamia* [Rome, 1960–1962]). On the problematic criteria for identifying animal names in the Sumerian–Akkadian lexical lists, see Benjamin R. Foster, "Animals in Mesopotamian Literature," *HAWANE,* pp. 272–74.

[22] Bodenheimer, *Animal Life in Biblical Lands*.

The present study does not reopen the discussion of these scholars' identifications. Instead, it relies on the existing assumptions of zoological investigations of the native fauna of the Syro-Palestinian region and on etymological comparisons with Semitic cognates. In cases where the animal's name is a *hapax legomenon*—e.g., the *zarzīr motnayim* (Prov. xxx 31) and the *śᵉmāmīt* (Prov. xxx 28)—my conjectured identification is based on a contextual and exegetical approach.

1.3.2 *The Zoological Dimension*

With regard to the zoological aspects of each image, we consider how the animal is perceived throughout the Bible and examine its integration into various rhetorical patterns in Proverbs. We look at how the literary conception of the animal emphasizes the wise teacher's didactic tendencies. For example, the chief characteristic of locusts, as found in the description of the Eighth Plague in Egypt (see Exod. x 4–20; cf. Ps. cv 34–35) and throughout the prophetic literature, is their destructiveness. The damage to crops caused by an invasion of locusts provides a concrete example of the severity of the threatened divine punishment (see Isa. xxxiii 4; Jer. xlvi 23, 51; Joel i 4; ii 2–12; Nah. iii 15–18). But the notion of locusts in Proverbs, "The locust have no king, yet all of them go out in ranks" (xxx 27), gives no hint of their baneful effect.

1.3.3 *The Literary Dimension*

The investigation of the word *māšāl* by Form-Critical study of biblical literature has uncovered a broad range of formal categories within the Wisdom literature. With regard to its various contexts in the Bible and in light of its etymology, a distinction needs to be made between *māšāl* as *popular saying* (*Volkssprichwort*) and as *wisdom saying* (*Weisheitsspruch*). Scholars who appeal to the semantic range of *mṯl* in Arabic insist on the sense of *resemblance;* a *māšāl*, for them, is a simile. Others believe that *māšāl* is better understood as *model*, *exemplar,* or *paradigm.*[23] Fox argues that it means "proverbs that are cur-

[23] O. Eissfeldt, *Der Maschal im Alten Testament* (BZAW 24; Berlin and New

rent in public wisdom."[24] Because it is ultimately impossible to define the word *māšāl* based on its semantic development or etymology, and also because it is applied to several literary genres, including allegory (Ezek. xvii 3–12), satire (Isa. xiv 4–23), prophetic vision (e.g., Num. xxiii 7–18), and proverbial sayings (mainly in Proverbs), in each case we must interpret *māšāl* according to the specific context.

Our study analyzes the use of *parallelismus membrorum*, a stylistic feature of biblical poetry that relates the clauses of the verse in some kind of parallel structure (synonymous, antithetic, and synthetic).

The simile is an explicit and concise figure. The relationship between its two terms may be that between the abstract and the concrete, between the general and the individual, and so forth.[25] The comparison between two distinct semantic fields challenges readers to search for the underlying analogy/contrast (or similarities or dissimilarities), thereby evoking ideas, feelings, values, and stereotypes.

The use of similes that employ animal imagery to make a statement about human conduct reflects the sage's educational demands.

Our literary inquiry delves into the interrelationship of three rhetorical elements: the *comparandum* (equivalent to the *tenor* of a metaphor), the *comparatum* or object to which it is compared (the *vehicle* of a metaphor), and the literary form.[26]

The two terms of the simile or metaphor have some common feature (the *tertium comparationis*) that readers are supposed to discern in order to appreciate the teacher's lesson. We must note, however, that what this is can be somewhat enigmatic, because the original author and the readers are not necessarily contemporaries and frequently do not share the same cultural sign-context.[27]

York, 1913), pp. 12–13, 33–51. For the etymology of *māšāl*, see A. R. Johnson, "משל," SVT 3 (1955), pp. 162–69. For a critical survey of methodologies of the study of traditional sayings in the Bible, see C. R. Fontaine, *The Use of the Traditional Saying in the Old Testament* (Sheffield, 1982).

[24] M. V. Fox, *Proverbs 1–9* (AB 18A; New York, 2000), pp. 54–55.

[25] See Alonso Schökel, *A Manual of Hebrew Poetics*, pp. 96–97.

[26] The general format of a metaphor is "Caruso [tenor; Hebrew *nimšal*] is an Alpha-Romeo [vehicle; Hebrew *mašal*]." When this is written as a simile, we have "a great singer [comparandum] is like a luxury automobile [comparatum]." The rhetorical style of Proverbs frequently inverts the order of the clauses: e.g., "Like a sparrow wandering from its nest is a man who wanders from his home" (xxvii 8); "like a gold ring in the snout of a pig is a beautiful woman bereft of sense" (xi 22); "a roaring lion and a prowling bear is a wicked man ruling a helpless people" (xxviii 15).

[27] See S. J. Brown, *Image and Truth: Studies in the Imagery of the Bible* (Rome, 1955), p. 48; Strawn, *What is Stronger than a Lion?* pp. 12–16. On metaphors and

The aesthetic rules of the literary form in which the animal image appears provides the rhetorical foci of the model; conversely, every deviation from the formal model indicates some variation in the rhetorical emphasis.

For example, an application clause about an adulterous woman (xxx 20) is tacked on to a Numerical-Sequence Saying that consists of four mysterious phenomena (the ways of a vulture, serpent, ship, and maiden). The formal deviation takes place on two levels: on the structural level there is a stylistic shift from the enumerated example to the application clause (a pattern found most often in the admonition); on the thematic level, there is a shift from experience to moralizing.

My hermeneutic and literary discussion of the image in its context is holistic in nature.[28] The enlarging focus on words, phrases, images, sentences, sequences, and literary units uncovers the relationship of the whole to its parts, and vice versa.[29]

1.3.4 *The Conceptual Dimension*

The present study focuses on animal images in the book of Proverbs as a lens through which we can share the teacher's viewpoint. His main concern is not the national history of Israel or the people's fidelity to its covenant with the Lord. Instead, the teacher addresses individuals, urging them to internalize behavioral values to promote integration into the social order. The lessons of Proverbs do not just offer moral advice and guidance for practical conduct; they also raise theological and philosophical issues, such as the Lord as Creator (e.g., iii 19–20), "Fear of the Lord" (e.g., i 7), reward and punishment (e.g., x 6), and human impotence in the face of the Divine will (e.g., xix 21).[30]

---

similes, see Watanabe, *Animal Symbolism in Mesopotamia*, pp. 16–21.

[28] On the literary approach to Bible studies and especially the hermeneutic principle "unity of form and content," see L. Alonso Schökel, "Hermeneutical Problems of a Literary Study of the Bible," *Congress Volume Edinburgh 1974* (SVT 28; Leiden, 1975), pp. 1–15.

[29] For an in-depth survey of the method of Total Interpretation (i.e., Werkinterpretation, New Criticism, Close Reading) in the history of the study of literature and its impact on biblical scholarship, see Meir Weiss, "Die Methode der 'Total Interpretation': Von der Notwendigkeit der Struktur-Analyse für das Verständnis der biblischen Dichtung," SVT 22 (1972), pp. 88–112; idem, *The Bible from Within: The Method of Total Interpretation* (Jerusalem, 1984), pp. 1–46.

[30] On the theological worldview of Proverbs, see L. Boström, *The God of the*

The teacher's dicta do not claim to have the same authority as the Commandments and the Law of God. Although his precepts are referred to as *miṣwâ* 'injunction/teaching' (x 8) and, implicitly, as *leqaḥ* 'internalized teaching' (i 5; x 8), they are counsels (*ʿēṣâ*) rather than categorical injunctions. As Zimmerli noted, wisdom structures such as the admonition and "better-than" saying can be read as reflections of an anthropocentric viewpoint, because they emphasize progressive clarification through reasoning and appeals to common sense and deliberation.[31]

Even though the wise instructions, which concern a broad domain of life, call for human consultation, reflection, and independent decision, they are nevertheless based on a religious perspective, ranging from the dogmas of "fear of the Lord" and divine recompense (iii 5–12) to the pragmatic doctrine known as the *Tat-Ergehen Zusammenhang* or "deed-consequence nexus" (vi 27), which asserts a mechanical association between the quality of the action and the quality of its result.[32]

In this study I investigate the animal image as found both in discrete sayings and in extended passages. In the didactic framework of the book of Proverbs—a collection of practical counsels, exhortations, and moralistic admonitions—the animal imagery reinforces the wise man's empirical observations and worldviews, which give meaning and direction to the daily conduct of human beings.

Sages: The Portrayal of God in the Book of Proverbs (CB; Old Testament Series 29; Stockholm, 1990).

[31] See Walther Zimmerli, "Concerning the Structure of Old Testament Wisdom," in J. L. Crenshaw (ed.), *SAIW* (New York, 1976), pp. 175–207 [= "Zur Struktur der Alttestamentlichen Weisheit," *ZAW* 51 (1933), pp. 178–204]; idem, "The Place and the Limit of the Wisdom in the Framework of Old Testament Theology," in Crenshaw, *SAIW*, pp. 314–26; Roland E. Murphy, "Wisdom—Theses and Hypotheses," in J. G. Gammie et al. (eds.), *Israelite Wisdom: Theological and Literary Essays in Honor of Samuel Terrien* (New York, 1978), pp. 35–42; James L. Crenshaw, "Prolegomenon," in Crenshaw, *SAIW*, pp. 1–60; idem, "Wisdom," in J. H. Hayes (ed.), *Old Testament Form Criticism* (San Antonio, 1977), pp. 225–64; R. N. Whybray, *The Intellectual Tradition in the Old Testament* (BZAW 135; Berlin and New York, 1974), pp. 44–74; Fox, *Proverbs 1–9*, pp. 79–80.

[32] On the "concept of built-in and inherent connection between an action and its consequences as the logical paradigm that outlines many proverbs" (p. 61), see Klaus Koch, "Is there a Doctrine of Retribution in the Old Testament," in J. L. Crenshaw (ed.), *Theology in the Old Testament,* trans. T. H. Trapp (Philadelphia, 1983), pp. 57–87 [= *ZTK* 52 (1955), pp. 1–42]. Van Leeuwen raises the contradictory evaluation of wealth in Proverbs as an example of divergent points of view; see Raymond C. Van Leeuwen, "Wealth and Poverty: System and Contradiction in Proverbs," *Hebrew Studies* 33 (1992), pp. 25–36. See also Bruce K. Waltke, *The Book of Proverbs Chapters 1–15* (NICOT; Grand Rapids, MI, and Cambridge, 2004), pp. 73–76.

1.4 The Book of Proverbs: Introductory Remarks

The book of Proverbs mentions many members of the animal kingdom. These include birds (sparrow, eagle/vulture, brook-raven), insects (ant, locust), reptiles (serpent, viper), wild mammals (bear, lion, pig, dog, deer, rock-cony), domesticated animals (ox, goat, donkey, horse), and animals whose identification is problematic (e.g., *śᵉmāmīt* and *zarzīr motnayim*).

Although animal imagery is found within most of the separate collections of proverbs (defined by their section headings),[33] there are notable concentrations in several sections, such as chapter 26, which mentions the sparrow, swallow, donkey, horse, dog, and lion (vv. 2, 3, 11, 13, 17), and chapter 30, which refers to the brook-raven, young vultures, ants, the rock-cony, locusts, *śᵉmāmīt*, the lion, *zarzīr motnayim,* and the he-goat (vv. 17, 19, 25–28, 30–31).

As we shall see, the style of the animal images, like that of images drawn from other spheres of life (vegetation, climate, aquatic cycles, metallurgy, and precious stones), conforms to the typical pattern of each collection of proverbs. For example, the parable of the ant and the sluggard (vi 6–11) has the structure of the admonition speech, which is characteristic of the first collection (chs. 1–9). The animal images in the second collection (x 1–xxii 16) are incorporated in a variety of forms characteristic of proverbs and aphorisms, such as comparison and analogy, antithetical couplets, direct speech, metaphorical proverbs, and "better-than" sayings. Similarly, the animal images in the sixth collection (ch. 30) take the form of the Numerical Saying (cf. xxx 18–20, 24–28, 29–31). Animal imagery also appears in the "double sayings" of the second collection (e.g., x 1 = xv 20; x 2 = xi 4), in which a fixed recurrent clause is paired with a variable clause.[34]

[33] The division of Proverbs into separate collections is based on the titles and arrangement in the Masoretic text. All biblical citations are from the NJPS translation unless otherwise indicated.

[34] The phenomena of doubles or repetitions indicate "that the book has been formed by the combination of collections of various dates and origins." See C. H. Toy, *The Book of Proverbs* (ICC; Edinburgh, 1959 [1899]), vii–viii; D. C. Snell, *Twice-Told Proverbs and the Composition of the Book of Proverbs* (Winona Lake, IN, 1993).

Imagery borrowed from the animal kingdom and from other natural phenomena is presented in a rich variety of rhetorical patterns that offer an empirical perspective aimed at providing guidance concerning the appropriate conduct (practical, legal, or ethical) in diverse life situations. In these similes (explicit and implicit) the relationship between the animal term and the term drawn from human life is one of identity or correspondence, or, alternatively, of antithesis or non-identity. The animal image stimulates the recipient of the admonition—whether boy, idler, fool, simpleton, or hothead—to reflect upon it and to extract relevant, immediate, and personal implications from the figurative expression.

Chapter 1 introduces the combined methodology—zoological, literary, and conceptual—of analyzing animal imagery, and surveys the literary forms in which it is used.

Chapter 2 focuses on what we have been discussing above: the literary and artistic uses of animal imagery.

Chapter 3 juxtaposes animals and humans and their behavioral vices: bear and fool (xvii 12), lion and sluggard (xxii 13; xxvi 13), dog and fool (xxvi 11), dog and meddler (xxvi 17). The comparison of human being and animal evokes reflection, and then mockery and sarcasm.

Chapter 4 considers the notion of animals' qualities as virtues to be emulated in human behavior, both individual and social. For example, the idler is entreated to imitate the ant (vi 6–11). Small creatures—ants, locusts, the rock hyrax, and the *ś*^{e}*māmīt* (house gecko?) (xxx 25–28)—are incorporated into a numerical saying and praised highly: "Four are among the tiniest on earth, Yet they are the wisest of the wise" (xxx 24). Animal examples incorporated in numerical patterns reflect the author's encyclopedic knowledge, but readers and hearers are expected to reflect on their didactic implications. The link between the lesson to be learned and the animal image induces cognitive and emotional processes that turn an empirical observation into a moral norm.

The appendices examine two other Wisdom compositions—the dialectical debate of Qoheleth and the didactic and reflective writing of Psalms—employing the same methods as in the body of the book. Zoological, literary, and conceptual aspects introduce the dynamic hermeneutic into the animal image, its literary form, and the conceptual framework of each work.

1.5 Literary Forms

James G. Williams lists three dynamic elements that power the rhetoric of the literary proverb: (1) intensification of the rhetoric through antithetical parallelism and heightening the ambiguity of the opening clause by strengthening or sharpening the second clause (xi 11, xii 11); (2) narration to express a process of acts, events, or experiences in the extremely compact and controlled form of the proverb (xix 24); and (3) metaphoric play within the frames of reference of the referents (abstract and concrete) of each part of the proverb and their combination as a whole (xiv 11; xviii 21).[35]

The sayings in the book of Proverbs can be classed, roughly speaking, into two types: long and short. My discussion of the short forms—the comparison, the antithesis, direct speech, the "better-than" saying, and the metaphorical saying—examines how their rhetoric concretizes ideas (xi 12; xxvi 11; xxvii 8) and presents didactic messages (xiv 4; xix 12; xx 2; xxvi 2,3; xxviii 1,15) and ethical values (xv 17; xxi 30–31; xxx 17).

The long forms include the admonition and exhortation (e.g., i 10–19), the biographical speech (xxiv 30–34), the numerical saying (xxx 24–28), and the graded numerical sequence (xxx 29–31). In the admonition, the animal image offers a concrete illustration that promotes internalization of virtues and wise counsels such as diligence and efficiency (vi 6–12), avoiding the company of criminals (i 10–19), not going surety for others (vi 1–5), moderation in the pursuit of wealth (xxiii 4–5), and sobriety (cf. xxiii 29–35). Here the animal imagery is found in the motive-argument clause (i 17; xxiii 4–5), the circumstance clause (vi 1–5; vii 22–23) and the result-consequence clause (xxiii 29–35).

[35] See James G. Williams, "Proverbs and Ecclesiastes," in R. Alter and F. Kermode (eds.), *The Literary Guide to the Bible* (Cambridge, MA, 1987), pp. 273–76. On "metaphor," see Benjamin Hrushovski, "Poetic Metaphor and Frames of Reference," *Poetics Today* 5 (1984), pp. 5–43.

1.5.1 *Short Forms*

According to many scholars, the folk proverb that express life experiences evolved into sayings of a relatively didactic nature that have undergone clear secondary elaboration of their stylistic and structural components.[36] Thus form criticism distinguishes the popular proverb (*Volkssprichwort),* with its clear, prosaic, and concise style, which expresses a generalized truth based on common experience or a particular incident, from the wisdom saying (*Weisheitsspruch*), which employs more sophisticated rhetorical means and syntax, such as *parallelismus membrorum* and intensification and explication. An example of the former is "Like Nimrod a mighty hunter by the grace of the Lord" (Gen. x 9); of the latter, "A scoffer seeks wisdom in vain, but knowledge is easy for a man of understanding" (Prov. xiv 6).[37]

Gerhard von Rad included practical knowledge in the domain of wisdom and traced the evolution from an early focus on nature and agriculture to the legal and social framework of clan-tribal society and then the royal court.[38]

William McKane classified the individual sayings in Proverbs according to their moral and religious intention, ignoring their actual order in the text. He defined three stages of development in the Israelite wisdom tradition, from the secular to the sacred:

1. Sayings that draw on ancient wisdom and seek to guide individuals to a successful and harmonious life
2. Sayings that concern the community, rather than the individual, and offer advice on proper conduct that adheres to social norms while avoiding anti-social behavior
3. Sayings taken from ancient wisdom that have been subjected to moralistic Yahwistic reinterpretation. These can be identi-

[36] See Robert B. Y. Scott, "Folk Proverbs in the Ancient Near East," in *SAIW*, pp. 417–26 [=*Transactions of the Royal Society of Canada* 15 (1961), pp. 47–56]; Fontaine, *Traditional Saying,* pp. 6–41.

[37] On folk proverbs and wisdom sayings, see Eissfeldt, *Der Maschal,* pp. 12–13, 43–51; Johnson, "משל," pp. 162–64; H. J. Hermisson, *Studien zur israelitischen Spruchweisheit* (WMANT 28; Neukirchen and Vluyn, 1968), pp. 36f.

[38] G. von Rad, *Old Testament Theology* I, trans. D. M. G. Stalker (Edinburgh, 1962), pp. 418–41.

fied by the presence of the name of God and the use of a moralistic and pietistic vocabulary.[39]

In opposition to these evolutionary conceptions, other scholars advance thematic and poetic links and the use of catchwords to link adjacent proverbs as signs of the editorial process of combining individual sayings into groups or collections.[40]

1.5.1.1 *The Comparative Saying*

The use of similarity and analogy is the hallmark of the comparative saying. In comparative sayings, the explicit or implicit simile offers a concrete illustration of the message.

Some comparative sayings focus on negative social types such as the sluggard, fool, or quarrelmonger; others describe negative traits of a ruler or host; still others refer to common social values and beliefs, such as the virtues of nomadism and the effectiveness of curses.

Although the two terms of the simile represent different levels of abstraction, the conjunction of different objects and categories stimulates our curiosity and gets us to look closely at the significance of their correspondence.[41]

Consider several parabolic proverbs, of which all but the last employ animal imagery:

a. Like a sparrow wandering from its nest is a man who wanders from his home (xxvii 8).

b. As a sparrow must flit and a swallow fly, so a gratuitous curse must backfire (xxvi 2).

c. As a dog returns to its vomit, so a dullard repeats his folly (xxvi 11).

d. A whip for a horse and a bridle for a donkey, and a rod for the back of dullards (xxvi 3).

[39] William McKane, *Proverbs, A New Approach* (OTL; London, 1970), pp. 10–22.

[40] For comprehensive survey of theories of literary development in Proverbs, see R. C. Van Leeuwen, *Context and Meaning in Proverbs 25–27* (SBLDS 96; Atlanta, GA, 1984), pp. 5–19; R. N. Whybray, *The Book of Proverbs: A Survey of Modern Study* (Leiden, New York, and Cologne, 1995), pp. 54–61.

[41] On the parabolic proverb see F. Delitzsch, *Biblical Commentary on the Proverbs of Solomon* I, trans. M. G. Easton (Grand Rapids, MI, 1960), pp. 7–11; A. Kahana, *Sefer Mishley* (Miqraʾ meforash; Tel Aviv, 1968), p. 21. Von Rad explains the distance between parabolic elements as the factor stimulating the reader's noetic function (G. von Rad, *Wisdom in Israel,* trans. J. D. Martin [New York, 1972], p. 120).

e. [Like] a gold ring in the snout of a pig is a beautiful woman bereft of sense (xi 22).

f. A roaring lion and a prowling bear is a wicked man ruling a helpless people (xxviii 15).

g. A passerby who gets embroiled in someone else's quarrel is [like] one who seizes a dog by its ears (xxvi 17).

h. Charcoal for embers and wood for a fire and a contentious man for kindling strife (xxvi 21).

Here we may distinguish several modes of comparison:[42]

1. The two terms are linked as metaphor—*a* is *b*—without the prosthetic comparative *kāp* 'as, like' introducing the comparatum (d, e, f, and g).
2. The comparative *kāp* introduces the first clause and the adverb *kēn* 'thus, so' introduces the second clause consequential clause of the saying (a and b).
3. In a three-clause comparative saying, the comparative *kāp* precedes the first two clauses and the particle *kēn* introduces the final clause (b again).
4. A two-clause saying in which the comparative *kāp* is missing from the first clause and the second clause is introduced by the comparative *wāw* (*wāw adaequationis*) instead of the particle *kēn* (d, h).

1.5.1.2 *The Antithetical Saying*

The two clauses of the statement may have a contrasting or antithetical relationship. The truth stated in the first clause is emphasized by its contrary in the second clause.[43] In one common antithetical pattern,

[42] The discussion here relates to the syntax of the Hebrew; translations tend to level all these different rhetorical forms into similes, softening, for example, "a beautiful women is a pig" into "… is *like* a pig."

[43] See Delitzsch, *Proverbs of Solomon* I, pp. 7–8. For a careful consideration of the difference between the antithetic parallel and the negative see Moshe Held, "The Action-Result (Factitive-Passive) Sequence of Identical Verbs in Biblical Hebrew and Ugaritic," *JBL* 84 (1965), pp. 275, 282 n.71; Edward L. Greenstein, "Two Variations of Grammatical Parallelism in Canaanite Poetry and their Psycho-Linguistic Background," *JNES* 6 (1974), pp. 96–105; J. L. Kugel, *The Idea of Biblical Poetry* (New Haven and London, 1981), p. 14; W. G. E. Watson, *Classical Hebrew Poetry: A Guide to its Techniques* (JSOTSup 26; Sheffield, 1983), pp. 214–21; A. Berlin, *The Dynamics of Biblical Parallelism* (Bloomington, 1985), pp. 56–57; Chaim Cohen,

the prepositional *bet* prefixes the negative particle *ʾên* in the opening clause, while the adversative *wāw* and the prepositional *bet* are prefixed to the adjectival *rōb* 'many' in the second clause (cf. v 23; xi 14; xv 22).

There are several stylistic variations here:

1. The negative *b^{e}ʾên* 'in the absence of' can be delayed to the second half of the first clause (xv 22), or *b^{e}rōb* can be displaced to the second half of the second clause (xi 14).
2. *B^{e}rōb* may stand at the beginning of the saying (xiv 28), with the negative *b^{e}ʾên* replaced by its poetic synonym *b^{e}ʾepes* at the start of the second clause.

1.5.1.3 *The "Better-Than" Saying*

The "better-than" saying or "ṭôb-proverb" is a formal variant of the comparative saying. In the "better-than" saying, the item in clause A is stated to be qualitatively superior to the item in clause B. For example: "My fruit is better than gold, fine gold, and my produce [is better] than choice silver" (Prov. viii 19).

In the simplest form, the combination of the initial *ṭôb,* which functions as a predicative, and the *mêm* of comparison prefixed to the second noun creates the analogical relation between the two terms[44]—one of inequality (see Prov. xv 17; xvii 1, 12; xxii 1; xxvii 5; xxviii 6; and more).

On a higher level of complexity, the inequality is buttressed by a clause or clauses that specify the reason and/or particular circumstances of the greater (or lesser) merit or value; e.g., "Better a meal of vegetables where there is love than a fattened ox where there is hate."(Prov. xv 17)

The system of arguments enables the listener/reader to consider and re-evaluate the expected relation between the two options. Nevertheless, the absolute conviction with which the saying is formulated corroborates the wisdom teacher's selection of the appropriate behavior.[45]

"The Phenomenon of Negative Parallelism and its Ramifications for the Study of Biblical Poetry," *Beer-Sheva* 3 (1988), pp. 69–107 [Hebrew]; B. K. Waltke and M. O'Connor, *An Introduction to Biblical Hebrew Syntax* (Winona Lake, IN, 1990), pp. 130–32.

[44] For the various functions of the prepositional *mem*, see GKC, §133b; P. Joüon and T. Muraoka, *A Grammar of Biblical Hebrew* I (*SubBi* 14/1; Rome, 1996), §103d.

[45] See von Rad, *Wisdom in Israel*, p. 115; Glendon E. Bryce, "Better-Proverbs: An

1.5.1.4 *Direct Speech*

Some sayings employ direct speech; e.g., "The lazy man says, 'There's a lion in the street; I shall be killed if I step outside' " (Prov. xxii 13; cf. xxvi 13). The simple speech attributed to a particular social type adds a ring of authenticity for listeners/ readers, while placing the statement in the mouth of a negative character produces a sense of disbelief, similar to the reaction to the trickster's lame declaration, "I was only joking" (Prov. xxvi 19).

1.5.1.5 *The Metaphorical Saying*

In the metaphorical saying the two terms merge, thereby creating a single conceptual picture. The metaphor functions within the aphoristic language by employing the various referents (concrete or abstract) of the comparative components as mutual frame of references.[46] For example, in "The eye that mocks a father and disdains the homage due a mother—the ravens of the brook will gouge it out, young eagles will devour it" (Prov. xxx 17), the synechdochal eye that represents filial scorn of parents merges with the implicit real eye of the second clause, creating a symbolic illustration of the retribution visited on wayward children (cf. Prov. xix 24 and xx 5).

1.5.2 *Long Forms*

1.5.2.1 *Admonition and Exhortation Speech*

The instructional speeches (*Lehrreden*) in the prophetic and legal literature of the Bible have several essential rhetorical elements. The speaker may use the imperative to instruct his audience in the behavior appropriate to the societal and cultural norms of the times, or

---

Historical and Structural Study," *SBLSP* 108, 2 (1972), pp. 343–54; Graham S. Ogden, "The 'Better' Proverb (Ṭôb-Spruch), Rhetorical Criticism and Qoheleth," *JBL* 96 (1977), pp. 489–505.

[46] See Hrushovski, "Poetic Metaphor," pp. 5–43. See also Alonso Schökel, *A Manual of Hebrew Poetics*, pp. 108–109. For a critical historical survey of the change in definition of "metaphor," see Ch. Perelman, *L'empire rhétorique-rhétorique et argumentation* (Paris, 1977), pp. 95–96 (ch. 10).

admonitory and prohibitive forms to exhort them to avoid wrong-doing.[47]

Wolfgang Richter points to the literary pattern of apodictic biblical laws and links the admonition "workshop" of Proverbs with the courts.[48] John Bright compares the development of the admonition pattern with that of apodictic laws and notes the main difference between them: the role in the admonition speech of the motivation clause, which is not part of apodictic laws. He discusses the use of the prohibitive *ʾal* as a warning, guidance, and directive, unlike the one-time prohibition of apodictic laws (e.g., Prov. xx 13; xxii 24, 26).[49] The didactic admonitions in Proverbs, too, employ the imperative or jussive in positive and asseverative formulations, and the vetitive or prohibitive in negative formulations.

Walther Zimmerli maintains that the wisdom exhortation is anthropocentric, whereas the prophetic exhortation is theocentric. This can be seen in the frequent inclusion in the former of a motive clause derived from practical experience.[50] The invocation of experience to ground the injunction reflects the essentially human context. Human beings and society, not the Lord, are the focus of the admonition, and the emphasis is on satiety, wealth, security, and honor. The exhortatory pattern suggests a definite mode of behavior to the listener, probably formed by the authoritative figure of the father or the wisdom teacher in the context of court or school.[51]

The admonitions in Proverbs (e.g., i 10–19; vi 1–5, 6–11; xxiii 4–5, 6–8, 29–35) employ a sophisticated style in which a father or teacher

[47] On the varied forms of the jussive and the imperative vs. the prohibitive or vetitive, see Roland E. Murphy, "Form Criticism and Wisdom Literature," *CBQ* 31 (1969), pp. 475–83.

[48] W. Richter, *Recht und Ethos: Versuch einer Ortung des Weisheitlichen Mahnspruches* (SANT 15; Munich, 1966), pp. 68ff.

[49] John Bright, "The Apodictic Prohibition: Some Observations," *JBL* 92 (1973), pp. 189–201.

[50] See Zimmerli, "Concerning the Structure," pp. 182–87.

[51] See André Lemaire, "The Sage in School and Temple," in J. G. Gammie and L. G. Perdue (eds.), *The Sage in Israel and the Ancient Near East* (Winona Lake, IN, 1990), pp. 165–81. Perdue suggests the term "liminality," meaning the stage in which "the 'son' is leaving his former status and is to be reincorporated into society at an elevated status" (Leo G. Perdue, "Liminality as a Social Setting for Wisdom Instructions," *ZAW* 93 [1981], p. 125). For a summary of scholarly debate of the existence of schools in Israel, see Michael V Fox, "The Social Location of the Book of Proverbs," in M. V. Fox and V. A. Hurowitz et al. (eds.), *Texts, Temples, and Traditions: A Tribute to Menahem Haran* (Winona Lake, IN, 1996), pp. 227–39.

preaches to his son or pupil.[52] Although the length and extent of the admonition varies, it comprises two essential rhetorical elements: the direct speech and the motive clause. The syntax of the latter determines the formal structure of the exhortation. It may be phrased as a protasis that introduces the rhetorical unit (see vi 2), or as a consequence of the conduct to be avoided (xxiii 21). The motive clause is frequently introduced by the particle *kî* (i 16, 17), but it may be phrased asyndetically. The addition of other elements to the basic jussive/imperative and motive clauses expands the exhortation into a literary unit and sometimes into a larger unit composed of smaller blocks.

The stylistic markers of the admonition include direct address ("my son"), terms of prohibition ("do not," "cease," "avoid"), cautionary words ("if," "lest," "for," "so as to"), logical connectives ("for," "because," "in order to" followed by the infinitive), the interrogative *heh* and other interrogative patterns ("how long," "when," "to whom"), and final (simple or compound) prepositions or conjunctions ("for the sake of," "until").[53]

Animal imagery may appear in any part of an admonition. The image often illustrates the addressee's concrete predicament at the time, as in the case of the lad who follows the loose woman: "Suddenly he follows her, like an ox going to the slaughter" (Prov. vii 22a). More often, however, the figure is used to describe the likely consequences of an action that contravenes decorum and order: "Its end is like a serpent that bites, and like a viper that secretes [venom]" (Prov. xxiii 32). In the didactic relationship of teacher and student, the motive clause seeks to improve the addressee—lad, sluggard, dullard, or fool; all the structural devices of the admonition are employed to help him internalize the teacher's message.[54]

[52] For a comparative study of Egyptian wisdom teachings/counsels and the admonitory pattern in Proverbs 1–9, see Crista Kayatz, *Studien zu Proverbien 1–9* (WMANT 22; Neukirchen and Vluyn, 1966), pp. 15–75.

[53] See McKane, *Proverbs*, p. 11. Philip Nel uses the term "ethos" to define the close relation between the structure and interpretation of the admonitions in Proverbs. He examines the syntactical link between the admonition and motive clauses and concludes that they should be defined not as genres (*Gattungen*) but as structural options. See P. J. Nel, *The Structure and Ethos of the Wisdom Admonitions in Proverbs* (BZAW 158; Berlin and New York, 1982), pp. 3–7.

[54] On the "deed-consequence nexus" (*Tun-Ergehen Zusammenhang*) as an expression of dogmatic thinking, which shapes the application and result clauses in the admonition speech, see John A. Emerton, "Wisdom," in G. W. Anderson (ed.), *Tradi-*

1.5.2.2 *First-Person Narrative*

In the first-person narrative, the speaker states his opinion as the fruit of his own experience (Prov. vii 1–27; xxiv 30–34; Ps. xxxvii 25, 35; Sir. li 13–16). This immediacy lends authority to the statement, as in, "I observed and took it to heart; I saw it and learned a lesson" (Prov. xxiv 32). Sometimes the speaker contemplates his past and draws conclusions from childhood to arouse the listener's sympathy and convince him of the truth of his position: "I have been young and now am old, but I have not seen a righteous man abandoned, or his children seeking bread" (Ps. xxxvii 25); "when I was young and innocent, I kept seeking wisdom. She came to me in her beauty, and until the end I will cultivate her. ... For from earliest youth I was familiar with her" (Sir. li 13–16). At other times, the speaker acts as an eyewitness and vividly records his observations in the first person. In the wisdom teacher's admonition against the seductive wiles of the "strange woman," he peers out the lattice-window of his home and describes what he sees in bold, unmediated strokes of color (Prov. vii 6–23). The chronological descriptive report is occasionally replaced by the teacher's personal evaluation of the object's behavior as in the case of the adulterous woman: "She sways him with her eloquence, turns him aside with her smooth talk" (vii 21).

1.5.2.3 *The Numerical Saying*

A numerical saying consists of a heading followed by a list of phenomena drawn from various categories. The heading enumerates the number of phenomena or elements and specifies the trait they have in common.[55]

The development of this pattern may be associated with the tendency to improve instructional methods by referring to models drawn

---

tion and Interpretation: *Essays by Members of the Society for Old Testament Study* (Oxford, 1979), pp. 216–221. Zimmerli ("Concerning the Structure," pp. 178–184) claims that a wisdom admonition does not have an authoritative character and does not make a categorical demand; instead it stimulates reflection and independent decision.

[55] W. M. W. Roth, *Numerical Sayings in the Old Testament* (SVT 13; Leiden, 1965), pp. 5–9.

from natural science and empirical knowledge. The number in the heading makes it easier for students to remember the lesson.[56]

1.5.2.4 *The Graded Numerical Sequence*

The Graded Numerical Sequence, widespread in the literature of the ancient Near East and found in both the poetry and prose of the Bible,[57] employs binary parallelism. The two sequential numbers are assigned to the two halves of a verse in increasing order, first *x* and then *x+1*.[58]

The relationship between the two halves of the verse can be expressed through contents, syntax, or rhythm (alone or in combination). Kugel reevaluates this relationship as following: "B always comes after A, not simultaneously; so B always completes, comments on, or explains, particularizes, or as here, 'goes one better' "[59] (see Prov. xxx 18–19; 21–23).

In the graded numerical sequence of Prov. vi 16–19, the second number is relevant to the examples: "Six things there are that the Lord hates, seven his soul does loath: (1) arrogant eyes, (2) a lying tongue, (3) hands that spill innocent blood, (4) a heart that crafts wicked plans, (5) feet that hasten to run to evil, (6) a lying witness who breathes deceit, and (7) a fomenter of strife among brothers." Thus "seven" represents the true number of examples[60] or emphasizes the climactic seventh item, which is the most severe crime of all.[61]

[56] On the mnemotechnic role of the number in Proverbs and Ben Sira, see William B. Stevenson, "A Mnemonic Use of Numbers in Proverbs and Ben Sira," *TGUOS* 9 (1938/39), pp. 26–38. For numbers as mnemonic devices used in rabbinic traditions, see Roth, *Numerical Sayings*, p. 72.

[57] See Y. Zakovitch, "The Pattern of the Numerical Sequence Three-Four in the Bible," (Ph.D. dissertation, Hebrew University of Jerusalem, 1979), pp. 3, 29 [Hebrew].

[58] The graded numerical sequence occurs 38 times in the Bible and Ben Sira; see Wolfgang M. W. Roth, "The Numerical Sequence X/X+1 in the Old Testament," *VT* 12 (1962), pp. 301–307. See the pattern 6/7 in Prov. vi 16–19 and 3/4 in Prov. xxx 15b–16; 18–20; 21–23; 29–31. On the roots of 2/3 and 7/8 in Ugaritic literature, see U. Cassuto, "Biblical and Canaanite Literature," in *Biblical and Oriental Studies* 2, trans. I. Abrahams (Jerusalem, 1975), pp. 16–59. On the use of paired sequences as a regular poetic schema in the Bible, in Ugaritic poetry, the *Maqlû* tablets, and the Gilgamesh epic, see S. Gevirtz, *Patterns in the Early Poetry of Israel* (SAOC 32; Chicago, 1963), pp. 15–25.

[59] Kugel, *The Idea of Biblical Poetry*, pp. 52–54.

[60] Haran termed the second number "the corrector of the first," as if it displaces the first number and leaves it with no role other than the essence of the lyrical experience. See Menachem Haran, "Biblical Categories, the Pattern of the Numerical Sequence,

The heading of another graded numerical sequence in Proverbs, "Three things are beyond my comprehension, four I do not understand" (xxx 18),[62] uses the *x/x+1* pattern to juxtapose two natural phenomena from the animal kingdom—"The way of a vulture in the sky" and "the way of a serpent on a rock"—with two phenomena of human civilization—"the way of a ship on the high seas" and "the way of a man with a maiden." Here too the four examples match the second number and the number pair is best understood as a word pair distributed between parallel lines.[63]

---

its Forms and Relations to the Formal Types of Parallelism," *Tarbiz* 29 (1970), pp. 109–136 [Hebrew]; idem, "The Graded Numerical Sequence and the Phenomenon of 'Automatism' in Biblical Poetry," SVT 22 (1972), pp. 238–67.

[61] Weiss proposes considering the "three" and "four" sequence in the prophecies of Amos as a unique stylistic element found only in that book. He holds that "three plus four" equals the typologically complete number seven. The stylized use of two sequential numbers undoubtedly stems from the frequent Northwest Semitic poetic technique of parallelism, in which the same thought is doubled by being stated in two ways. See Meir Weiss, "On Three ... and on Four," *Scriptures in their own Light: Collected Essays* (Jerusalem, 1987), pp. 24–25; ibid., *The Book of Amos* I (Jerusalem, 1992), pp. 21–25 [Hebrew].

[62] In the Septuagint, the header to Proverbs xxx gives the first number as a cardinal number and the second as an ordinal: "Moreover there are three things impossible for me to comprehend, and the fourth I know not" (xxx 18b; cf. 29b). Scholars hypothesize that this pattern attests the original formula in the Hebrew text. See Roth, "The Numerical Sequence," p. 302 n. 1.

[63] For a broader discussion of Prov. xxx 18–20, see §4.2.3. Lindblom asserts that the numerical pattern is grounded "in the teaching of 'the wise' " (Johannes Lindblom, "Wisdom in the Old Testament Prophets," SVT 3 [1960], pp. 202–203).

CHAPTER 2

ANIMAL IMAGERY AS A LITERARY AND ARTISTIC DEVICE

2.1 ADMONITIONS

2.1.1 *Animal Imagery as a Concretizing Device in the Motive Clause*

2.1.1.1 *Baʿal Kānāp 'Winged Creature'*

> My son, if sinners entice you, do not consent; If they say, "Come with us, let us lie in wait for blood; let us wantonly ambush the innocent; like Sheol let us swallow them alive and whole, like those who go down to the Pit. We shall obtain every precious treasure; we shall fill our houses with booty. Throw in your lot among us; we will all have one purse." My son, do not walk in their way, keep your foot from their paths; for their feet run to evil, and they hurry to shed blood. For in the eyes of every winged creature the net is outspread in vain; but they lie in wait for their own lives. Such are the ways of all who are greedy for gain; it takes the life of its possessor. (Prov. i 10–19; free translation)

The Animal

The Bible uses various terms to designate flying creatures: *ʿôp kānāp* 'winged birds' (Gen. i 21; Ps. lxxviii 27); *ṣippôr kānāp* 'winged bird' (Deut. iv 17); *ʿôp hārîm* 'bird of the mountains' (Ps. l 11); and, the most frequent term (36 occurrences), *ʿôp haššāmayim* 'birds of the sky' (e.g. 1 Sam. xvii 44). The collocation *baʿal kānāp* 'winged creature' (lit. "possessor of a wing") occurs only once in the Bible. The similar construction *baʿal kᵉnāpayim* (Qere) ("possessor of wings") is found in Qoheleth x 20, where it parallels *ʿôp hašāmayim*. The noun phrase in Prov. i 17b, *kōl baʿal kānāp,* is an inclusive designation for birds, similar to *kōl ṣippôr kōl kānāp* (Gen. vii 14). These inclusive terms for winged creatures are part of the basic classification of the animals of earth, air, and water—fish of the sea, beasts of the field, cattle, and reptiles.[1]

The Text

Proverbs i 10–19, in which sinners tempt a young man, coincides with the didactic purpose announced in the opening verses of the book; namely, that these Proverbs are meant "for endowing the simple with shrewdness, the young with knowledge and foresight" (i 4). The structural and stylistic components of this passage are typical of admonitions: The speaker employs direct address, "My son," and begins with a hypothetical scenario: "if sinners entice you" (v. 10). The exhortation is expressed by a blunt prohibition: *ʾal tōbēʾ* 'do not consent', appropriate to his authoritative standing.[2]

In the second conditional clause (vv. 11–14), the criminals' plans are described in vivid detail, with boastful verbiage enunciating both the fate of their victims and the rich loot they expect to share among themselves.[3]

The speaker uses the vocative "my son" a second time in v. 15, where he repeats his opening admonition that the youth not "walk in their way" and follow the evildoers' wicked path.

The last section of the passage offers two motives for heeding the speaker's admonition. One proposes a moral reason for not joining the sinners' company: "For their feet run to evil, they hurry to shed blood" (v. 16; cf. Isa. lix 7). The second explains their ultimate failure: "For in the eyes of every winged creature the net is outspread in vain; but they lie in wait for their own lives." (vv. 17–18).[4]

The passage concludes with a result clause that invokes the principle of divine retribution: "Such are the ways of all who are greedy

[1] The use of *baʿal* as the nomen regens of *kānāp* reflects Aramaic influence. See Avi Hurvitz, "Studies in the Language of the Book of Proverbs: Concerning the use of the Construct Pattern *baʾal* x," *Tarbiz* 55 (1986), p. 12 [Hebrew].

[2] BHK³ reads the problematic MT *ʾl tbʾ (tōbēʾ)* as the initials of *ʾal̲ t̲ēlēk b̲ᵉderek ʾittām* "do not walk in the way with them" [RSV: v.15]. Fox (*Proverbs 1–9*, p. 85) explains the MT *tbʾ* (*tōbēʾ*) as an apocopated form of *tʾbh* (*tōʾbeh*), from *ʾ-b-h* 'be willing', with elision of the *aleph*. The writing of the final vowel with *-ēʾ* is apparently an Aramaism (cf. *yôreʾ* in Prov. xi 25; see GKC §75*hh*.).

[3] On casting lots or throwing dice to divide up loot and inheritance, cf. Prov. i 14 with Joel iv 2–3. For the biblical meaning of *kîs* 'purse' (Prov. xvi 11; Deut. xxv 13; Mic. vi 11; Isa. xlvi 6), cf. Akk. *kīsu*(*m*) II, *CAD* K, pp. 431–32.

[4] Richard Clifford claims that v. 16, which appears also in Isa. lix 7, is a late interpolation by a copyist of Proverbs who did not understand v. 17. See R. J. Clifford, *Proverbs* (OTL; London and Leiden, 1999), p. 39.

for gain; it takes away the life of its possessor" (v. 19); i.e., the life of the perpetrator.

The animal image in v. 17 grounds the motive of the admonition in this passage. At first glance, the image of winged creature and net seems to interrupt the syntactic and conceptual flow between v. 16, "For their feet run to evil, and they hurry to shed blood," and v. 18, "but they lie in ambush for their own blood," since the latter completes the former with the principle of divine retribution.[5]

But the image of the bird that is oblivious to its peril in v. 17, clearly inserted as a motive for eschewing the sinner's evil ways, challenges readers to understand the complex relation between the image and its symbolic meaning or moral lesson. There are two possibilities: the net laid for the winged creature may represent the trap set for innocent victims; or the criminals may be thought of as falling victim to their own evil plot.[6]

In order to understand the enigmatic parable and the interrelations between the image and its moral, we must first clarify the sense of the phrase *mᵉzōrâ hārešet* 'the outspread net'. The outspread net is a frequent metaphor for the attempt to entrap a designated victim. The verbal component is usually from the root *p-r-ś*, as in "I will spread My net over him and he shall be caught in My snare … for the trespass which he committed against Me" (Ezek. xvii 20; cf. xii 13, xix 8, xxxii 3; Hos. vii 12); or the root *ṭ-m-n* (Ps. ix 16, xxxi 5, xxxv 7). The use of *mᵉzōrâ* here is a hapax. Reading *mᵉzōrâ* as an active participle of the secondary root *m-z-r,* derived from *z-w-r/z-r-r* 'tighten, shrink', is not plausible, because the action—which would be that of fastening the net on the victim—is described as a possible deterrent to it; and this action is said to be *ḥinnām* 'in vain'. In other words, the hunted creature is not conscious of the possibility that the net will close in on it.[7] If, accordingly, we take *mᵉzōrâ* to refer to spreading out the net,

[5] See Kahana, *Mishley*, p. 5; David W. Thomas, "Textual and Philological Notes on Some Passages in the Book of Proverbs," SVT 3 (1955), p. 282 n. 3; B. Gemser, *Sprüche Salomos* (HAT 16; Tübingen, 1963), p. 20; McKane, *Proverbs,* pp. 270–71.

[6] Delitzsch (*Proverbs of Solomon* I, pp. 65–66) explores the solution of the *applicatio similitudinis* of the birds and the net parable: "The net leads us to think only either of the net of the malicious designs, or the net of the alluring deceptions." He concludes that those who are warned should apply the image and stay away from evildoers, just as the bird flees the net. The application of "for the net is outspread in vain *(ḥinnām*)" is to avoid their ensnarement.

[7] Driver vocalizes the word as *mūzārā* (*hopʿal* participle of *z-w-r* or *qal* passive participle of *m-z-r*), glossing both roots as "tighten, constrict" (cf. *z-w-r (z-r-r)* 'com-

from the root *z-r-h* or *m-z-r,* as in the vocalized verb *m*^e*zūrāh* 'stretched out', the bird still does not perceive the net as a threat.

The motive clause, "For in the eyes of every winged creature the net is outspread in vain," might refer to the behavior of killers: because nothing deters them from their wicked deeds, the warning addressed to them is in vain (cf. Ps. xxxv 7; Lam. iii 52; Job ii 3). Rashi interprets *mᵉzōrâ* as meaning both baiting the net with grain and spreading it out as a snare. He clarifies the puzzling *ḥinnām* through reference to parable about the innocence of fish that do not discern the hook as a trap, but perceive the bait as food and swallow it to their ruin.[8] Just as the winged creatures are victims of their own hunger, the highwaymen's appetite for plunder causes them to fling caution to the winds and fall into the very snare they set for others.[9] Rashi's comment reflects a realistic approach, based on empirical observation of the behavior of birds, which often remain oblivious of the dangers of the net and the trapper's cunning. This simpleminded behavior of birds is reflected in the wilderness stories of the Israelites, in which quail alighting on land after a long sea journey were probably caught in nets (Num. xi 31–32; Exod. xvi 13; Ps. lxxviii 26–28).[10] It seems, then, that the net here will ensnare the sinners who lie in wait for the youth and threaten his innocence. The young man is exhorted to avoid the company of sinners, saving himself from their fate and thereby saving his own life.

Here the LXX is phrased in the negative, as if the Hebrew were *kî lōʾ lᵉḥinnām:* οὐ γὰρ ἀδίκως ἐκτείνεται δίκτυα πτερωτοῖς ("nets are not without cause [*lit.* unjustly] spread for birds." In this reading, the folly of the lad, if he allows himself to be seduced by the criminals, is compared to the innocence of the victimized winged creature.[11] The young man is called on to act with caution and avoid the immediate

press', as in "he squeezed the fleece" [Judg. vi 38]). See Godfrey R. Driver, "Problems in the Hebrew Text of Proverbs," *Bib* 32 (1951), p. 173. Cf. BDB, *z-w-r* III, pp. 266–67.

[8] *Midrash Shoher Tov on Proverbs* (Jerusalem: Midrash Publishing, n.d.), 5. For the synonyms *z-r-h* (*z-w-r*) and *p-ṣ-h* (*p-w-ṣ*) 'scatter' see Ezek. xxii 15, xxix 12.

[9] Most modern scholars reject Rashi's "strewn [with seed]" (Thomas, "Textual and Philological Notes", pp. 281–82), because there is no mention of grain in the text. See Delitzsch, *Proverbs* of Solomon I, p. 65; Fox, *Proverbs 1–9*, pp. 88–89.

[10] See also Isa. xix 8. For an illustration of the mechanism of netting birds, see O. Keel, *The Symbolism of the Biblical World: Ancient Near Eastern Iconography and the Book of Psalms,* trans. T. J. Hallett (Winona Lake, IN, 1997), pp. 89–95.

[11] See Isaac Arama in his commentary on Proverbs, in I. Freimann (ed.), *Yad Avshalom* (Leipzig, 1858–59), p. 8.

danger to himself. His situation is precisely that of the lad who follows the adulterous woman, who is "like a bird rushing into a trap, not knowing his life is at stake" (Prov. vii 23b).

We find a similar stylistic and conceptual pattern in Ps. xxxv 7:

Ps. xxxv 7	Prov. i 17a
kî ḥinnām *ṭām*^{e}*nû lî šaḥat* ***riš***^{e}***tām*** *ḥinnām ḥāp*^{e}*ru l*^{e}*napšî*	***kî ḥinnām*** *m*^{e}*zōrâ* ***harešet*** *bᶜênêy baᶜal kānāp*
For in vain they hid a net to trap me, in vain they dug a pit for me.	For in the eyes of every winged creature the net is outspread in vain.

In Psalms, the adverb *ḥinnām* appears as an anaphora in both clauses of the synonymous parallelism to emphasize the vain striving of the evildoers. Here *ḥinnām* has a double meaning: their plots are both unjustified and in vain—the victim is innocent and will come through unscathed. In Proverbs, too, the text speaks of the casting of the net over the innocent victims *nāqî ḥinnām* (v. 11c) of the evildoers (although, as we shall soon see, it does so ironically).

In Proverbs i 10–19 the key word *nepeš* 'life' is transferred from the innocent victim to the perpetrator of violence, shaping a circular conception of the principle of retribution. The ensnared victim is, in fact, the evildoers caught in their own web: "They lie in wait for their own lives" [*l*^{e}*napšōtām*] (v. 18b) and their way "takes the life of its possessor" [*nefeš b*^{e}*ᶜālāyw*] (v. 19b). The same idea of the "sophisticated" net that turns from its target and traps the ensnarer instead of the victim appears in the Psalm just referred to: "For in vain they hid a net to trap me [*lî*], for in vain they dug a pit for my life [*l*^{e}*napšî*] (Ps. xxxv 7). The bird as a metaphor for the trapped soul is found in another psalm, too: "We are like a bird escaped from the fowler's trap; the trap broke and we escaped" (cxxiv 7).[12] The similarity of the stylistic components in Psalms helps us understand the figure in Proverbs i 17.

In the didactic rhetoric of the admonitory speech, the metaphor of trapping birds has turned into a moral lesson that offers the honest victim an escape route, while the wicked man is ensnared by the trap that he himself has set. The image of the outspread net makes the dangers that attend the lad tangible and is transformed into a figurative illustration of the principle of retribution.[13]

[12] On the circular perception of divine retribution, see Ps. ix 16; xxxv 8; lxvii 7; Job xviii 8; Prov. i 24–33; ii 21–22; iii 7–11.

[13] On retribution and character-consequence nexus in Proverbs, see Waltke, *The Book of Proverbs Chapters 1–15*, pp. 73–76, 197.

2.1.1.2 *Nešer 'Vulture'*

> Do not toil to gain wealth; Have the sense to desist. You see it, then it is gone; it grows wings and flies away, like a vulture, heavenward. (Prov. xxiii 4–5)

The Animal

The noun *nešer* occurs in various Semitic languages: e.g., Ugaritic *nšr* 'bird of prey', conventionally rendered "eagle" or "falcon," widely attested in the Aqhat Legend;[14] *nešrāʾ* in various Aramaic dialects; Arabic *nasrum;* Ethiopian *nesr.* In Akkadian, *zību* is vulture and *erû* is eagle. Only once is *našru* given as a gloss to *erû* in the Sumerian-Akkadian lexical lists *ura=ḫubullu* (Tablet XVIII).[15]

The *nešer* is mentioned 28 times in the Bible, more than any other impure bird. The references and images of the *nešer* in biblical sources seem to indicate the griffon vulture (*Gyps fulvus*), rather than the eagle (*Aquila spp.*) The book of Micah invokes the *nešer*'s bald neck in a powerful image of exile and desolation: "Shear off your hair and make yourself bald, for the children you once delighted in; make yourself as bald as a *nešer*, for they have been banished from you" (Mic. i 16).[16] In Job, too, the *nešer* is described as a carrion-eater, peering down from its aerie at the battlefield in search of food: "From there he spies out his food; From afar his eyes see it. His young gulp blood; Where the slain are, there is he" (xxxix 29–30; cf. Prov. xxx 17; Hab. i 8).[17]

[14] In Ugaritic, *nšr* occurs in parallel with *diy* (hawk*)* or in pl. *nšrm//[ḥbl d]/iym* 'eagles//a flock of kites' (Aqhat, *CAT* 1.18, Tab. II, Col. IV, lines 17–18, 19–21), but the contexts offer no hint as to its specific identity. See Simon B. Parker, *Ugaritic Narrative Poetry* (SBLWAW 9; Atlanta, 1997), pp. 65–66. See also the discussion of *nšr* in the Aqhat legend by Militarev and Kogan, *SED*, No. 166.

[15] *Našru* (Hg. C I 26, in MSL 8/2 172) is probably a late replacement for *erû* 'eagle', borrowed from the Northwest Semitic languages. See *CAD* N/2, p. 79.

[16] The attempt to link *nešer* with the root *n-š-r* 'fall off', explained by the bird's bald neck and head mentioned by Micah, is incompatible with the original *śîn* of the Semitic root of *nešer*; if derived from *nĕšîrâ* 'falling out' the *šîn* would be transcribed as a *tāw*.

[17] The motif of birds of prey feeding on dead warriors on the battlefield is frequent in ancient Near Eastern literature, related to the sanctity of corpses and the importance of proper burial. Cf. 1 Sam. xvii 44–46; Ps. lxxix 2–3 and the Ugaritic story of Aqhat, in which a flock of hawks circles over the slain body of Danʾil (*CTA* 19.1: 32–33). The motif of unburied corpses is echoed in the biblical curses against violators of the

The *nešer* comes first in the lists of impure birds in Lev. xi 13–19 and Deut. xiv 12–18. Following the principle that the most important and widespread item is the first to be listed in any category, we should identify *nešer* as the vulture, which is one of the most common birds of prey in the region of Israel.[18]

The biblical references to the *nešer* allude to its impressive qualities that aroused admiration among the ancients. Its large size and wingspan are mentioned in an allegorical passage of Ezekiel: "The great *nešer* with the great wings and the long pinions" (xvii 3; cf. Jer. xlix 22). The *nešer* glides lightly despite its weight (Deut. xxviii 49; Isa. xl 31; Jer. iv 13, xlviii 40, xlix 15, 22; Ezek. xvii 3, 7; Lam. iv 19; Prov. xxx 18–19; Job xxxix 26). The way its soars easily and freely symbolizes the renewal of youthful strength (2 Sam. i 23; Isa. xl 31; Jer. iv 13; Hab. i 8; Lam. iv 19; Ps. ciii 5). The vulture builds its nest high up in the crannies of cliffs: "Building his nest high, dwelling in the rock, lodging upon the fastness of a jutting rock" (Job xxxix 27–28; cf. Jer. xlix 16; Obad. 4), whereas the eagle nests on trees. The *nešer* is also depicted as especially devoted to its young and providing its young with food (Hab. i 8; Job ix 25). The image of the *nešer* carrying its young on its wings, instead of holding them in its claws (cf. Exod. xix 4), however, should be regarded as folklore and without foundation in reality.[19]

The Text

Structurally and stylistically, Prov. xxiii 4–5 is an admonition.[20] The unit is introduced by two prohibitions: "Do not toil to gain wealth; Have the sense to desist." The warning against acquiring wealth is followed by an appeal to act deliberately and intelligently when com-

---

Covenant (Deut. xxviii 26; 1 Kgs xiv 11; xvi 4; xxi 24; Jer. xvi 4; xix 7; xxxiv 20, et passim), see M. Weinfeld, *Deuteronomy and the Deuteronomic School* (Oxford, 1972), pp. 129, 132–140. Cf. the Maqlû curses, G. Meier, *Die Assyrische Beschwörungssammlung Maqlû,* AfOB 2 (1937), 56, Col. VIII, 85; D. R. Hillers, *Treaty Curses and the Old Testament Prophets* (BibOr 16; Rome, 1964), pp. 54–56.

[18] See Godfrey R. Driver, "Birds in the Old Testament," *PEQ* 86 (1955), p. 8. On *nešer* = vulture see: Tristram, *The Natural History of the Bible*, pp. 95–96, 172–79, 182–86; Y. Feliks, *Animals in the Bible* (Tel Aviv, 1954), p. 66 [Hebrew]; Menahem Dor, "Hannešer Vehaʿayit," *Leš* 27–28 (1963/4), pp. 290–92 [Hebrew]; David Talshir, "The Semantic Shift of *Nesher ʿAyit and Dayah* in Hebrew," *Leš* 62 (1999), pp. 107–27 [Hebrew].

[19] See *Mekilta de Rabbi Yišmʿael, Beḥodesh Yitro* 2, ed. H. S. Horowitz and I. A. Rabin (Frankfurt, 1928), pp. 207–8; *b. B. Bat.* 16b.

[20] On the admonition pattern, see §1.5.2.1.

plying with this warning. The passage concludes with a simile that equates riches with a bird: "It grows wings and flies away, like a vulture heavenward."

This admonition warns against striving excessively for wealth: "Do not toil to gain wealth."[21] Such an effort is perceived as conduct that is contrary to the ideal ethos of the sage as well as incompatible with the righteous and the faithful believer in God: "He who trusts in his wealth shall fall, but the righteous shall flourish like foliage" (Prov. xi 28; cf. xiii 7, xxii 1, xxviii 11, 20; Qoh. ix 11). Exertion in pursuit of wisdom is valued to the same extent as that in pursuit of riches: "The ornament of the wise is their wealth" (Prov. xiv 24a). But striving in vain and for no concrete achievement characterizes the fool: "A fool's exertions tire him out, for he doesn't know how to get to a town" (Qoh. x 15).

The chiastic placement of the prohibitive forms *ʾal* 'do not' and *ḥădāl* 'desist' sets up a paradoxical link between the exhortation to abstain from pursuing riches, a negative value, and that to draw back from understanding, a positive value. The asyndeton does not clarify the association of ideas. The best way to resolve the paradox is to merge the two terms of prohibition into a single syntactical and conceptual clause: Do not toil; desist from using your intelligence in order to gain wealth—hence rendering the *mem* as instrumental rather than as privative.[22]

The rhetorical question, *hătāʿīp* (Q) *ʿênêkā bô wᵉʾênennû*, rendered as a conditional clause, "[If] you see it, then it is gone" (xxiii 5a), provides logical justification for the prohibition.[23]

Rashi glosses *hătāʿīp* as "doubling the eye," i.e., blinking rapidly: riches pass away in the blink of an eye. This is a plausible interpretation, because in Job the same idiom is applied to the transience of life:

[21] The root of *tîgaʿ*, *y-g-ʿ* 'toil, be fatigued', is a synonym of *ʿ-y-p* (see Deut. xxv 18; Isa. xl 28). The LXX reads "If you are poor, do not measure yourself against a rich man," rendering the infinitive *lᵉhaʿăšīr* 'to acquire wealth' as if it were *lᵉheʿāšīr* 'to the rich man'. Hitzig reconstructs a conjectural Hebrew *ʾal tiggaʿ lᵉheʿāšīr* 'Do not approach the rich man' (cf. Tg). See A. J. Baumgartner, *Etude critique sur l'état du texte du Livre des Proverbes* (Leipzig, 1890), p. 205.

[22] Ibn Ezra merges the two prohibitions into one consecutive idea: "Cease using your intelligence for the purpose of gaining wealth."

[23] The interrogative particle *hă-* can be understood as introducing a rhetorical question that expresses surprise—"[if] you see it"—or as an idiomatic expression, "you blink your eyes at it and it is gone."

"The eye that gazes on me will not see me: your eye will seek me, but I shall be gone" (Job vii 8).[24]

The Qere *hătāʿīp* is addressed to the hearer, with "your eyes" the object of the verb. Toy holds that the text is corrupt and that *hătāʿûp*/*hătāʿīp* in the first clause is a scribal insertion from the nearly identical *yaʿûp* (Q) in the second clause; restoring the original text, without it, yields "your eye [is] on it, and it is gone" (cf. Job vii 8). He also emends the reduplication of the root *ʿ-ś-h,* correcting *ʿāśoh* to *ʿōšer* 'wealth'; i.e., "... wealth grows wings and flies away." McKane understands *tāʿīp ʿênêkā* as "cast a glance."[25]

The simile that winds up the passage, "like a vulture it flies (*yaʾûp* [Qere]) heavenward" (v. 5c),[26] illustrates the notion that riches may vanish as fast as a vulture soaring aloft. The rhetorical impact of the simile is reinforced by the word play of *hătāʿīp* and *kᵉnāpayim,* which foreshadow, phonetically and pictorially, the vulture that soars heavenward and vanishes. However, the object pronouns *bô* (v. 5a) and *lô* (v.5b) draw attention to the main issue of wealth, introduced in v. 4.

Except for the fact that the bird depicted here is a predator, a Sumerian adage presents a similar notion of the fickleness of wealth and material possessions: "Possessions are small birds flying around, unable to find a place to settle."[27] The biblical passage also has a close parallel in the instructions of *Amenemope*:

[24] Ibn Ezra assumes that *tāʿīp* derives from the hapax *tāʿūpâ* "lights up" (3rd fem. sg., according to the Masoretic pointing), and interprets the clause: "If you light up your eyes by gazing on riches," (cf. "You will shine, you will be like the morning," Job xi 17). Other commentators compare *tāʿīp* to *ʿêpātā* (Job x 22) or *ʿêpā* (Amos iv 13) as a semantic antonym of "light" i.e., "darkness," synonym of *ʿêpātā* and *ʾōpel.* See E. Dhorme, *A Commentary on the Book of Job* (trans. H. Knight; Leiden, 1967), pp. 157, 165–66, and for the semantic antonym of *tāʿīp* in Proverbs see R. Menachem ben Shelomo Hameʾiri, *Pêrûš Hameʾiri ʿal Seper Mišley.* ed. Menachem Mendel Meshi-Zahav (Jerusalem, 1969), p. 222; A. B. Ehrlich, *Psalmen, Sprüche und Hiob* in *Randglossen zur hebräischen Bibel* (Leipzig, 1913; repr. Berlin, 1968), pp. 51, 56.

[25] Toy, *Proverbs*, p. 429; McKane, *Proverbs,* pp. 382–83.

[26] The Qere *yaʿûp* is attested also by the Targumic version. The reading *wᵉʿôp* appears in a few Hebrew MSS. See *BHS.*

[27] This translation is that of Black, "The Imagery of Birds in Sumerian Poetry," pp. 35–36; see Heimpel, *Tierbilder*, pp. 451–52; Gordon translates: "possessions are migratory flocks of birds, unable to find a place to stay." E. I. Gordon, *Sumerian Proverbs: Glimpses of Everyday Life in Ancient Mesopotamia* (Museum Monographs; Philadelphia, 1959), p. 50 Coll. 1.18. Landsberger (*Die Fauna des Alten Mesopotamien*, pp. 18, 122) rendered $buru^{5}$ as *eribu*, "locusts." Lambert renders $buru^{5}$ ^{mušen} as "sparrows". Maurice Lambert, "Le signe $\underline{bur}_5$ et sa signification 'moineau,'" *RA* 48 (1954), pp. 29–32.

IX (10) Cast not thy heart in pursuit of riches,
(For) there is no ignoring Fate and Fortune.
Place not thy heart upon externals,
(For) every man belongs to his (appointed) hour.
Do not strain to seek an excess,
(15) When thy needs are safe for thee.
(16) If riches are brought to thee by robbery,
(17) They will not spend the night with thee;
(18) At day break they are not in thy house:
Their places may be seen, but they are not.
The ground has opened its mouth...that it might swallow them up,
X (1) And might sink them into the underground.
(Or) they have made themselves a great breach of their (own) size and are sunken down in the storehouse.
(Or) they have made themselves wings like geese
(5) And are flown away to the heavens.[28]

In both the biblical and the Egyptian admonitions, wealth is pictured as a winged creature that flies away—the vulture in Proverbs, and geese, common in Egypt, in *Amenemope*.[29]

Both the biblical and Egyptian sayings are clearly framed as admonitions, in direct address, with imperatives, motive clauses, and a consequential clause. Both perceive wealth as something negative that humans should not tax themselves to achieve. But whereas the Egyptian text warns against becoming rich through crime, for Proverbs the ways of acquiring wealth are irrelevant. *Amenemope* invokes up "Fate and Fortune" as a theological argument: "Every man belongs to his (appointed) hour." Thus fate and fortune are not in human hands.

Egyptian Wisdom literature associated its teachings with the goddess Ma'at, who played an important role in the Egyptian perception of life. Ma'at was the central concept behind the cosmic and social order; thus living in harmony with Ma'at meant obeying the laws of the land and fulfilling human destiny.[30] In the didactic speech of biblical Wisdom literature, on the other hand, we may discern the individual's

[28] *Amenemope*, Chapter 7, ix, lines 10–18; x, lines 1–5, in *ANET*, p. 422; see McKane, *Proverbs*, pp. 6, 103, 382–83.

[29] Egyptian artists often portray geese. See, e.g., the humoristic drawing on the ostracon from Deir el-Medina, in Patrick F. Houlihan, "Animals in Egyptian Art and Hieroglyphs," *HAWANE*, p. 125.

[30] H. H. Schmid, *Wesen und Geschichte der Weisheit* (BZAW 101; Berlin, 1966), p. 17; Kayatz, *Studien zu Proverbien* 1–9, pp. 15–75. For a summary of the difference between Ma'at and the biblical concept of Wisdom, see Whybray, *The Book of Proverbs*, pp. 65, 130.

cautious efforts to make use of his own powers of observation and understanding. In this setting, wealth is not considered to be the main goal toward which individuals should strive and true stability comes from wisdom: "A house is built by wisdom, and is established by understanding; by knowledge are its rooms filled with all precious and beautiful things" (Prov. xxiv 3–4).

Thus despite their different worldviews and conceptual backgrounds, both texts use birds to illustrate the ephemeral condition of those who exhaust themselves to acquire wealth and the transience of riches.

The Book of Proverbs challenges the teacher's competence by his capacity to discern the appropriate opportunities for using his intellect and refraining from using it in certain cases: "Trust in the Lord with all your heart, and do not rely on your own understanding" (Prov. iii 5). Other sayings recommend marshalling all one's mental faculties in pursuit of wisdom: "The beginning of wisdom is—acquire wisdom; with all your acquisitions, acquire discernment" (Prov. iv 7).[31]

2.1.2 *Animal Imagery in the Consequence Clause*

2.1.2.1 *Nāḥāš* 'Serpent' and *Ṣipᶜônî* 'Viper' in a Satirical Poem

> Who has woe? Who has sorrow? Who has strife? Who has complaining? Who has wounds without cause? Who has redness of eyes?
> Those who tarry long over wine, those who go to try mixed wine.
> Do not look at wine when it is red, when it sparkles in the cup and goes down smoothly.
> Its end is like a serpent that bites, and like a viper that secretes [venom].
> Your eyes will see strange things, and your mind utter perverse things.
> You will be like one who lies down in the midst of the sea, like one who lies on the top of a mast.
> "They struck me," you will say, "but I was not hurt; they beat me, but I did not feel it. When shall I awake? I will seek another drink."[32] (Prov. xxiii 29–35)

[31] *Bînâ* can mean both the contemplative faculty and the intellectual ability to discern and deduce. The root *b-y-n* designates careful observation, as in "When you sit down to dine with a ruler, consider well (*bīn tābīn*) who is before you" (Prov. xxiii 1). See Fox, *Proverbs 1–9*, p. 30.

[32] The translation follows the RSV, except for a free rendering of v. 32.

The Animal

Ṣipʿônî represents the entire family Viperidae; the *ṣepaʿ* has been identified with *Vipera palestinae*, a yellow poisonous snake prevalent in Israel.[33] The viper lives near human habitats and its bite is considered dangerous. Its hollow fangs inject its victims with the venom secreted by the poison glands, as indicated here by the verb *p-r-š* 'secrete' (Prov. xxiii 32b).

Ṣipʿônî occurs in biblical literature parallel to *peten* 'asp, viper', which presumably represents the family Elapidae (Isa. xi 8), as well as to the general term *nāḥāš* 'snake' (Prov. xxiii 32; Isa. xiv 29). The plural *ṣipʿônîm* appears as an adjective modifying *nᵉḥāšîm* (Jer. viii 17), thus indicating its use as a generic term.

Biblical sources tell us that the *ṣipʿônî* lives in a den (Isa. xi 8) and bites its victims (Jer. viii 17; Prov. xxiii 32). Isaiah's portrayal of the *ṣipʿônî* as an egg-layer (lix 5a) is consistent with the behavior of *Vipera palestinae* and of most snakes in Israel, although in Europe the members of the family Viperidae are ovoviviparous, giving birth to live young after the eggs develop within the mother's body.[34]

The identification of snake names according to particular characteristics is problematic. The ancient translators were not sure about the identification of these snakes. The Aramaic translations use the same equivalent *ḥūrmānāʾ* for *ṣipʿônî* (Prov. xxiii 32), *šěpîpōn* (Gen. xlix 17), *haněḥāšîm haśěrāpîm* (Num. xxi 6), and *ʾepʿeh* (Job xx 16).

In folklore, the snake has been the enemy of humankind since time immemorial, as in the divine chastisement of the serpent in Eden: "They shall strike at your head, and you shall strike at their heel" (Gen. iii 15; cf. Ps. xci 13). Snakes are sworn enemies of human beings, lying in ambush for them on the road (Gen. xlix 17). Hence snakes' venom symbolizes the malicious intentions of evildoers and is turned against them in retribution: "His food in his bowels turns into asps' venom within him" (Job xx 14).

[33] See Tristram, *Natural History*, pp. 275–76; Feliks, *Animals in the Bible*, p. 104; R. G. Murison, "The Serpent in the Old Testament," *AJSL* 21 (1905), p. 119; I. Löw, *Fauna und Mineralien der Juden* (Hildesheim, 1969), p. 33. Dor (*Animals in the Days of the Bible, the Mishnah and the Talmud*, p. 159) identifies the *ṣipʿônî* with the viper, i.e., the *ṣepaʿ* (*Vipera xanthina palestinae*).

[34] See Dor, *Animals in the Days of the Bible, the Mishnah and the Talmud*, p. 160; Karen R. Joines, "The Serpent in the Old Testament" (Ph.D. diss., Southern Baptist Theological Seminary, 1966), p. 10.

The Text

Proverbs xxiii 29–35 is an exhortation against drunkenness and the drunkard's bad habits. The passage opens with a string of six short rhetorical questions, linked by the anaphoric interrogative *lĕmî* 'to whom?' or 'who has?' In the Hebrew these questions constitute a rapid-fire staccato pattern: the first four questioned are two words each; the last two, three words each. The onomatopoeic expressions of grief and despair, *ʾôy* 'woe' and *ʾăbôy* 'sorrow', are borrowed from the lament *Gattung;*[35] "strife," "complaining,"[36] and "wounds" are terms taken from the semantic field of quarrel and dispute.

The noun *mādôn* occurs frequently in Proverbs (18 of its 22 occurrences in the Bible) as a synonym for *rîb* 'strife, conflict' (xv 18; xxvi 21).[37] A tendency to provoke quarrels is perceived as characteristic of mischief-makers, whose malevolent intentions are to cause strife and separate friends (see Prov. vi 14; xvi 28). The drunkard is considered to be a potential quarrelmonger. Proverbs warns against the company of hot-tempered persons who are quick to provoke fights (cf. Prov. xv 18, xxviii 25, xxix 22), causing physical confrontations and injuries for no purpose. The solution to the riddle is provided by the final question: "Who has redness of eyes?" (v. 29d). The idiom *ḥaklīlût ʿênāyim* alludes to the dark red wine.[38] The sense of *ḥaklīlût ʿênāyim* is picked up later in the poem, in connection with wine itself: "Do not look at wine when it is red, when it sparkles in the cup and goes down smoothly" (v. 31).

An explicit answer to the barrage of questions is provided by two clauses introduced by the attributive *lamed*: "Those who tarry long over wine, those who go to try mixed wine" (v. 30). These two answers portray the typical behavior of the drunkard, as described elsewhere by Isaiah: "Ah, Those who chase liquor from early in the morning, and till late in the evening are inflamed by wine!" (Isa. v 11; cf. v. 22).

[35] *ʾôy* 'woe' appears in laments (Jer. iv 13, xiii 27, xv 10; Lam. v 16). *ʾăbôy* is a hapax, probably formed to rhyme with *ʾôy*.

[36] For *śîaḥ* as "complaint" see 1 Sam. i 16 and Job xxiii 2.

[37] The plural *midyānîm* also occurs in Prov. vi 14 [Qere].

[38] Rashi and Ibn Ezra interpreted *ḥaklīlût ʿênāyim* (here and in Gen. xlix 12) as redness of eye, usually linked with wine-drinkers. The Targum uses the root *s-m-k* 'be red'. Compare Akkadian *ekēlu* 'be(come) dark' applied to the sun or mood (see *CAD*, E, p. 64 iv). See McKane, *Proverbs*, p. 393.

The sarcastic description of the drunkard is molded by words borrowed from lexicon of the sage. In Wisdom Literature, the infinitive *laḥqōr* 'to search, examine' (v. 30) refers to the mysteries of creation and its wonders (see Job xxviii 27) or to human intellectual discernment (see Prov. xxviii 11); here it mocks the intellectual effort invested in mixing intoxicating beverages.

In v. 31 the speaker makes the transition from posing riddles to the direct-address style of the exhortation, but he continues to employ figures of speech that maintain the ironic overtone: "Do not look at wine when it is red, when it sparkles in the cup and goes down smoothly."

The adverbial *mêšārîm* (v. 31d), contextually interpreted "smoothly," often comes in combination with *ṣedeq* 'justice' (Prov. i 3, ii 9; Isa. xi 4, xxxiii 15, xlv 19) to convey the idea of a moral path. Here *mêšārîm* is associated ironically with the smooth passage of wine over the palate (v. 31b), similar to the description of the loving wife in the love poem: "And your mouth like choicest wine, let it flow (*lᵉmêšārîm*) to my beloved as new wine gliding over the lips of sleepers" (Song vii 10).

The drunkard's ultimate destiny is dramatized by two separate images: one exemplifies the consequences of drinking wine as like the sensation of the bite of a poisonous viper; the other compares him to a man sleeping in mid-ocean on the top of a mast during a violent storm.

The consequential clause of the warning employs the term *ʾaḥărit,* which does not necessarily indicate the end of life or even the future in general,[39] but rather "aftereffect"—the effect of drinking wine to the point of intoxication. The simile of "like a viper that secretes" is defective; the Septuagint and Vulgate insert the accusative "venom" as the object of the verb. It is certainly possible that *rōʾš* or *rôš* 'venom' has dropped out by haplography, due to the proximity of *yap**rīš**.*[40]

The other image evokes what the drunk feels, which is compared to the experience of someone who sleeps on a wildly rocking vessel or atop a mast (cf. Ps. cvii 23, 27). The hapax legomenon *ḥibbēl* 'mast'

[39] Cf. Prov. xxiii 18; xxiv 14. See Fox, *Proverbs 1–9*, p. 197.

[40] *Rōʾš/rôš* occurs in various compounds; see Deut. xxxii 32c, 33b. Rashi glosses *yaprīš* as "sting" or as from the root *p-r-š* 'separate [from life]'. Gemser (*Sprüche Salomos*, p. 88) understands the verb as meaning "puncture and inject." McKane (*Proverbs,* p. 395) opts for "prick, puncture," by analogy to Arabic *paraṯa* 'wound in the liver or stomach'.

(v. 34)—a noun rather than a verb in the *piʿel*—is derived from *ḥebel* 'rope', and probably refers to the ropes tied to the masthead.[41]

The images of snake and viper are ironically related to the interpretation of the term *ʾaḥărît*. The moral retribution awaiting the drunkard is articulated in the conceptual paradigm of the wrong and right ways of conducting life in Proverbs: "A road may seem right to a man, but in the end (*ʾaḥărît*) it is a road to death" (Prov. xiv 12, xvi 25).[42] However, the sarcasm about the toper does not end with the sage's rebuke and moral lesson, but with the pathetic confession of the drunkard himself, who, sobering up, says: "They struck me, but I was not hurt; they beat me, but I did not feel it" (v. 35). This conclusion deviates from the standard pattern of the admonition, which usually offers its moral in the final clause, as in: "Such is the fate of all who pursue unjust gain; It takes the life of its possessor." (i 19; cf. vi 11, ix 36, xxiii 5). We may conjecture, then, that the direct warning (vv. 31, 33–34) and ultimate consequence (v. 32), stylistic components of the admonitory speech, were deliberately interpolated into a satire on those who drink excessively (cf. Isa. v 21–22, lxv 11), like the New Kingdom Instruction of Ani, which uses the exhortation pattern rather than satire.

> Don't indulge in drinking beer, / lest you utter evil speech / And don't know what you are saying. / If you fall and hurt your body, / None holds out a hand to you: / Your companions in the drinking / Stand up saying: "Out with the drunk!" / If one comes to seek you and talk with you, / One finds you lying on the ground, / As if you were a little child (4.7–10).[43]

[41] The Septuagint renders verse 34b "as a sailor in a great wave," reading *ḥōbēl* (cf. Ezek. xxvii 8, 29; Jonah i 6).

[42] *ʾAḥărît* is also mentioned with hope (Prov. xxiii 18; xxiv 14; Jer. xxxi 17). *ʾAḥărîtô* is either an accusative adverb ("at the last" [RSV]) or is a noun clause to which the following clause functions as virtual predicate: "Its end is: like a serpent it bites" (cf. the same syntactic relation in Prov. xxix 21). See Delitzsch, *Proverbs of Solomon* II, pp. 122–123, 255–256. The frequency of biblical warnings against intoxicating wine proves the existence of a widely known literary tradition cautioning against wine (cf. Isa. v 11; xxviii 7–8).

[43] See "The Instruction of Ani" IV 6–11, in A. Erman, *The Literature of the Ancient Egyptians,* tr. A. M. Blackman (New York, 1927), p. 236; Nili Shupak, "The Sitz im Leben of the Book of Proverbs in the Light of a Comparison of Biblical and Egyptian Wisdom Literature," *RB* 94 (1987), pp. 98–119; Clifford, *Proverbs*, p. 214. Ben Sira (xxxi 25–31) condemns excessive intoxication and recommends drinking wine in moderation.

The exhortation against drunkenness in the ancient Egyptian wisdom literature employs the stylistic elements of the admonition (direct speech, imperatives, conditional clause, and comparative clause), whereas the biblical passage is a mixed genre. The alternating mode of address, from a direct appeal to the drunkard to third-person speech and back again to the second person creates a dynamic movement suitable to the drunkard's unsteadiness. It changes again, switching from direct address to the drunkard, "You will be like one who lies down in the midst of the sea, like one who lies on the top of a mast" (v. 34), to a confession placed in his mouth: "'They struck me,' you will say, 'but I was not hurt; they beat me, but I did not feel it. When shall I awake? I will seek another drink'" (v. 35). His pathetic confession heightens the sense of his absurdity and lack of reliability.[44]

2.1.3 *Animal Imagery as an Exemplification in a Situational Clause*

2.1.3.1 *Ṣᵉbī 'Deer' and Ṣippôr 'Bird'*

> My son, if you have stood surety for your fellow, given your hand for another, You have been trapped by the words of your mouth, snared by the words of your mouth. Do this, then, my son, to extricate yourself, for you have come into the power of your fellow: Go grovel—and badger your fellow; give your eyes no sleep, your pupils no slumber. Save yourself like a deer out of the hand [of a hunter], like a bird out of the hand of a fowler['s trap]. (Prov. vi 1–5)

The Animals

The noun *ṣᵉbī* 'deer' is attested in other Semitic languages: Akkadian *ṣabītu*, Ugaritic *ṯby*, Aramaic and Syriac *ṭabyā*, Arabic *ḏaby*.[45] The

[44] Parallel to "'They struck me,' you will say, 'but I was not hurt'" (v. 35a) is "You have struck them, but they sensed no pain" (Jer. v 3b). Rather than "hurt" or "illness," Driver explains *ḥālîtî* on the analogy of Ethiopic *ḥallaya* 'look out for, be concerned' (cf. 1 Sam. xxii 8). See Godfrey R. Driver, "Some Hebrew Words," *JTS* 29 (1928), p. 392; McKane, *Proverbs*, p. 396.

[45] The Hebrew spelling with *ṣ*, from an etymological ṯ, is a common shift (see Militarev and Kogan, *SED*, No. 242). Pace medieval commentators like David Qimḥi, *ṣᵉbī* 'deer' derives from the proto-Semitic *ṯ-b-y* and is not related to the *ṣ-b-y* that connotes beauty or the precious and desirable (see Isa. xxviii 5; Jer. iii 19), as in "the land of *ṣᵉbī*" (Dan. xi 16, 41), an epithet for the Land of Israel. See Elqanah Billiq and Shmuel E. Loewenstamm, "*Ṣᵉbī*," *EM* 6: 661–63 [Hebrew].

local species (mountain gazelle, Dorcas gazelle) probably roamed freely during the biblical period, before large tracts of wooded land had been ravaged by domestic ruminants.[46]

The *ṣᵉbī* is a clean animal that may be eaten (Deut. xii 15, xiv 5, xv 22), but it is not acceptable as a sacrifice. It appears as part of the menu in Solomon's household (1 Kgs v 3 [RSV iv 23]).[47]

In the Bible, the *ṣᵉbī* and *ṣᵉbīyyâ* are symbols of grace, beauty, and erotic love (Song iv 5; vii 4). The deer's noble appearance inspired the poet of the Song of Songs (cf. ii 9, 17; viii 14), while its supple body and fleet-footedness provided a perfect image of swiftness: "Asahel was swift of foot, like a gazelle in the open field" (2 Sam. ii 18; 1 Chr. xii 8).[48]

Ṣippôr 'bird' is a collective noun for fowl (see Gen. vii 14; Deut. iv 17, xiv 11). It appears as the *nomen rectum* governed by *ᶜayīṭ* to indicate the zoological category of the latter: "and I will give you as food to carrion birds (*ᶜêṭ ṣippôr*) of every sort and to the beasts of the field" (Ezek. xxxix 4b). It also appears as a general noun in parallel with a particular species or category, such as *bᵉnôt haššîr* 'daughters of song' (Qoh. xii 4), *dᵉrôr* (Ps. lxxxiv 4), and *yônâ* (Hos. xi 11).

The Text

This passage is a warning against going surety for another. *Tᵉkîᶜat kap* 'striking the hand' (Prov. vi 1; xvii 18; xxii 26) or *yād lᵉyād* 'hand to hand' (Prov. xi 21)—a handshake—is a conventional gesture for ratifying an agreement. The verbal phrase *ᶜārabtā lᵉ-* generally indicates accepting responsibility (cf. Gen. xliii 9; Ps. cxix 122), but here this is specifically responsibility for the repayment of a loan in the event of default, either "giving surety to" the lender or "going surety for" the borrower. The identity of the two parties to the loan, the *rēaᶜ* 'fellow, neighbor' and the *zār* 'another, stranger', and their legal status is crucial for an understanding of the socioeconomic background of the verse. Who are they?

Here *zār* does not necessarily mean an alien or a stranger, but rather designates a person more distant than the *rēaᶜ*. According to one

[46] Firmage, "Zoology (Fauna)," pp. 1141–1142.

[47] On further discussion of clean animals in relation to cultic sacrifice, see Oded Borowski, "Animals in the Religions of Syria-Palestine," *HAWANE*, p. 412.

[48] Cf. *CAD* L, p. 105a, *lusma kīma ṣabīti* 'swift like a gazelle' (Köcher BAM 248 iv 2).

approach, the case is of going surety for a friend or neighbor who is the borrower; that is, of providing a guarantee to the "foreign" lender. In the other reading, it is a case of guaranteeing to one's friend, who is the lender, that the "foreign" borrower will pay his debt. The guarantor is told to go importune his neighbor: "Do this, then, my son, to extricate yourself, for you have come into the power of your fellow: Go grovel—and badger your fellow" (v. 3). Whether the *rēaᶜ* is the borrower or the lender, the victim is always the person who pledges to pay someone else's debts.[49]

The admonition opens with the formula "my son," which indicates a teacher-pupil relationship and not necessarily a true father-son relationship.

The conditional clause refers to taking on a particular legal and financial obligation: "My son, if you have stood surety for your fellow, given your hand for another" (vi 1).[50] This practical business-like statement leads into a metaphor borrowed from the world of the hunt: "You have been trapped by the words of your mouth, snared by the words of your mouth" (v. 2).[51] The addressee is described as a naïf whose own words have caused him to fall into the trap of assuming the obligation of guarantor. Furthermore, as a result of this rash *tᵉkîᶜat kap* 'handshake', he is told, *bāʾtā bᵉkap rēᶜekā*—"you have come into the hand [i.e. power] of your fellow" (v. 3), an echo of the expression *bᵉkap ʾōyēb* 'into the hands of the enemy' (Judg. vi 13; Jer. xii 7). The multiple repetitions of terms related to entrapment —"the words of your mouth" (v. 2a, b), "save yourself" (vv. 3, 5), "your hand," "the

[49] Delitzsch (*Proverbs of Solomon* I, pp. 135–36) claims that *zār* and *rēaᶜ* are synonyms (see Prov. xi 15) that refer to the same person; *zār* is equivalent to *ʾaḥēr* and means some third party (see Prov. v 10; xx 16); *rēaᶜ* is not a friend, but one who stands in any kind of relation, including legal or judicial (Prov. xxiv 28). The phrase *ᶜarab lᵉ*- is problematic unless the *lāmed* is *dative commodi,* with the meaning "giving surety for anyone" (cf. Prov. xvii 18; xxii 26). The customary usages are *ᶜārab bᵉᶜad* (cf. Prov. xx 16; xxvii 13) and *ᶜārab miyyād* (Gen. xliii 9). Snijders' view that *zār* means not foreigner but "outsider" (i.e., one who does not follow the normative rules of society) is linked to his theory of the "strange woman"; see L. A. Snijders, "The Meaning of *zār* in the Old Testament: an exegetical Study," *OtSt* 10 (1954), pp. 82–84. Boström (cited by McKane) opts for *zār* = "foreigner" to support his theory. For different interpretations of *zār* and *rēaᶜ* as legal terms, see: McKane, *Proverbs*, pp. 321–22; Fox, *Proverbs 1–9*, pp. 211–212; Waltke, *Proverbs 1–15*, pp. 331–33.

[50] The gesture of *tᵉkîᶜat kap* or *yād* 'shaking hands' denotes a legal undertaking of providing surety (Prov. xvii 18, xxii 26; Job xvii 3). Gemser (*Sprüche Salomos*, p. 36) mentions "give me your hand" (2 Kgs x 15) said by Jehu to Jehonadab son of Rechab, as referring to surety for fulfilling a promise.

[51] For the pair "trapped" and "snared" see Isa. xviii 15 and Jer. l 24.

hand of your friend" (vv. 1, 3), "from the hand" (v. 5a, b)—create a dramatic atmosphere of the crisis in which the young man finds himself.

The speaker urges his listener to action through his repeated calls to "save yourself." The first time this immediately follows the description of the young man's situation: "Do this, then, my son, to extricate yourself" (v. 3). The second time it appears in the simile that follows the series of staccato imperatives: "Do this," "Extricate yourself," "Go," "Grovel," "Badger your fellow," "Give your eyes no sleep, Your pupils no slumber" (vv. 3, 4).

The speech closes with hunt imagery to illustrate the seriousness of the guarantor's situation and persuade him to act as quickly as possible. This sense of urgency is enacted phonetically in the voiceless velar sibilant *ṣādê* that is repeated in rapid-fire succession in the words *hināṣṣēl*, *ṣ*^{e}*bî,* and *ṣippôr* (v. 5).

The synonymous parallelism in v. 5 proposes a conceptual link between the deer and the bird, both of them targeted by the hunter. But whereas the method employed (a snare) is specified in the case of the bird, no details are provided about the deer hunt.

The first clause, *hinnāṣēl kiṣ*^{e}*bî miyyād,* "Save yourself like a deer out of the hand" (v. 5a) lacks the *nomen regens* that should be governed by "out of the hand," leaving hanging the question of whose hand is meant. Early translations attest to a reading *mimmāṣōd* 'from a snare', which would have fallen out of MT by a double haplography: *mem-mem* and *ṣade-yod* (in the archaic Hebrew script). Nahmias suggests supplying a missing word: *hinnāṣēl kiṣ*^{e}*bî miyyād* [*ṣayyād*], "Save yourself like a deer out of the hand of [a hunter]" (v. 5a).[52] Perles proposes a lesser corruption: the MT's *miyyād* as the relic of an original *miṣṣayyād* 'from the hunter'.[53]

[52] Quoted by Fox, *Proverbs* 1–9, p. 214. The figure of hunter appears many times in the Bible; e.g., "a skillful hunter, a man of the outdoors" (Gen. xxv 27); "if any Israelite or any stranger … hunts down an animal or a bird that may be eaten" (Lev. xvii 13).

[53] F. Perles, *Analekten zur Textkritik des Alten Testaments* (Leipzig, 1922), p. 52. LXX reads ἐκ βρόχων = "from meshes [of the net]." For a recent discussion of the Septuagint variant to Prov. vi 5, see Michael V. Fox, "LXX-Proverbs as a Text-Critical Resource," *Textus* 22 (2005), pp. 106–107. The Aramaic and Syriac agree with the conjectural Greek variant, filling in the indirect accusative *min nišbāʿ* 'from a snare'. Delitzsch (following Hitzig) supports the reading of *hinnāṣēl miyyād* as a complete predicate with the sense of entrapment (cf. 1 Kgs xx 42). See Delitzsch, *Proverbs of Solomon* I, p. 139; McKane, *Proverbs*, p. 323; R. E. Murphy, *Proverbs* (WBC 22; Nashville, 1998), p. 34.

The second clause, with its image of the bird (v. 5b), repeats *miyyād* and attaches it to the passive participle *yāqûš* 'ensnared, trapped'—syntactically problematic. In Hosea we find the form *yāqôš,* a gerund with the sense of the noun "fowler," modifying the noun *paḥ*: "Fowlers' snares are on all his paths" (Hos. ix 8; the collocation of *paḥ* with the verb is also found in Ps. xci 3, civ 7, and ci 9). It thus seems preferable to read here *k^eṣippôr miyyād paḥ yāqôš* 'like a bird out of the hand of a fowler' or to take the MT as an elliptic expression that omits the nomen regens *paḥ* 'snare'.[54]

The use of imagery borrowed from hunting emphasizes the grave condition of a person who goes surety for another, because he may well become the hapless victim of both creditor and debtor.

Ben Sira employs the same image of the hunted birds and deer, but uses their escape as a simile for the irretrievable damage caused by betraying the confidence of a good friend.

> Whoever betrays a secret destroys confidence; he will never find an intimate friend. … Like a bird released from the hand, you have let your friend go and you cannot recapture him. Follow him not, for he is far away; he has escaped like a gazelle from the snare (xxvii 16–21).[55]

2.1.3.2 Šôr *'Bull, Ox' and* Ṣippôr *'Bird' in a First-Person Narrative*

> She sways him with her eloquence, turns him aside with her smooth talk. Suddenly he follows her, like an ox going to the slaughter, like a stag being bound to the stocks, until the arrow pierces his liver; he is like a bird rushing into a trap, not knowing his life is at stake. (Prov. vii 21–23; free translation)

The Animal[56]

Šôr denotes a single bovine (as distinct from the collective *bāqār*), but is also a general term for "oxen" (cf. Gen. xxxii 6).[57] The noun is

[54] For the compound *paḥ yāqôš* (Hos. ix 8) or *paḥ yāqûš* (Ps. xci 3), see GKC, §72r. On hunting terminology in the Bible see Aaron Kampinski, "Hunting and Fishing," *EM* 6:716–17 [Hebrew].

[55] Alexander A. Di Lella, *The Wisdom of Ben Sira,* trans. P. W. Skehan (AB 39; New York, 1987), pp. 354, 357–58. Cf. the admonitions in Proverbs against gossip, garrulity, and revealing intimate secrets by those who are incapable of holding their tongue (xx 19; xxv 9–10); cf. *Amenemope*, chapter 21, xxii, *ANET*, p. 424. See McKane, *Proverbs,* pp. 537–38.

[56] For a discussion of birds, see §2.1.3.1.

[57] Militarev and Kogan (*SED*, No. 341) define *šor* as a *nomen unitatis*. If so, the

attested in cognate Semitic languages: *šūrum* in Akkadian, *ṯr* in Ugaritic; *tōrāʾ* in Jewish Aramaic, *tawrā* in Syriac, and *ṯawr* in Arabic. *Šôr* appears in the Bible three times parallel to *r*ᵉ*ʾēm* 'aurochs' (*Bos primigenius*), a frequent symbol of divine power and strength (cf. Ps. xcii 11).[58]

Among the common domestic livestock of biblical times, oxen were employed for various agricultural tasks such as plowing and threshing (see Deut. xxii 10, xxv 4; Hos. x 11). The ox was also employed as a beast of burden and harnessed to carts (see Num. vii 3; 1 Sam. vi 7; 1 Chr. xii 41; Prov. xiv 4). Cattle might be led out to pasture for grazing (see Num. xxii 4) or fed hay, straw, and mixed fodder in the manger (cf. Prov. xiv 4; Isa. xi 7; xxx 24; Job vi 5, xl 15).

The Text

Proverbs vii 1–4 calls on the youth to internalize the precepts of wisdom as part of the process of developing the appropriate approach to life. The common formula "my son"[59] and the sequence of imperatives—"keep," "store," "bind," and "write"—emphasize the didactic authority of the sage. The specific concrete exhortation against seduction by a strange woman is introduced in verse 5 by the infinitive *lišmōrkā* 'to guard you', followed by the conjunction *kî* 'for' in verse 6, thus linking the admonition with the first-person narrative that follows. Here the formal structure of the admonition is interrupted by a vivid report of an erotic encounter, a nocturnal tryst that the sage saw when he looked out his window.[60] He shares with his readers his impressions, whose moral is the goal of his teaching and is strikingly similar to another first-person monologue in Proverbs: "I passed by the field of a lazy man, by the vineyard of a man lacking sense" (xxiv 30). The first-person narrative ultimately yields a moral lesson: "I

plural form *š*ᵉ*wārîm* in Hos. xii 12 is not usual and probably due to textual corruption.

[58] See Borowski, "Animals in the Literatures of Syria-Palestine," *HAWANE,* pp. 299–300.

[59] On the formulas "my son" or "sons" applying to pupils in the Bible and in Egyptian didactic literature, see Gemser, *Sprüche Salomos*, p. 21. Cf. Sir. ii 1; iii 7, 11, 16; iv 1; the Syriac Ahiqar ii 23. For the relationship between teacher and pupil as that of father and son in Proverbs and ancient Near Eastern wisdom literature, see: Wilfred G. Lambert, "Counsels of Wisdom," *Babylonian Wisdom Literature* (Oxford, 1960), p. 96; M. Weinfeld, *Deuteronomy and the Deuteronomic School*, p. 305 n. 3.

[60] The LXX renders the verbs and the suffixes of the possessive pronouns in vv. 6–7 in the third instead of the first person ("she looks ... out of her house") of the MT.

observed and took it to heart, I saw it and learned a lesson" (xxiv 32).[61]

The framework in which the passage is set (vii 1–5 and 24–27) calls on the youth to internalize the teachings of wisdom for use as a weapon against the allures of the seductive woman.

The narrator spurs the reader's imagination with a finely etched tableau. We are introduced to the adulterous woman as she lures on the foolish youth with her seductive actions and words of enticement. The narrative interweaves details of the woman's fine bedcovers of dyed Egyptian linen, the hushed voices of courting, and perfumed spices (myrrh, aloes, and cinnamon).[62]

The youth who consorts with the strange woman is described as following her "suddenly" (*pitʾōm*); in the context, "impulsively" might be a better rendering. In Proverbs, the adverb *pitʾōm* is associated with unexpected disaster that falls upon the evildoer: "You will not fear sudden terror or the disaster that comes upon the wicked" (Prov. iii 25; cf. vi 15, xxiv 22). Here, though, the person involved is a thoughtless youth rather than an evildoer. In fact, the ancient versions render the term as if related to the Hebrew *petî* 'simpleton' or the plural *pᵉtāʾîm* (v. 7) or *pᵉtayût* 'in a naive manner' (Prov. ix 13).[63] The biblical writers seem to pun on *pitʾōm* and synonyms of *petî*. Examples are *tām* 'innocent' and *pitʾōm* in Psalms lxiv 5 (RSV 4): "To shoot from hiding at the blameless man; they shoot him suddenly and without fear"; *ʾĕwîl* 'fool' and *pitʾōm* in Job v 3: "I myself saw a fool who had struck roots, impulsively, I cursed his home." Our verse may similarly be playing *pitʾōm* against *pᵉtāʾîm* in v. 7.

[61] See Tova Forti and Zipora Talshir, "Proverbs 7 in MT and LXX: Form and Content," *Textus* 22 (2005), pp. 142–44. On the autobiographical narrative style of Prov. iv 3–4; xxiv 30–34; Ps. xxxvii 25, 35; Sir. li 13–16 (cf. xxxiii 16–19), see Von Rad, *Wisdom in Israel*, pp. 37–38.

[62] Some scholars have adopted the LXX version (above, n. 60) to support their hypothesis that the strange woman is a cult prostitute of the fertility goddess Ishtar. For a summary of the various proposals (Albright, Snijders, Boström) see McKane, *Proverbs*, pp. 334–36. On the motif of the queen peering through the lattice in ancient Near Eastern literature, see M. Cogan and H. Tadmor, *II Kings* (AB 11; New York, 1988), pp. 111–12.

[63] The LXX renders the conjectured *pᵉtāʾîm* by the peculiar κεπφωθείς 'bird-brained': hence "he followed her being easily cajoled" (cf. Job xxxi 9). On the Greek idiom, see Fox, *Proverbs 1–9*, p. 406; D. M. d'Hamonville, *La Bible d'Alexandrie: Les Proverbes* (Paris, 2000), p. 203. The Aramaic version has "he goes after her without paying attention" (i.e., without concern or worry); the Syriac has "like a lad."

The youth walking after her is compared to an ox *yābōʾ* '[that] will go'—i.e., "is going"—to the slaughter. The ancient versions render this in the passive, similar to the description of the sacrificial lamb in the prophetic literature, "like a sheep (*yûbāl*) being led to slaughter" (Isa. liii 7b) or "like a docile lamb led (*yûbal*) to the slaughter" (Jer. xi 19a).[64]

The second simile, *ûkʿekes ʾel mûsar ʾĕwîl* ("... like a stag being bound to the stocks [?]"), is incomprehensible as it stands. The various attempts to render the enigmatic *ʿekes* 'anklet' in this context and in relation to the construction *mûsar ʾĕwîl* 'obedience of the fool' seem forced and implausible. For example, the KJV translates: "or as a fool to the correction of the stocks"; similarly the NJPS: "like a fool to the stocks for punishment." Both ignore the conceptual background of the passive behavior of the animals being victimized.

The collocation *mûsar ʾĕwîl* incorporates the standard didactic term *mûsar,* which refers to obedience and discipline in heeding the instructions of the sage (cf. xvi 22). It expresses the negative traits of immorality and disobedience, as in the adage "A fool spurns the discipline of his father, but one who heeds reproof becomes clever" (Prov. xv 5). But this sense of *mûsar ʾĕwîl* does not seem to fit the theme of the seduction of the youth by the adulterous woman.

The sequence of animals in the unit (ox, bird) seems to have led the ancient translators to look for more of them, even at the cost of borrowing from their own cultural milieu. The reading of the LXX, καὶ ὥσπερ κύων ἐπὶ δεσμοὺς "and as a dog to bonds," is based on the reading *môsēr* 'bond' (from the root *ʾ-s-r*) rather than the MT vocalization *mûsar* 'teaching'.[65] The enigmatic *ʿekes* is turned into a dog, while *ʾĕwîl* 'fool' metamorphoses into *ʾayyāl* 'stag' (a plausible emendation) and is linked to the start of the next verse: "as a hart shot in the liver with an arrow." The Vulgate renders *ʿekes* as "agnus" = lamb.

Revocalizing the noun *k*ᵉ*ʿekes* 'like an anklet' as the absolute infinitive *k*ᵉ*ʿākōs* 'in the state of being bound' would emphasize how the fool goes towards his *môsēr* 'bond' or, better, 'imprisonment' (cf. Job xiii 27; xxxiii 11).[66]

[64] Cf. the compound *šor ṭābûaḥ* 'slaughtered ox' in Deut. xxviii 31. For *ṭebaḥ* = slaughter, cf. Prov. ix 2; Jer. li 40; Ps. xliv 23; 1 Sam. xxv 11.

[65] *Mûsar* is frequent in Proverbs (30 occurrences), but occurs only four times in Job and never in Qoheleth. See Whybray, *The Intellectual Tradition*, p. 128.

[66] This is the reading suggested by Fox (*Proverbs 1–9*, 249–50). *ʿEkes* 'anklet'

This string of similes exemplifies both the passive attitude of the young naïf who is led astray by the temptress as well as his anticipated tragic outcome.

Although the result clause introduced by the preposition *ʿad*—"until the arrow pierces his liver" (v. 23a)—might refer to the hunted hart, it does not fit well in the sequence of images that represent the lad's behavior (vv. 22, 23b); the passivity of the victim does not easily lend itself to the sophistication of hunting methods. If, however, we consider "until the arrow pierces his liver" (v. 23a) in light of the first clause that describes the youth who "suddenly follows her" (v. 22a), and remember that the liver was considered to be the seat of the emotions,[67] *ʿad* can be understood as denoting the end-result of the process. Thus the image of the arrow closes the cycle of the lad's seduction.

The bird rushing into a trap (v. 23b), introduced by the comparative *kāp,* adds another simile for the victim's behavior and should be integrated into the sequence of animal images—all of which are comparative clauses (vv. 22b, 22c, 23b). Moreover, it seems that the sage deliberately accumulates images drawn from the field of trapping and slaughter. The result clause, "until the arrow pierces his liver" (v. 23a), seems to be out of sequence and should follow "suddenly he follows her" (v. 22a), leading to the sage's reflection, "not knowing his life is at stake" (23c). This establishes a narrative framework (vv. 22a, 23a, 23c) for the sequence of images. The pictures that flash before the reader's eyes, one after another, evoke a dramatic sensation of unavoidable disaster. In fact, the ancient versions (LXX, Targum, and Peshitta) all have a uniform structure of four independent scenes, ignoring the preposition *ʿad* of the result clause and presenting a

appears in the plural in Isa. iii 18 as an ornamental accessory worn on the leg (see Gersonides). The denominative verb *ʿakkēs* occurs two verses earlier and is usually interpreted as "shaking bangles, rattling, tinkling." In *Sefer Hashorashim*, David Qimḥi explains *ʿakkēs* as "the way that women sway and clack with their bracelets" and the noun *ʿekes* as a chain wound around the leg. See David Qimḥi (Radaq), *Sefer Hashorashim*, ed. J. H. R. Biesenthal and F. Lebrecht, (Berlin, 1847; repr. Jerusalem, 1967). Ibn Ezra (comm. on Prov. vii 22) says that *ʿekes* is a kind of chain. Driver associates *ʿakkēs* with Arabic *ʿākasa* 'tie (a camel) with a rope' and understands *ûkʿekes ʾel mûsar ʾᵉwîl* as "and like a hart that is tied to a cord" (Godfrey R. Driver, "Problems in Proverbs," *ZAW* 50 [1932], p. 143). Later, still referring to Arabic, he suggested "as a hart skips into a noose" (idem, "Hebrew Notes," *VT* 1 [1951], p. 241). On the Arabic *ʿākasa* see E. W. Lane, *An Arabic-English Lexicon* (London, 1863–1893; repr. 1968), Book I, 5:2121.

[67] Cf. Lam. ii 11.

different animal in each image. In free translation, we can harmonize all three as follows:

(22b) As an ox led to the slaughter
(22c) As a dog to bonds
(23a) As a hart shot in the liver with an arrow
(23b) As a bird rushing into a trap

The last image of "a bird rushing into a trap" emphasizes the rapidity of the victim's capture. The bird is depicted as a creature that does not fall into its fate passively, but rather actively assists its own downfall. Similarly, the youth's innocence contributes to his own undoing, "not knowing his life is at stake,"[68] and leads him to Sheol.

The image of the innocent and unsuspecting creature that hastens its own end takes the place of the warning and threat usually found in the admonition. The sequence of images designating the fate of those who associate with the strange woman evokes the urgency of internalizing the moral lesson. The inexperienced addressee is repeatedly warned against rushing headlong into the net spread out around him.[69]

After this sequence of images, which exemplify the dismal fate to which the lad devoid of sense is running heedlessly, the sage reverts to the admonition pattern, combining a general appeal to heed his advice with a concrete exhortation to stay away from the strange woman whose house leads to Sheol (vv. 24–27).

2.2 Proverbial Sayings

2.2.1 *Animal Imagery to Exemplify an Idea*

2.2.1.1 *Ḥăzîr 'Pig' in a Simile*

Like a gold ring in the snout of a pig is a beautiful woman bereft of sense. (Prov. xi 22)

[68] The preposition in *b^e^napšô* is the *bêt* of price; i.e., he pays "with his life." cf. "if broaching this matter does not cost Adonijah his life!"(1 Kgs ii 23b).

[69] The image of entrapped birds crops up frequently (e.g., Amos iii 5; Ps. cxxiv 7; Qoh. ix 12; Lam. iii 52), as does that of birds escaping from the snare (e.g., Prov. i 17; vi 5b; Ps. xci 3; cxxiv 3, 7).

The Animal

The noun *ḥăzîr* has cognates in other Semitic languages: Ugaritic *ḫzr*,[70] Akkadian *ḫuzīrum (šeḫû)*, Aramaic *ḥăzîrāʾ*, and Arabic *ḫinzîrun.*

In Psalms we find *ḥăzîr miyāʿar* (Ps. lxxx 14 [RSV 13]) 'boar from the forest', evidently meaning the wild boar *(Sus scrofa)* and its natural habitat. It gnaws indiscriminately, trampling and destroying cultivated lands: "wild boars gnaw at it, and creatures of the field feed on it" (ibid.).[71] Wild boars were abundant in forests and marshes and even in the bare desert.[72] The Mishnah (Ḥul. 9:2) refers to both wild and domesticated swine.

Ancient Near Eastern cultures differed in their attitude to swine.[73] Hittite religious practice, for instance, prescribed the sacrifice of piglets (and dogs) in rites of atonement and purification.[74] But Hittite instructions for temple officials also instruct the kitchen staff to keep dogs and pigs away from the sacrificial utensils so as to avoid contamination of the gods' food.[75] Evidence of pigs and dogs scavenging in the streets comes from Babylonian literature and Esarhaddon's revenge on the murderers of Sennacherib: "I fed their corpses, cut into small pieces, to dogs, pigs, *zîbu*-birds, vultures, the birds of the sky and (also) to the fish of the ocean."[76]

In two loci the Septuagint interpolates pigs where they are not found in the MT. Pigs, and not only dogs, lick the blood of the corpse in Elijah's curse of Ahab and its fulfillment (1 Kgs xxi [xx in the LXX] 19 and xxii 38). In 2 Sam. xvii 8, a wild boar is added to the bereaved bear of Hushai's metaphor for David's desperation.[77]

[70] Militarev and Kogan (*SED*, No. 111) argue that "*ḫnzr* and *ḫzr* do not denote an animal but rather a profession or an administrative function."

[71] Several commentators emend the text to *ḥăzîr miyyᵉôr* 'the boar of the Nile' and associate the enemy with Egypt (e.g., Charles A. Briggs and Emilie G. Briggs, *The Book of Psalms* II [ICC; Edinburgh, 1976 (1907[1])], p. 206).

[72] See Tristram, *Natural History of the Bible*, pp. 54, 145; Firmage, "Zoology," p. 1130.

[73] The pig is depicted as a submissive and obedient creature in Sargon's annals (Winckler, Sar. 56:336). See Marcus, "Animal Similes in Assyrian Royal Inscriptions," pp. 91–92.

[74] Firmage, "Zoology," pp. 1131–32.

[75] See *ANET*, p. 209 (14.65); G. McMahon, "Instructions to Priests and Temple Officials," in W. W. Hallo (ed.), *The Context of Scripture, Volume 1: Canonical Compositions from the Biblical World* (Leiden, 1997), p. 220.

[76] See *ANET*, p. 288 (iv 65–82).

[77] The pig is also added when the NT cites the proverbial saying about the dog

The biblical dietary laws define two characteristics for distinguishing clean from unclean mammals: "Every animal that parts the hoof and has the hoof cloven in two, and chews the cud, among the animals, you may eat" (RSV; Deut. xiv 6; Lev. xi 3). The biblical list of impure animals that may not be eaten (Leviticus xi; Deut. xiv 3–21), which includes birds of prey and scavengers, explicitly lists the pig among the unclean mammals, because it is not a ruminant and does not chew its cud (Lev. xi 7; Deut. xiv 8). There is no distinction between wild and domesticated pig. Isaiah denounces the eating of pork an abomination: "...who eat the flesh of swine, with broth of unclean things in their bowls" (lxv 4b; cf. lxvi 17). He also lists breaking a dog's neck and offering swine's blood as examples of loathsome rituals associated with idol worship (lxvi 3).[78]

The Text

This comparative saying[79] consists of two clauses in which concepts from different semantic fields are equated, but without the comparative *kāp* and applicative particle *kēn*. The same "stripped down" syntax is found in "a roaring lion and a prowling bear is a wicked man ruling a helpless people" (xxviii 15; cf. xxvi 17). To extricate the author's meaning we must identify the common denominator of the two images—the direct or indirect association between them.

The first clause presents a curious association: a gold ring and a pig's snout. The image is absurd, because a *nezem* 'nose ring' is an ornament worn by women (Gen. xxiv 22, 47; Judg. viii 24; Isa. iii 21; Ezek. xvi 12; Job xlii 11). The contrast between a woman's fine jewelry and the ungainly garbage-eater, with its bristles and snout, produces ridicule and astonishment.

Of all animals, the swine seems to have been chosen because of its repulsive habits, such as its wallowing in mud and thriving on scraps of vegetable and flesh. But the use of the pig in the simile depends primarily on the cultic-religious tradition that reflects a longstanding aversion to swine.[80]

(Prov. xxvi 11a): "As a dog returns to his vomit and the sow that was washed to her wallowing in the mire" (2 Pet. ii 22 [KJV]). See further below, §3.3

[78] On religious rituals that employ pigs, and the prohibition of pork in Israel, see: Firmage, "Zoology," pp. 1124–1125, 1130–1135; Billie J. Collins, "Animals in the Religions of Ancient Anatolia," *HAWANE*, pp. 322–23.

[79] On the comparative saying, see §1.5.1.1.

[80] In addition to the biblical references given above, see 1 Macc. i 44–50; *b. Soṭah*

Here the comparandum or tenor is the beautiful woman who lacks *ṭāʿam* 'taste, sense'. In this context *ṭāʿam* does not indicate the sense of taste (cf. Job xii 11) but mental discernment, as in "Teach me good sense and knowledge" (Ps. cxix 66; cf. Prov. xxvi 16); *ṭāʿam* also denotes practical understanding, as in David's praise of Abigail's conduct: "Blessed be your good sense (*ṭaʿmēk*)" (1 Sam. xxv 33).[81] A similar appreciation of a woman's practical intelligence is echoed in the panegyric of the Woman of Valor: "She perceives (*ṭaʿămâ*) that her merchandise is profitable" (Prov. xxxi 18; NRV); "Her mouth is full of wisdom, Her tongue with kindly teaching." She is also lauded for her wisdom and moral judgment: "Grace is deceptive; beauty is illusory; it is for her fear of the Lord that a woman is to be praised" (xxxi 30).[82]

We may therefore consider the saying in Proverbs to be a moral statement about the advantage of intellect over beauty. Beauty in a woman who lacks the additional qualities of intelligence, discernment, and understanding, is a combination as ridiculous as a golden nose-ring in a pig's snout.

2.2.1.2 Ṣippôr *'Sparrow' in a Comparative Saying*[83]

> Like a sparrow wandering from its nest is a man who wanders from his home. (Prov. xxvii 8)

This saying compares a man's wandering from his home to a bird's wandering from its nest. The Bible applies the root *n-d-d* to both human beings and animals. Some of its occurrences refer to destruction and exile, which cause people to wander, and are best rendered as *flight*: "For they have fled (*nâdâdû)* before swords, before the whetted

---

49b; *b. B. Qam.* 82b.

[81] On the semantic development of *ṭaʿam* from palatal sensation to aesthetic taste and thence to prudent wisdom and intelligence, see Gemser, *Sprüche Salomos*, p. 56; McKane, *Proverbs*, p. 430; Murphy, *Proverbs*, p. 83.

[82] The LXX renders Prov. xxxi 30 "Charms are false, and woman's beauty is vain: for it is a wise woman that is blessed, and let her praise the fear of the Lord" (Eng. translation follows Brenton), thus adding the epithet "wise" to the ideal of woman. See Alexander Rofé, "The Valiant Woman, γυνὴ συνετή, and the Redaction of the Book of Proverbs," in *Festschrift Rudolf Smend,* ed. Ch. Bultmann et al. (Göttingen, 2002), pp. 145–155. Cf. Syriac Aḥiqar, II.19: "A woman of wisdom is the one to be praised" (free translation).

[83] On *ṣippôr,* see §2.1.3.1.

sword, before the bow that was drawn, before the stress of war" (Isa. xxi 15). The depiction of wandering often involves famine, whereas permanent settlement is associated with satiety: "Some lost their way in the wilderness ... hungry and thirsty. ... He showed them a direct way to reach a settled place. ... For He has satisfied the thirsty, filled the hungry with all good things" (Ps. cvii 4–9). In Jeremiah's vivid depiction of the Day of Judgment, the migration of birds is identified with the hasty abandonment of the country by the inhabitants of the land: "I look: no man is left, and all the birds of the sky have fled" (Jer. iv 25). The victims of exile, a punishment imposed by the Lord, are compared to birds driven from their nest: "Like the fugitive (*nôded*) birds, like nestlings driven away, Moab's villagers linger at the fords of the Arnon" (Isa. xvi 2). In Jeremiah's lament on the exile, the national catastrophe extends to animals as well: "Birds of the sky and beasts as well have fled (*nâd^{e}dû)* and are gone" (Jer. ix 9).[84]

The hermeneutic tradition associated with our verse from Proverbs reflects the influence of the prophetic literary tradition just surveyed, in which birds that leave their nest and flee are metaphors for the desolation of the land.[85] This exegetical bent tries to reconstruct the circumstances of the wanderer, including war, exile, destruction, and hunger (cf. Gen. xii 10; Ps. cvii 4–7; Job xv 23). In our verse, however, there are no hints of any socio-historical background or sermons, as in the prophetic literature. The image of the bird's flight is not used to depict destruction as punishment for sin (cf. Jer. iv 25; Isa. xvi 2). The saying does not offer a detailed description of individual or societal circumstances that compel a person to leave his home.[86] Nevertheless, the concluding *mimm^{e}qômô* 'from his place', where *mâqôm*

[84] Cf. the use of the stem *n-d-d* for the exile of the Ephraimites (Hos. vii 13; ix 17) and in the prophecy of the destruction of the Ammonites (Jer. xlix 6). *N-d-d* is also used of insomnia (see Esth. vi 1; Gen. xxxi 40).

[85] Rashi glosses *nôded/et* 'wandering' as a state of being dragged from place to place. Ibn Ezra explains that bird and man wander "in search of sustenance." Isaac Arama understands *nôdedet* as the bird's being driven out of the nest and forced to wander the wide world to seek its own prey. Delitzsch (*Proverbs of Solomon* I, pp. 203–204) understands *nôdedet* as roaming without any direction and goal, similar to the idiom *nāʿ wānād* of Cain's destiny as "a ceaseless wanderer on earth" (Gen. iv 12b), and not as migration to warmer countries. LXX renders *n-d-d* differently in the two stichs and adds the notion of human slavery: "As when a bird flies down from its own nest, so a man is brought into bondage whenever he estranges himself from his own place."

[86] Gemser (*Sprüche Salomos*, p. 96) posits sociocultural circumstances for traveling, such as trade or a search for knowledge (cf. Sir. xxix 24; xxxix 5).

means "home and family" (cf. 1 Sam. ii 20) or "homeland" (cf. Gen. xviii 33, xxx 25; Judg. xi 19; Ezek. xii 3), may indicate the attitude of the wise towards the phenomena of wandering, similar to abandoning one's secure habitat. The general formulation of the saying presents a universal perception of the phenomenon of wandering in a person's life, which is similar to a bird's urge to migrate.

The various phenomena drawn from the avian world that appear in the Bible reflect daily experience of and familiarity with their lives and habits; for example, "Even the stork in the sky knows her seasons, and the turtledove, swift and crane keep the time of their coming" (Jer. viii 7). Here we see how people in ancient times were attuned to birds' seasonal migration. The Song of Songs notes the species associated with the seasons of the year: "For now the winter is past, the rains are over and gone. The blossoms have appeared in the land, the time of pruning has come; the song of the turtledove is heard in our land" (Song ii 11–12). In Job we encounter the ancients' knowledge that birds migrate to warmer lands: "Is it by your wisdom that the hawk grows pinions, spreads his wings to the south?" (Job xxxix 26).

To sum up, in the equation bird = human being and driven from the nest = leaving one's home, the accent is on wandering in the bird's life and human migration, without particular attention to personal or societal circumstances. The concision of the saying scarcely allows us to divine the teacher's own evaluation of wandering (e.g., Prov. xxiii 4–5, xxvi 2). But the two locatives, "from its nest" and "from the home," do suggest that wandering is perceived as especially evocative of uprootedness and alienation from home.[87]

[87] McKane (*Proverbs,* p. 612) interprets this wandering as a metaphor not only for transience and insecurity, but also for rootlessness and loss of identity, which prevent a person from integrating in society. Murphy (*Proverbs,* p. 207) raises the possibility of interpreting the wandering bird "as a symbol of the fluctuations and inconsistencies in human existence."

2.2.2 *Animal Imagery as a Rhetorical Device in the Moral of an Instruction*

2.2.2.1 *ʾĂlāpîm 'Oxen, Cattle' and Šôr 'Ox' in an Antithetical Saying*[88]

> Without oxen, there is no grain; [but] a rich harvest comes through the strength of an ox. (Prov. xiv 4)

The Animals[89]

The singular noun *ʾelep,* which is not found in the Bible, is attested in Ugaritic *ʾalp* '[head of] cattle, bullock, yearling calf'; in Phoenician *ʾelep* 'ox, bull', and in Akkadian *alpu* 'bull, ox, beef'.[90]

The plural *ʾălāpîm* indicates livestock, cattle, as in the verse "as for the cattle and the asses that till the soil they shall partake of salted fodder" (Isa. xxx 24), and, in poetry, as the governed noun in a construct, "the calving of your herd" in parallel with "the lambing of your flock," i.e., offspring of your large and small cattle (Deut. vii 13; cf. xxviii 4, 18, 51).[91]

The Text

Some of the sayings in the book of Proverbs encourage farmers to be diligent; for example, "He who tills his land shall have food in plenty, but he who pursues vanities is devoid of sense" (xii 11). The teacher praises the clever herdsman who knows how to make fullest use of his herds: "Mind well the looks of your flock, pay attention to your herds. ... The lambs will provide you with clothing, the he-goats the price of a field. The goats' milk will suffice for your food" (xxvii 23–27). He

[88] On the structure of the antithetical saying, see §1.5.1.2.

[89] On *šôr* 'ox' see §2.1.3.2.

[90] See Militarev-Kogan, *SED*, No. 4.

[91] See BDB, *ʾelep,* p. 48,. The collocation *kebeś ʾallûp* 'docile (?) lamb' (Jer. xi 19; cf. xiii 21) means the bellwether. The technical term *ʾallûp* may have been borrowed from the semantic field of domesticated animals to indicate the head of the family or chief of the tribe, as in Gen. xxxvi 15: "These are the chiefs of the sons of Esau" (RSV). Militarev-Kogan (*SED*, No.4) claim that *ʾallûp* = "cow, bull" (Ps. cxliv 14; Sir. xxxviii 25) "is probably rebuilt after a secondary derivational pattern" and should not be related to the proto-Semitic root *ʾlp* 'domesticate' and Hebrew *ʾlp* 'learn, teach', since the noun is much more widely attested in Semitic languages than the verb.

also praises the wise farmer who knows how to make best use of the vegetation on his plot throughout the seasons of the year: "Grass vanishes, new grass appears, and the herbage of the hills is gathered in" (xxvii 25). Economic planning to take maximum advantage of the productive capacity of one's land and livestock merit the sage's praise as guarantors of the farmer's prosperity. In contrast, the lazy man is denounced for not being bright enough to take proper care of his vineyard and obtain a proper vintage from it (xxiv 30–32).

Our saying, which extols planning ahead and maintaining a balance between consumption and production, is formulated as the antithetical juxtaposition of two economic options: The rendering of the word *bār* is crucial for understanding this adage. If it is understood to mean "grain," as in Gen. xli 35 and Prov. xi 26, the first clause means that the absence of cattle explains why the granary remains full, while the second clause proposes a direct relation between the strength of the ox and the size of the harvest.[92]

Read this way the statement is enigmatic. What profit can the owner gain from a crib full of grain because he has no cattle, if without oxen he will have no harvest?

To get around this, the ancient versions and some medieval commentaries understand *bār* to mean, not "grain" but "clean," from the root *b-r-r* (cf. Job xi 4; Ps. xxiv 4) in the sense of "emptiness."[93] This resolves the logical difficulty, in that we now have antithetical circumstances that produce antithetical results: without oxen the crib is *empty,* but it takes the strength of only one ox to *fill it*. This contrast of depletion and plenitude highlights the advantage of the second option. But *bār* 'clean, pure' is a strange adjective to apply to an empty crib.[94]

Gersonides, who took *bār* to mean "grain," read the verse as presenting two different pictures of agricultural life. In the first, the granary remains full because of a lack of oxen; in the second, the strength

[92] Compare *ʾēbûs* with the Akkadian *abūsu* 'storehouse, crib' [*CAD* A, p. 92]). For occurrences of *ʾēbûs* 'crib', see Jer. l 26; Isa. i 3; Job xxxix 9. *Bar* can mean "grain" as opposed to straw (see Jer. xxiii 28). Stored-up grain indicates prosperity and blessing (cf. Gen. xli 49; Amos viii 6; Ps. lxv 14; lxxii 16); a shortage of grain is considered to be a curse (see Prov. xi 26).

[93] See *HALOT* 1:153, s.v. II *bar*.

[94] Ibn Ezra holds that the solution lies in the distinction between "the crib is clean" in singular, and "rich harvest" in plural. Many commentators follow the sense of *bar* as "empty," see e.g., Gemser, *Sprüche Salomos*, p. 66; Toy, *Proverbs*, pp. 282–83; Murphy, *Proverbs,* p. 103.

of the oxen increases the supply of grain. According to Gersonides, we must distinguish between cattle that are being readied for slaughter and remain in their stalls from draft animals that graze in the field. Our saying describes a situation of the first type that enables the farmer to enjoy the second type, where the strength of the work ox increases his harvest.[95]

Yosef Ibn Kaspi resolves the difficulty of the first clause in a different way. He proposes emending the text and replacing the *yôd* of *b*^{e}*ʾên* with a *wāw,* yielding *b*^{e}*ʾôn* 'with the strength' (cf. Gen. xlix 3); as he puts it, "through the strength of the oxen a man acquires a crib of grain."[96] This turns the verse into a chiastic synonymous parallelism:

Through the strength [*b*^{e}*ʾôn*] of oxen ***there is a crib of grain***

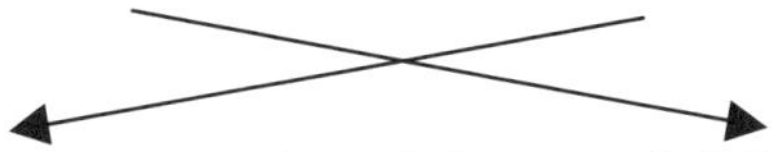

And a rich harvest comes through the strength [*b*^{e}*kōaḥ*] of the ox.[97]

This interpretation, attractive as it is on its own, does not suit the larger context of the chapter, which consists almost entirely of verses based on antithetic parallelism (xiv 1–35, except for vv. 17, 19, 26, 27).

Another suggested emendation, of *ʾēbûs* to *ʾepes,* seems plausible, and preserves the antithetical relation between the two clauses: without oxen, there is no (*ʾepes*) grain; [but] a rich harvest comes through the strength of an ox. Such a contrast between *ʾepes* and *rōb* is found in "A numerous [*b*^{e}*rob*] people is the glory of a king; without [*b*^{e}*ʾepes*] a nation a ruler is ruined" (Prov. xiv 28).[98]

2.2.2.2 *K*^{e}*pîr 'Lion' in an Antithetical Saying*

> The rage of a king is like the roar of a lion; his favor is like dew upon the grass. (Prov. xix 12)

[95] Ad loc. in Gersonides, Commentary, in *Mikraʾot gedolot.*

[96] Yosef Ibn Kaspi, *Ḥăṣoṣ*^{e}*rot Kesep* (Trumpets of Silver), in *ʿĂśārâ K*^{e}*lê Kesep* (Ten Instruments of Silver), ed. Isaac Last (Pressburg, 1903; repr. Jerusalem, 1969/70).

[97] Cf. Kahana, *Mishley*, p. 64; N. H. Tur Sinai, *Pešuṭo šel Miqraʾ* 4/1 (Jerusalem, 1967), p. 98.

[98] Cf. *ʾepes* in Isa. xli 12 and the emended reading of *ʾapaʿ* to *ʾepes* in v. 24 (*BHS*; cf. v. 29). For the proposed emendation of *ʾēbûs* to *ʾepes*, see Toy, *Proverbs*, p. 282; *BHS* ad loc.

The Animal

The consensus among medieval Jewish grammarians, based on contextual exegetics, is that *k^{e}pîr* is *ʿûl yāmîm* 'infant'; that is, a young lion larger than a cub and to be distinguished from the other words for lion: *ʾaryēh* (*ʾărî*), *layiš, lābîʾ*, and *šaḥal. K^{e}pîr* occurs as the nomen regens in *k^{e}pîr ʾărāyôt* 'young lion of lions' (Judg. xiv 5), a construction similar to *g^{e}dî ʿizzîm* 'kid of she-goats'. It also occurs in parallel to lion cubs: "Like lions (*kakk^{e}pirîm*), they roar together, they growl like lion cubs" (Jer. li 38). The main source for this meaning, however, is the verse "And she brought up one of her whelps; he became a young lion, and he learned to catch prey; he devoured men" (RSV; Ezek. xix 3).[99] It is hard to interpret *k^{e}pîr* as a young lion in other contexts where it is parallel to *ʾaryēh, šaḥal,* and *lābîʾ* (see Job iv 10; xxxviii 39), but that can be understood as poetic license.

The image of the lion, monarch of the animal kingdom, was commonly utilized to represent human kings. The lion's roar appears three times in the Book of Proverbs (xix 12, xx 2, xxviii 15), introduced in two of these cases by the comparative *kāp*. The first two occurrences involve the simile "like the roar of a lion" occurs twice, likened respectively to a king's rage and the dread caused by him.

The literary image of the lion's roar is often associated with its hunger: it roars before it leaps on its prey: "Their roaring is like a lion's, they roar like the great beasts; When they growl and seize a prey, they carry it off and none can recover it" (Isa. v 29). Intense cruelty characterizes the hungry lion, while the verb "roar" is used metaphorically for human mental distress: "I roar because of the turmoil in my mind" (Ps. xxxviii 9b).[100]

The Text

Our present saying compares two regal creatures: the lion, "king of the beasts" and the ruler of a human society. The lion's roar and the king's rage symbolize the temperament of rulers who react angrily to

[99] See: David Qimḥi, *Sefer Hashorashim*, s.v. *k-p-r;* BDB, p. 498. In *k^{e}pîr ʾărāyôt* (Judg. xiv 5), Tur-Sinai proposes emending *k^{e}pîr* to *kabbîr* 'great' (*bêt* replacing the *pê*), indicating the lion's large size rather than young age (*Halašon vehasefer* I [Jerusalem, 1948], pp. 380–82).

[100] The noun *naham* 'growl, roar, moan' also pertains to bears (Isa. lix 11), waves (Isa. v 30), and human voices in distress (Prov. v 11; Ezek. xxiv 23).

their subjects, whom they seek to keep under their control. Because the ruler's policy and decisions are unpredictable, the king's subjects must act with extreme caution so as not to arouse his fury and seal their fate: "The terror of a king is like the roar of a lion; he who provokes his anger risks his life" (Prov. xx 2).

Kings are likened to beasts of prey from whom it is difficult to escape: "A roaring lion and a prowling bear is a wicked man ruling a helpless people" (Prov. xxviii 15; cf. Hos. xiii 8). It follows that the ability to pacify an enraged king is highly valued: "The king's wrath is a messenger of death but a wise man can appease it" (Prov. xvi 14).

The second clause of our saying, "his favor is like dew upon the grass," conveys an ideal pastoral scene: "his favor" means the king's grace and good will toward his subjects.[101] The phrase "the king's favor" recurs in Proverbs (xiv 35, xvi 13) with precisely this meaning and is similar to the use of *rāṣôn* 'favor' with regard to God, in the prayers of the righteous: "A good man earns the favor of the Lord" (Prov. xii 2); "The prayer of the upright pleases Him" (Prov. xv 8).[102]

The "dew upon the grass" to which the king's favor is compared is an image of natural renewal, used several times in the Bible as a simile for divine grace and blessing—"like dew from the Lord, like droplets on grass" (Mic. v 6b; cf. Hos. xiv 6a; Zech. viii 12). The withholding of dew is a curse: "That is why the skies above you have withheld [their] moisture and the earth has withheld its yield" (Hag. i 10).

A parallel simile compares the king's favor to a "rain cloud in spring" (Prov. xvi 15). The verse describes the sunny countenance of the king, whose face shines like a farmer's rejoicing at the sight of the clouds that augur the coming of the first rain. Similarly, the expression on the king's face makes his subjects happy.

Returning to our verse, the conjunction of lion and king in the first stich, where the king is angry, with the image of "dew upon the grass" in the second stich, where he is not, presents some difficulty. To

[101] Delitzsch (*Proverbs of Solomon* II, p. 27) interprets *rāṣôn* as a mental disposition toward kindness, opposed to *zaʿap* "ill-humor," based on the LXX τὸ ἱλαρόν 'favor, cheerfulness'. Hameʾiri (*Proverbs*, p. 188) interprets *rāṣôn* as placating the king.

[102] On the wisdom of doing what pleases God, a behavior typical of the righteous, cf. Prov. x 32; xv 8; Ps. xix 15. Ibn Ezra draws a circular argument of retribution: the king's rage rewards those who make him angry, while his goodwill rewards those who please him, in the same way that grass thirsts for the dew.

create thematic unity between them, Arnold Ehrlich would emend *kakk*^{e}*pîr* ‘like a lion’ to *kik*^{e}*pôr* ‘like frost’ (cf. Job xxxviii 28–29) and delete *naham* ‘roar’ as a secondary interpolation influenced by the common idiom *naham kakk*^{e}*pîr* ‘roar like a lion’ (cf. Prov. xx 2). This produces “The rage of a king is like frost; his favor is like dew upon the grass,” with the two poles of the king’s rage and favor balanced by two antithetical natural phenomena—the frost that damages crops and the dew that nourishes them.[103] In the context of all the “king sayings,” however, Ehrlich’s proposed deletion of *naham* ‘roar’ seems inappropriate. “His favor,” a common idiom in Proverbs, fits the moral of the saying. There is no need to harmonize the different semantic fields, fauna and climate, because each functions as a separate illustration associated with the didactic message.

To sum up, by linking the human monarch with the king of the animals the sage suggests the ideal conditions of good will and peace between subject and ruler. His admonition draws the reader’s attention to the king’s “favor” as opposed to the dire effects of his “rage.”

2.2.2.3 *K*^{e}*pîr ‘Lion’ in a Synthetic Saying*[104]

> The terror of a king is like the roar of a lion; he who provokes his anger risks his life. (Prov. xx 2)

Here the second clause complements the first. The first clause likens dread of a king to a lion’s roar; the second clause explains that a person who provokes the king’s wrath endangers his own life.

This saying is one of those about the norms of conduct between kings and their subjects.

The first clauses of Prov. xix 12 and xx 2 are similar in form and style,[105] except that the royal rage in the former is replaced by terror of him in the latter.[106] The second stich of the latter verse adds the complementary parallelism of the response that awaits one who arouses

[103] Ehrlich, *Psalmen, Sprüche und Hiob*, p. 110.

[104] On *k*^{e}*pîr* ‘lion’ see §2.2.2.2.

[105] The LXX^{A} varies the pattern: instead of ὁμοία ‘is like’ (xix 12a) it has οὐ διαφέρει ‘does not differ from’ (xx 2a).

[106] For the Hebrew *ʾêmâ* ‘terror’ (xx 2a) the LXX has ἀπειλή ‘threat’. The Syriac replaces “terror of the king” with “the king’s rage,” similar to the MT *ḥămat/zaʿap melek* (xvi 14 and xix 12). The *BHS* proposal to read here *ḥămat melek* ‘wrath of the king’ (cf. Prov. xvi 14), instead of *ʾêmat melek* (Prov. xx 2), parallel to *zaʿap melek* ‘rage of a king’ (Prov. xix 12) seems plausible, but the MT also suits the context.

the king's wrath, instead of the antithetical relation between the king's wrath and his favor proposed in xix 12b.

Despite the differences, both sayings have the same didactic goal of making courtiers' aware of the royal power and king's capriciousness. The terror inspired by a king, who intimidates his subjects, is exemplified by the impression created by the roars of the "king of the jungle."

The sage discusses the consequences for a courtier who has provoked the king's wrath. The verb *mitʿabbēr* 'provoking anger' is in a reflexive conjugation because of the reflexive effect of the doer's action: by arousing the king's wrath he brings harm upon himself.[107] *Mitʿabbēr* is a denominative, from *ʿebrâ* 'arrogance, fury' (cf. "raging anger" in Job xl 11). Some would emend *mitʿabbēr* by metathesis to *mitʿārēb* 'be involved', emphasizing that a subject's intrusion where he does not belong is liable to bring disaster on his own head.[108]

The Book of Proverbs instructs readers to conduct themselves carefully and with restraint when in the presence of the king. The short-tempered person is one of the principle targets of the sage's advice: "An impatient man commits folly; A man of intrigues will be hated" (xiv 17; cf. v. 29). The ideal is the calm person who controls himself and reacts carefully, thinking clearly and speaking reasonably. But the hot-tempered man stirs up strife and is soon drawn into situations of conflict and fighting: "A hot-tempered man provokes a quarrel; A patient man calms strife" (xv 18).[109]

The sayings that condemn negative behaviors are often marked by the notion of reward and punishment, as in the case of the adulterer: "Only one who would destroy himself does such a thing" (vi 32b). Those who ignore wisdom destroy themselves (viii 36). Here too the courtier who provokes the king's anger "risks his life" (xx 2b).[110]

[107] The reflexive meaning of the *hitpaʿel* form *mitʿabber,* from *ʿ-b-r* II (*HALOT,* 3: 737), refers to a person who brings his anger upon himself. On this aspect of the *hitpaʿel*, see Joüon and Muraoka, *A Grammar of Biblical Hebrew* I, pp. 157–60, §53. Gemser (*Sprüche Salomos*, 112) suggests the reading *mitʿabber weḥoṭēʾ*, explaining the *wāw* of *mitʿabberô* as the *wāw adaequationis*; i.e., the irritator of a king is likened to a person who sins against himself.

[108] On the alternative reading *mitʿārēb* 'meddling', see below, §3.4. Baumgartner believes that this alternative, attested in LXX^{A}, represents the interpolation of a marginal note by a later copyist. See Baumgartner, *Etude critique sur l'état du texte du Livre des Proverbes*, p. 183.

[109] On the hot-tempered type see §3.4.

[110] Ibn Ezra interprets *ḥôṭēʾ napšô* (xx 2b) as self-mischief done by a person who does not respect royalty and establishes a link to the word *kābôd* 'honor' in the next verse.

The principle of reward and punishment aims to preserve the social values and the social order. It accentuates the wisdom of obeying authority in its various forms, whether parents or king. A person's ability to control his own drives and to adopt moderate and prudent behavior suited to his social environment is a mechanism that preserves the social order and solidarity (cf. xv 18, 23, 27, 28, xvii 27).

2.2.2.4 *ʾĂrî 'Lion' and Dōb 'Bear' in a Comparative Saying*[111]

> [Like] a roaring lion and a growling [*or:* prowling] bear is a wicked ruler over a poor people. (Prov. xxviii 15; free translation)

In this analogy (which many translations render as a simile, although the comparative particle is missing in the Hebrew), a bad ruler is equated with two predatory beasts, a lion and bear.[112]

The Animals

The noun *dōb* 'bear' (*Ursus arctos*) appears in cognate Semitic languages: *dabû* in Akkadian (fem. *dabītu*), *db* in Ugaritic, *dubbāʾ* in Aramaic, *debbā* in Syriac, and *dubbun* in Arabic.

In the Bible, *dōb* indicates both males and females (*dubbāh* 'she-bear' is attested only in post-Biblical literature). It is always treated as a masculine noun, even when the context clearly refers to a female—e.g., *dōb šakkûl* 'a she-bear deprived of her cubs'[113]—except for 2 Kgs ii 24, where both the adjective *štayim* and the verbs are in the feminine.[114]

In the Bible the bear, one of the indigenous carnivores of Palestine, is a paradigm of the dangerous animal from which there is no escape.[115] It is frequently mentioned, along with the lion, as a particularly dangerous animal (2 Kgs ii 24; Hos. xiii 8; Lam. iii 10). It is described as a ferocious animal in one of Daniel's visions (vii 5). It appears among the wild animals in the dramatic scene of the Day of the Lord, as foreseen by the prophet Amos: "Ah, you who wish for the

[111] On the comparative saying see §1.5.1.1.
[112] Instead of a bear, the LXX has λύκος διψῶν 'a thirsty wolf'. The Vulgate restores the MT animal, but makes him *esuriens* 'hungry'.
[113] On the idiom *dōb šakkûl*, see §3.1.2.
[114] See Joüon-Muraoka, *A Grammar of Biblical Hebrew* II, p. 493, §134.
[115] Tristram (*The Fauna and Flora of Palestine*, p. 7) reported seeing a Syrian bear (*Ursus arctos syriacus*) in Wadi Hammam.

day of the Lord! Why should you want the day of the Lord? It shall be darkness, not light! As if a man should run from a lion and be attacked by a bear, or if he got indoors, should lean his hand on the wall and be bitten by a snake!" (v 18–19). The prophet Isaiah, on the other hand, describes the eschatological ideal world of peace and justice in which dangerous animals are no longer a threat: "The wolf shall dwell with the lamb, the leopard lie down with the kid; the calf, the beast of prey, and the fatling together, With a little boy to herd them. The cow and the bear shall graze" (xi 6–7a; cf. lxv 25).

The copresence of bear and lion in our proverb expresses a danger from which there is no possibility of escape, as in Lamentations: "He is a lurking bear to me, a lion in hiding" (iii 10; cf. Hos. xiii 8). In fact, the confrontation between a human being and lion and bear is considered to be the test of heroism and courage (cf. 1 Sam. xvii 37).

Although *ʾărî/ʾaryēh* is by far the most common term for the lion (*Panthera leo*), the Bible has more names for it than for any other wild animal: *layiš* [Akkadian *nēšu*; Aramaic *lētāʾ*; Arabic *layṯ*], *lābîʾ* [Akkadian *lābum*; Ugaritic *lbì*; Arabic *labuwatun*], *šaḥal,* and *k^epîr*. It is difficult to assign different stages of maturity to the different terms, except the construct *gûr ʾaryēh,* which apparently refers to the young lion still nursing from its mother (cf. Deut. xxxiii 22; Jer. li 38), and *k^epîr* 'young lion', mentioned in parallel to *gûr* 'whelp, young' (Ezek. xix 3).[116]

The Bible provides information about the lion's habitat and predatory activity in various parts of Palestine, including the hill country around Bethlehem (1 Sam. xvii 34), the environs of Bethel (1 Kgs xiii 24) and Timnah (Judg. xiv 5), near the headwaters of the Jordan (Jer. xlix 19, l 44), Samaria (2 Kgs xvii 25), Mt. Hermon and the Lebanon (Song iv 8), and the southern Negev on the road to Egypt (Isa. xxx 6).

The lion symbolizes boldness and audacity (cf. Amos iii 8). Human bravery is shown in turn by a man's willingness to face a lion (cf. Judg. xiv 6, 1 Sam. xvii 34, 2 Sam. xxiii 20).

The prophetic literature employs the folk motif of the lion sent by God to punish those who transgress His laws or disobey Him (1 Kgs xiii 24, xx 36; 2 Kgs xvii 25–26).

[116] For more on lions, and specifically the *k^epîr,* see §2.2.2.2.

The lion, king of the beasts, became the symbol of divine kingship.[117] Hence, its roar is compared to God's word to his prophets: "A lion has roared, who can but fear? My Lord God has spoken, who can but prophesy?" (Amos iii 8). Prophetic texts associate the Lord's might in his battle against adversaries with the image of the lion (Jer. li 38); in this context the lion's roar and teeth are used as metaphors for the enemy's threat (Isa. v 29 and Joel i 6, respectively).[118]

Like the bear, the lion will be tamed in the end of the days. Isaiah's juxtaposition of predator and prey, wild beasts and domesticated animals (wolf and lamb, leopard and kid, lion and calf, bear and cow, lion and ox) means that dangerous animals will no longer threaten others and that for Divine providence the preyed upon will have equal status with the strong (see Isa. xi 6–8).

The lion in his supremacy is closely associated with the king's royal status. Solomon's throne was flanked by two lions, while twelve more lions lined the six steps leading up to it (1 Kgs x 19–20). The lion is also one of the animals, along with the cherubim, that decorated the Ark that was Yahweh's symbolic throne in the Temple of Jerusalem (ibid.; cf. Ezek. i 10).[119]

The Text

The threatening aspects of a bad ruler are conveyed by the reference to a roaring lion. The same pattern appears in two other sayings about kings and rulers that refer to their tyrannical habits and the appropriate conduct in their presence (Prov. xix 12, xx 2; see discussion above).

The epithet attached to the second animal in the first stich, *dōb šôqēq* 'growling (*or* prowling) bear', is a hapax. The root *š-q-q* has been interpreted as referring to greedy thirst, as in "when a thirsty man dreams he is drinking and awakes faint, with his thirst not quenched" (Isa. xxix 8b [RSV]), where the idiom *nepeš šōqēqâ* (lit. 'pulsating throat') also appears in Psalms: "for He has satisfied the thirsty, filled

[117] For Mesopotamia, see Watanabe, *Animal Symbolism in Mesopotamia,* pp. 22–24, 42–53; for Egypt, literature see Emily Teeter, "Animals in Egyptian Literature," *HAWANE,* p. 267.

[118] See Keel, *The Symbolism of the Biblical World,* pp. 85–89.

[119] On the iconographic and symbolic uses of the lion, see Catherine Breniquet, "Animals in Mesopotamian Art," *HAWANE*, p. 161; Borowski, "Animals in the Religions of Syria-Palestine," *HAWANE*, pp. 405–7; Watanabe, *Animal Symbolism in Mesopotamia*, pp.112–16.

the hungry with all good things" (Ps. cvii 9).[120] Another interpretation is that *š-q-q* refers to the sound uttered by the bear about to attack, as suggested by Targum Jonathan's *dûbāʾ maṣrîāḥ* 'a female bear who raises her voice'.[121] Rashi agrees, observing that "*nehîmâ* for a lion and *šᵉqîqâ* for a bear are both terms of screaming." This rendering fits better with the image of the roaring lion.

Another possibility is that *š-q-q* means "charging." In the *hitpalpel* the verb is used to represent the frenzied movement of chariots through plazas—evidently as an onomatopoeic representation of the noise made by the wheels (Nah. ii 5).[122] Delitzsch combines the two meanings—the passionate desire for prey and the beast running back and forth as it yearns to pounce on its prey.[123]

These two ferocious beasts, lion and bear, are linked in another metaphor for unavoidable danger: "He is a lurking bear to me, a lion in hiding" (Lam. iii 10).

The saying in Proverbs offers a vivid picture of a lion and a bear hunting for prey. The beast's behavior is motivated by uncontrollable drives; the unpredictable behavior of the evil ruler resembles these urges. The second stich, "a wicked man ruling over a poor people," provides the reason for the condemnation of the ruler; namely that he takes advantage of his power and oppresses the poor. The equation of the wicked ruler with "a roaring lion" or a "growling [*or* prowling] bear" emphasizes his unrestrained appetite for power and the cruelty that produce a reign of terror for his subjects.

None of the sayings about kings in the book of Proverbs reflect any expectation of social reform or question their authority. They are, however, critical of the moral flaws of the ruler who exploits his authority to abuse the poor and weak. Ibn Ezra argues that the wickedness of the ruler in this saying is emphasized by its contrast with the

[120] Gemser (*Sprüche Salomos*, p. 114) supports the meaning "thirsty" from Ethiopian "to strive for, desire" (*š-q-q* II, *HALOT,* 4:1647), and Isa. xxix 8 and Ps. cvii 9.

[121] The Peshitta follows the Targum. For the semantic synonym of *h-m-h* 'murmur, growl', see Isa. lix 11; Song v 4; Jer. xxxi 20.

[122] In tannaitic Hebrew, the *hitpolel* of *š-q-q* means "desire strongly" (e.g., *b. Ketub.* 65a).

[123] Delitzsch, *Proverbs of Solomon* II, p. 231. Greenberg asserts a semantic link between *š-q-q* "yearning" and *š-q-q* "noisy," similar to the use of *ʿ-r-g* in Joel (i 20a) in association with both animal sounds and thirst. See Moshe Greenberg, "Noisy and Yearning: The Semantics of שק"ק and its Congeners," in M. V. Fox et al. (eds.), *Texts, Temples, and Traditions: A Tribute to Menahem Haran* (Winona Lake, IN, 1996), pp. 339–44.

benevolent ruler in the second half of the next verse: "A prince who lacks understanding is very oppressive; he who spurns ill-gotten gains will live long" (Prov. xxviii 16). He explains that the essence of the ruler's wickedness is that he is "very oppressive" and loves ill-gotten gains. Nevertheless, this wickedness is not an ingrained trait, but rather the lack of prudence of "he who lacks understanding" (v. 16a). The suffering of a people who groan under the yoke of a tyrant is invoked in the saying, "when the wicked dominate the people groan" (xxix 2b). The opposite of this picture is associated with reward, for "If a king judges the poor with equity, his throne will be established forever" (xxix 14; NRSV).

2.2.2.5 *K^e^pîr 'Lion' in an Antithetical Saying*

> The wicked flee though no one gives chase; but the righteous are as confident as a lion.[124] (Prov. xxviii 1)

The two clauses of this saying constitute an antithetical parallelism of the wicked with the righteous, connected by the adversative *wāw*.

The first stich incorporates a proverbial expression, "flee though no one gives chase," found in the literary tradition of imprecations: "You shall flee though none pursues" (Lev. xxvi 17b; cf. v. 36 and Deut. xxviii 7, 25). The disagreement in number between the singular subject and plural verb, in the first clause, and between the plural subject and singular verb, in the second clause, as well as the lack of clarity about the syntactical function of "wicked," require clarification. The early versions tend simply to restore the concord of subject and predicate here.[125] Another approach notes that the noun *rāšāʿ* 'wicked' is displaced to the end of the verbal clause: "[they] flee though no one gives chase—wicked." This suggests that it is intended as an appositive to the tacit subject of the verb *nāsû* 'they flee'.[126]

[124] On *k^e^pîr* 'lion' see above, §2.2.2.2.

[125] The LXX and Vulgate render the verb *flee* in the singular. *BHS* restores the verb to the singular by conjecturing that the *wāw* of *nāsû* is a dittograph from *w^e^ʾên*. In the second stich it reads "righteous" in the singular instead of the plural. The Targum renders the whole saying in plural.

[126] The perfect *nāsû* is not the past historical but a perfect denoting an action that, although completed in the past, extends its influence into the present and even into the future. See GKC, §106g.

The first clause depicts a wicked man who believes himself pursued despite the fact that no one is chasing him. The antithesis of the wicked person haunted by anxieties is the righteous man who is as confident as a lion. The root *b-ṭ-ḥ* occurs in formulas of the righteous man's trust in the Lord: "but he who trusts in the Lord shall be surrounded with favor" (Ps. xxxii 10b; cf. Prov. xvi 20, xxii 19).[127] The motif of trusting in divine grace is found in several contrasts between good and bad people in Proverbs: e.g., "A greedy man provokes quarrels, but he who trusts the Lord shall enjoy prosperity" (xxviii 25; cf. xxix 25).

The comparison of the righteous with the lion evokes the image of the crouching lion, the symbol of security and complacency. Similarly, the royal image of the lion is found in blessings, including Jacob's of Judah—"he crouches, lies down like a lion, like the king of beasts; who dare rouse them?" (Gen. xlix 9b)—and Balaam's of the Israelites—"They crouch, they lie down like a lion, like the king of beasts; who dare rouse them?" (Num. xxiv 9).

Confidence is also a trait of the mythological Behemoth in the Lord's speech in Job: "He is confident the stream will gush at his command" (Job xl 23b).

The crouching lion is a concrete illustration of the worry-free trust of the righteous man that informs the moral and religious perspective of our verse.[128] In contrast to the fearless lion and confident righteous man, the wicked man is assimilated to the sinner and the curse that befalls him: "the wicked flee though no one gives chase" (Prov. xxviii 1a). In its concision, the saying does not provide details of the reprehensible deeds committed by the wicked, who put their trust in violence and robbery (see Ps. lxii 11) and lose their faith in the Lord. Nor does it describe their flight as a response to a real pursuit, but rather as an metaphor of the contrast between the wicked and the righteous and their respective punishment and reward.[129]

[127] For the semantic development of the stem *b-ṭ-ḥ,* from "falling down" (Jer. xii 5) to "having confidence in somebody," see Samuel E. Loewenstamm and Joshua Blau, *Oṣar Lešon Miqra*ʾ, vol. II (Jerusalem, 1960), p. 153.

[128] On the dogmatic teaching of the saying, see McKane, *Proverbs*, p. 621.

[129] For the moral-religious sphere of this saying, see Hameʾiri, *Proverbs,* p. 262. Toy (*Proverbs*, p. 494) argues for the metonymic meaning of wicked and righteous as good conscience and bad.

2.2.2.6 *D^e^rôr 'Sparrow' in a Comparative Saying*[130]

> Like a bird (*ṣippôr*) in its flitting, like a sparrow (*d^e^rôr*) in its flying, a curse that is causeless does not alight. (Prov. xxvi 2; free translation)

The Animal

Ibn Ezra (Prov. xxvi 2) objects to identifying animal names—birds among them—stating that the identifications of birds offered by the early commentators are "like dreams without solutions." In fact, there is no consistency in how translators ancient and modern identify *ṣippôr* and *d^e^rôr*. For example, the same pair of *ṣippôr* and *d^e^rôr* is rendered by the Septuagint as "birds" and "sparrows" (in the plural!) in Prov. xxvi 2 and as "sparrow" and "turtle-dove" in Ps. lxxxiv 4. Modern English translators usually render *ṣippôr* as "sparrow" and *d^e^rôr* as "swallow" (e.g., RSV, NJPS and KJV of Ps. lxxxiv 4).[131]

For modern scholars, too, the identification of Hebrew words with particular species of birds is problematic, because in only a few cases do they have reliable Semitic cognates.[132] Nevertheless, it is commonly accepted that the *d^e^rôr* is the sparrow (*Domesticus passer*), a permanent resident of Palestine. The *d^e^rôr* nests near human habitations, in attics, gutters, windowsills, skylights, caves, crannies in rocks, and trees, but is not easily domesticated.[133]

The rabbis, who considered the collocation *ṣippôr-d^e^rôr* to be a single noun, gave the second element two meanings derived from folk etymology. The first associated it with *dûr* 'reside, dwell', corresponding to the habit of the *ṣippôr-d^e^rôr* to live near human habitations. The second derived it from the abstract noun *d^e^rôr* 'freedom, liberty', emphasizing the bird's trait of avoiding human authority (see *b. Bêṣah* 24a).

[130] On the comparative saying, see §1.5.1.1.

[131] Rashi identifies *d^e^rôr* (Prov. xxvi 2) as רונדלע, i.e. 'swallow' (=*s^e^nunit* in Hebrew). The ancient versions attach the same identification for other birds, such as *sûs*/*sîs* (e.g., LXX χελιδών and Vulgate *hirundinis*/*hirundo* in Isa. xxxviii 14; Jer. viii 7). For *ṣippôr* as a collective noun = "fowl," see above, §2.2.1.2.

[132] On the identification of animal names on the basis of Semitic cognates, see Firmage, "Zoology," pp. 1144, 1151, 1154; Militarev and Kogan, *SED*, No. 71.

[133] See Tristram, *Natural History of the Bible*, pp. 201, 204; Bodenheimer, *Animal Life in Biblical Lands* I, pp. 89, 183, 185; idem, *Animal Life in Palestine* (Jerusalem, 1935), pp. 156, 164; E. Smo'li, *Birds in Israel* (Tel Aviv, 1957), pp. 128, 170–71.

For the psalmist, the motif of the bird nesting near the temple altar is a poetic trope expressing the sense of protection and confidence felt by those who dwell near the Lord: "Even the bird (*ṣippôr*) has found a home, and the sparrow (*dᵉrôr*) a nest for herself" (Ps. lxxxiv 4a [RSV 3a]).[134]

Although *ṣippôr* and *dᵉrôr* appear as separate substantives here and in Psalms lxxxiv 4, in both cases the segregation of the elements of the compound into the parallel clauses is probably meant for poetic effect (cf. Ps. civ 17); thus we should understand both clauses refer to the same species.

In the Bible, the root *n-d-d* is generally applied to the migration of birds (cf. Isa. xvi 2; Prov. xxvii 8a) and the wanderings of human beings (Isa. xxi 15, xxxiii 3; Prov. xxvii 8b).[135] But the phrase *nōdēd kānāp* denotes also "moving/flapping a wing" (Isa. x 14), referring to movement or the fluttering of wings, and not seasonal migration.[136] Because the *dᵉrôr* is a permanent denizen of Palestine, the infinitive *lānûd* here should be understood as representing instead the root *n-w-d* 'move about'.[137]

The Text

The saying is composed of two consecutive images linked by the comparative *kāp* to a comparandum introduced by the adverb *kēn*. The second clause, which definitely refers to taking flight, clarifies and intensifies the tentative "flapping" or "flitting" of the preceding clause. This prepares us to find the link between the bird imagery of the first half of the verse and the moral lesson conveyed in its second half.

But what is the fate of the "causeless curse"? The Qere replaces the negative *lōʾ* with the object pronoun *lô*, which means that, instead of

[134] Cf. Isa. lx 8. For a similar perception among Eastern peoples, see Herodotus, *The Histories,* Book II, § 64.

[135] On the root *n-d-d,* see §2.2.1.2.

[136] *N-d-d* as motion is exemplified by *nāʿ wānād* (Gen. iv 12, 14); the same pair of verbs used to describe an earthquake in Isaiah (xxiv 20); and the swaying of a reed in the water (1 Kgs xiv 15).

[137] For the grammatical and semantic affinity between the geminate form *n-d-d* and *n-w-d* (i.e., ע"ע and ע"ו verbs), see Joüon and Muraoka, *A Grammar of Biblical Hebrew* I, pp. 212–22 (§80a) and 224–33 (§82a). Arama (*Yad Avshalom*, p. 85) distinguishes *lānûd* from *lāʿûp,* emphasizing the forced circumstances of the former, when a bird is thrust out of the nest for good, opposed to *lāʿûp*, which refers to seasonal migration.

harming its target, the curse will boomerang on the person who uttered it. This reading reflects a circular perception of divine retribution in which a vain curse returns to strike the person who utters it. But the bird image that is invoked as similar to the curse supports the Kethib, *lōʾ tābōʾ* 'will not arrive': the baseless curse hovers without ever alighting at its destination.[138]

A curse is uttered with the intent of bringing misfortune on its target. In the biblical view, any curse is endowed with magical powers that stalk the target (and his descendants) until it catches up with him; e.g., "All these curses shall befall you; they shall pursue you and overtake you, until you are wiped out. ... They shall serve as signs and proofs against you and your offspring for all time" (Deut. xxviii 45–46). The severity of the biblical punishment for cursing one's parents is evidence of the ancients' belief in the power of a curse: "Whoever curses his father or his mother shall be put to death" (Exod. xxi 17 [RSV]; cf. Lev. xx 9; Prov. xxx 11).

The wisdom context of our saying places curses in practical contexts and not merely in the religious and moral realm. The book of Proverbs warns against passing on to the master gossip about his servant, thus avoiding the latter's curse: "Do not inform on a slave to his master, lest he curse you and you incur guilt" (Prov. xxx 10). This practical advice is meant to reduce the friction between master and servant and to leave responsibility for household affairs (such as treating servants properly and avoiding their insults) to each master.[139] Qoheleth, too, warns against cursing a king or a rich man, because he will find out and, given his power, the curse will come back to haunt you: "Even in your thought, do not curse the king, nor in your bedchamber curse the rich; for a bird of the air will carry your voice, or some winged creature tell the matter" (Qoh. x 20 [RSV]).

Curses have real weight; but the authority of the wise may restrain the power of a *qilᵉlat ḥinnām*, an "unjustified and purposeless curse."[140] The analogy between the avian comparatum or vehicle and the comparandum or tenor, drawn from the ethical and magical sphere

[138] The ancient translations (LXX, Tg.) follow the Qere, i.e., the negative particle.
[139] McKane, *Proverbs*, p. 650.
[140] For the use of *ḥinnām* to mean "in vain, groundless," cf. Prov. i 11; iii 30; Ps. xxxv 7. On the potency of curses and blessings, cf. Gen. xxvii 33; Judg. xvii 2.

of life, tells us that just as the birds are in perpetual motion, so too an unjustified curse will not come to rest on its intended victim.[141]

2.2.2.7 *Ḥămôr 'Donkey' and Sûs 'Horse' in a Comparative Saying*

> A whip for a horse and a bridle for a donkey; and a rod for the back of dullards. (Prov. xxvi 3)

The Animals

The noun *ḥămôr* 'donkey' is attested in other Semitic languages; e.g., *imērum* in Akkadian, *ḥmr* in Ugaritic,[142] *ḥāmārā* in Aramaic, *ḥ*ᵉ*mārā* in Syriac, and *ḥimārun* in Arabic.

The Bible distinguishes among the male *ḥămôr* 'jackass', the female *ʾātôn* 'jenny', and the young male *ʿayīr,* as well as the wild ass or onager (*ʿārôd, pereʾ*). Donkeys are frequently mentioned in the Bible as beasts of burden and transport[143] and as work animals performing various agricultural tasks (see Deut. xxii 10; Isa. xxx 24, xxxii 20). The donkey's value in the ancient world is reflected by the laws that protected owners against the damage caused by its loss or injury.[144] Idioms like "saddle a donkey" (Gen. xxii 3; 1 Kgs xiii 23; 2 Kgs iv 24) and "dismount the donkey" (cf. Judg. i 14) are used to describe its daily use by the ancients; they often mark a turning point in the narrative or a crucial decision taken by the hero. E.g., "So Abraham rose early in the morning, saddled his donkey, and took two of his young men with him, and his son Isaac; he cut the wood for the burnt offering, and set out and went to the place in the distance that God had shown him" (Gen. xxii 3); or in the story of Achsah, Caleb's

[141] On the hermeneutic impact of the Qere *lô* see Delitzsch, *Proverbs of Solomon* II, pp. 174–75.

[142] Also "load" or a "measure of capacity" (like the Hebrew *ḥomer*). The Akkadian term *imērum* attested in Mari, MA, NA, and Nuzi, denotes too "ass-load". Firmage, "Zoology," p. 1156, n.2; Riede, *Im Spiegel der Tier*, p. 175.

[143] On the donkey as a means of transportation, see Exod. iv 20; Josh. xv 18; Judg. i 14; 1 Sam. xxv 20; 2 Kgs iv 24; as a beast of burden, see Gen. xlv 23; 1 Sam. xxv 18; 2 Sam. xvi 1; Neh. xiii 15. Domestic donkeys were probably present in the Levant during the-Chalcolithic period and their remains have been found in Arad, Israel, in the Early Bronze I-II levels. See Brian Hesse and Paula Wapnish, "An Archaeological Perspective on the Cultural Use of Mammals in the Levant," *HAWANE*, p. 470; Gilbert, "The Native Fauna," *HAWANE*, pp. 17–18.

[144] See Exod. xxiii 4, 5, 12; Deut. v 13; xxii 1–4, 10. Cf. the Code of Hammurabi in *ANET* (trans. Theophile J. Meek), pp. 163–77, §§7, 8, 244, 269.

daughter: "When she came [to him], she induced him to ask her father for some property. She dismounted from her donkey, and Caleb asked her, "What is the matter?" (Judg. i 14b) A similar pattern appears in the Ugaritic Legend of Aqhat, where "saddling a donkey" is an idiom for starting a journey: the hero's sister, Pagat, prepares the animal to carry their father to the drought-stricken field: "Weeping, she leads the donkey, weeping, ropes up the ass" (Aqhat, *CAT* 1.19, Tab. III, Col. II, lines 8–9).[145]

The donkey's typical obstinacy is a crucial element of the Balaam pericope (Num. xxii 21–30). His she-ass exemplifies the obedient animal who follows God's instructions and disobeys her master, as the story vividly depicts: "When the ass now saw the angel of the Lord, she lay down under Balaam; and Balaam was furious and beat the ass with his stick" (Num. xxii 27).

The noun *sûs* 'horse' has cognates in the Akkadian *sisûm*, Ugaritic *s̀s̀w*, and Aramaic *sûsyāʾ*.[146] Unlike the ox and donkey, which served primarily as beasts of burden, in the Bible the horse is used exclusively by the cavalry and chariots (see 2 Sam. viii 4, 1 Kgs x 26).[147] It is frequently depicted as drawing chariots in warfare (see Exod. xv 1; Isa. xxxi 1; Jer. xlvi 9). Its tackle—harness, bridle, and bit—are frequently invoked in metaphorical senses (Ps. xxxii 9; Isa. xxx 28).[148]

The war-horse provided an ideal image for human might and vanity, which lower moral standards and undermine the fear of God (cf. Isa. ii 7–10, xxx 15–17; Hos. xiv 4; Amos ii 15; Mic. v 9; Ps. xxxiii 17; Prov. xxi 31). We encounter close descriptions of the horse in various poetical passages that reflect the Israelites' familiarity with the animal. Thus the ancients speak with admiration of the horse's mane, its snorting nostrils, neigh, and beating hoofs, and, especially, its rapid gallop (cf. Job xxxix 17–25, 2 Kgs vii 6; Judg. v 22; Jer. viii 16; Isa. v 28).

[145] See Parker, *Ugaritic Narrative Poetry*, p. 69.

[146] The Sumerian word for horse, ANŠE.KUR.RA 'donkey of the mountains', supports the theory that the domesticated horse (*Equus caballus*) was introduced to the ancient Near East from–central Asia some time before the fourth millennium. See Gilbert, "The Native Fauna," *HAWANE*, pp. 16–17.

[147] Firmage, "Zoology," p. 1136. On the introduction of the horse to Palestine, see Bodenheimer, *Animal Life in Biblical Lands* II, pp. 363–67.

[148] Horse and chariot are metaphors of war (Jer. vi 23; Amos iv 10; Neh. iii 2; Ezek. xxxviii 4, 14; xxxix 20; Zech. x 3); their absence symbolizes the approach of peace (cf. Zech. ix 10).

The swiftness of the horse is likened to and considered even to exceed that of eagles, wolves, and leopards (cf. Jer. iv 13; Hab. i 8).[149]

The Text

The analogies in our verse appear in a verbless sentence composed of three noun phrases—two of two words each (in Hebrew), the third of three words—in which the prepositional *lāmed* serves as the copula between each beast and its corrective device. The comparative *kāp* is omitted before the two animal images. The third stich is introduced by the comparative *wāw* (*wāw adaequationis*) instead of the more common adverbial *kēn*, so that the tenor is the applicative clause. The lengthening of the third stich, by breaking the symmetrical structure of the first two, calls attention to the proverb's conclusion.[150]

The foolishness of the young and inexperienced boy passes as he matures into a young man. It is consequently crucial to educate him while he is still young so that he will not fall into immoral actions: "If folly settles in the heart of a lad, the rod of discipline will remove it" (Prov. xxii 15). Flogging with a stick is the standard educational method in the Book of Proverbs; in fact, *mûsār* means not only "instruction" but also a disciplinary beating, as in "He who spares the rod hates his son, but he who loves him disciplines him early" (xiii 24). A father must discipline his son to save him from sin: "Do not withhold discipline from a child; if you beat him with a rod he will not die. Beat him with a rod and you will save him from the grave" (xxiii 13–14).[151]

In contrast to the *ʾiwwelet* 'folly' of the boy, who needs a firm guiding hand because of his youthful gullibility, the *k*ᵉ*sîlût* 'stupidity,

[149] In Egyptian literature, the horse is "swift as a jackal" (*ANET*, p. 477a) and like "falcons in the midst of small birds" (ibid., p. 263a). The prophet Joel compares the invading locusts to horses harnessed to chariots (Joel ii 4).

[150] See Robert Gordis, "ʿal Mibneh Hashirah Haʿibrit Hakedumah," *Sefer Hashanah Lihude Amerikah* 5693 (New York, 1944), p. 146 [Hebrew].

[151] Whipping was perceived as an educational tool in Egyptian Wisdom Literature. The form *sb3y.t,* which semantically parallels *mûsār,* has the double meaning of instruction and corporal punishment. See Nili Shupak, *Where Can Wisdom Be Found?* (OBO 130; Fribourg, 1993), p. 31. On the association between beating with a stick and teaching in the Bible, see Prov. xiii 24; xix 18; xxii 15; xxiii 13; xxix 19; 1 Kgs xii 11; Sir. xxx 1–13; xxxiii 25–30. Three consecutive sayings in the Words of Aḥiqar support flogging as a method for educating the young; see Arthur E. Cowley, *Aramaic Papyri of the Fifth Century B.C.* (Oxford, 1967 [1923¹]), pp. 215, 222, col. VI [Sachau, plate 44], lines 80–82). Cf. Bezalel Porten and Ada Yardeni, *Textbook and Aramaic Documents from Ancient Egypt,* Vol. III: Literature, Accounts, Lists (Jerusalem and Winona Lake, IN, 1993), p. 49, Col. 12 [Sachau 53/44], lines 175–77.

foolishness, doltishness' of the *k^e^sîl* 'fool, dolt, dullard' is a pattern of behavior and thinking that depends on character. The *k^e^sîl's* stupidity perverts his moral values.[152] The *k^e^sîl* lacks intellectual keenness, as indicated by the following saying: "What good is money in the hand of a fool (*k^e^sîl*) to purchase wisdom, when he has no mind (*w^e^leb ʾāyin*)?" (xvii 16; cf. viii 5).[153] This type of *k^e^sîl* considers himself to be a wise person; because of his overconfidence he will not listen to reproof or counsel: "A wise man is diffident and shuns evil, But a dullard rushes in confidently" (xiv 16).

Complacency and mental sloth are the main characteristics of the *k^e^sîl*'s (lack of) judgment (i 32, x 23), thus causing failure (Qoh. ii 14, x 2, 15) and even self-destruction (Qoh. iv 5). The *k^e^sîl* becomes easily enflamed, invites blows, and picks fights (Prov. xviii 6–7, xix 1). He is unreliable, utters slander and lies (cf. x 18, 23, xiv 8) and hates knowledge (cf. xvii 16, xviii 2).

Because of the *k^e^sîl's* destructive influence on those around him, from both a social and legal perspective, he merits corporal punishment, in the hope of educating him: "A rebuke works on an intelligent man more than one hundred blows on a fool" (xvii 10). The same sanction is appropriate to the *ḥăsar lēb,* as in "Wisdom is to be found on the lips of the intelligent, but a rod is ready for the back of the senseless" (x 13; cf. xix 29).

Our saying invokes the technical terms *šôṭ* 'whip' and *meteg* 'bridle', used to curb and train beasts, in the context of the education of the *k^e^sîl*, thus placing the fool on the level of domestic animals. Strictly speaking, the *meteg* is the piece of metal or chain—the bit—placed in the animal's mouth, to which the reins are attached, e.g., "I will place My hook in your nose and My bit between your jaws; and I will make you go back by the road by which you came" (2 Kgs xix 28b, Isa. xxxvii 29). But it may also stand for the entire bridle, consisting of headstall, bit, and reins. *Meteg* 'bit' is joined to *resen* 'bridle' as means of controlling dumb animals: "Be not like a senseless horse or mule whose movement must be curbed by bit and bridle" (Ps. xxxii 9). The other devices used to train beasts, the *šēbeṭ* 'whip, rod' and its parallel, *šôṭ*, are also appropriate for those lacking in

[152] See Fox, *Proverbs 1–9*, pp. 41–42.

[153] The biblical idiom *ḥăsar lēb* 'one who lacks sense' and its Egyptian counterpart *iw.ty ḥ3.ty* both reflect the concept of the heart as the seat of thought and mind. See Shupak, *Where Can Wisdom Be Found?* pp. 199–200.

intelligence: "Wisdom is to be found on the lips of the intelligent, but a rod is ready for the back of the senseless" (Prov. x 13b; cf. xix 29).

Despite the existence in Aramaic of *mitgāʾ* 'bridle', the Targum has *maglᵉbāʾ* 'rod' for *meteg,* perhaps in an attempt to strengthen the parallel with the other two means of correction in the verse, *šôṭ* 'whip' and *šēbeṭ* 'rod'. Medieval Jewish commentators understood *meteg* as the bit in the animal's mouth and also as a whip. David Qimḥi (*Sefer Hashorashim*) suggested unlinking the meanings of *meteg* and *meteg śᵉpātayim* (2 Kgs xix 28): the *meteg*, like the *dorbān* 'goad' (cf. 1 Sam. xiii 21), is attached to the end of a wooden stick and used to spur the horse, whereas *meteg śᵉpātayim* is the iron bit placed in the animal's mouth. Because this is the only locus in the Bible that associates *meteg* with a donkey (Balaam uses a stick on his ass [Num. xxii 27]), some scholars suggest reading *meteg lasûs* and *šôṭ laḥămôr*. Others think that both devices are meant for application to both animals.[154]

The teacher uses the same terminology for training fools as for training animals, thus revealing his attitude towards the stupid pupil, who stands in sharp contrast to the gifted student who is aware of his surroundings. Although the teacher uses the terminology of physical control and corporal punishment, which is part of his conventional concept of education, his choice of devices that are primarily designed to control beasts gives the proverb about the *kᵉsîl* a sarcastic flavor.

2.2.3 *Animal Imagery as an Expression of Ethical Values*

2.2.3.1 *Šôr ʾĀbûs 'Fattened Ox' in a "Better-Than" Saying*

> Better a meal of vegetables where there is love, than a fattened ox where there is hate. (Prov. xv 17)

This saying employs the "better-than" pattern.[155] Its two parts present an object and its environmental condition—first the positive value and then the inferior one. It can be diagrammed as follows: A + 1 (the condition that makes *A* preferable) is *better than* B + 2 (the condition that make *B* unacceptable).

[154] See, e.g., Delitzsch, *Proverbs of Solomon* II, p. 175.
[155] On the "better-than" saying, see §1.5.1.3.

The saying juxtaposes material values—a simple meal of greens, a feast based on a fatted ox[156]—with moral values—love and hate. The moral value of love makes the modest meal of the poor outweigh a banquet accompanied by the unworthy moral value of hatred.

The Egyptian Instruction of Amenemope uses the "better-than" proverb in a similar context:

> Better is poverty in the hand of the god, than riches in a storehouse;
> Better is bread, when the heart is happy, than riches with sorrow.
>
> Better is praise as one who loves men, than riches in a storehouse;
> Better is bread, when the heart is happy, than riches with sorrow.[157]

Happiness, even in material poverty, is superior to the sadness of the wealthy. Feasting is perceived as a conducive to hatred and strife, whereas love lives among those who are satisfied with a meal of vegetables.

The phrase *šôr ʾābûs* 'fattened ox' does not refer to a crib-fed ox, but is a technical term for a delicacy served at a rich man's table.[158] It is contrasted to a "meal of vegetables," which is idiomatic for a poor man's meal. Indeed, the ancient versions and medieval Jewish commentators interpret this saying as a moral lesson, an appeal to host passers-by cordially and generously, despite a scarcity of food. Hate, associated with the fattened ox, refers to the host's insulting and scornful attitude.[159]

The saying presents a series of contrasting values on three levels, moral, emotional, and material. The "better-than" pattern preaches love and making do with modest means.[160] It is integrated thematically with two other sayings (vv. 16, 18) that speak of the avoidance of strife and the advantage of peaceful relations and modest means: "Better a little with fear of the Lord than great wealth with confusion" (v. 16; cf. xvi 8). The teacher wants his listeners to value domestic peace—"Better a dry crust with peace than a house full of feasting

[156] On the ox, see §2.1.3.2.

[157] Chap. 6, IX; chap. 11, XVI (*ANET*, pp. 422 and 423).

[158] Meat was considered to be food for the wealthy (1 Kgs i 19, 25; v 3 [RSV iv 22]; Neh. v 18). The root *ʾ-b-s* appears only in the *qal* passive present; for the plural form see 1 Kgs v 3 [RSV iv 22].

[159] The LXX renders *ʾărūḥâ* 'meal' as ξενισμός 'entertainment'. The technical term *ʾărūḥat tāmîd* 'a regular allotment of food' indicates the king's bounty to privileged subjects (2 Kgs xxv 30; Jer. xlii 34). McKane (*Proverbs*, p. 484) emphasizes the importance of hospitality as the main lesson of the saying.

[160] Murphy, *Proverbs*, p. 113.

with strife" (xvii 1; cf. xxi 9, xxvii 15)—and self-control, and denounces impulsive behavior that sets off strife: "A hot-tempered man provokes a quarrel, a patient man calms strife (xv 18).[161]

2.2.3.2 *Sûs 'Horse' in an Antithetical Saying*

> No wisdom, no prudence and no counsel can prevail against the Lord. The horse is readied for the day of battle, but victory comes from the Lord. (Prov. xxi 30–31)

The first part of the saying is composed of three consecutive short negatives, each introduced by the anaphoric *ʾên*—"no wisdom, no prudence and no counsel"—with the third linked directly to the predicate: "no counsel can prevail against the Lord." The second part offers a contrast across an adversative *wāw*: "The horse is readied for the day of battle, but victory comes from the Lord." The first sentence dismisses three intellectual qualities as of no avail against God's supremacy. The second sentence offers a concrete instance in which the Lord's strength overcomes the might of animals and His salvation frustrates human plans.

The war-horse symbolizes the vainglory of human striving against God's supremacy.[162] The human trust in military might, in cavalry and chariots, is perceived as a challenge to faith in God's power of salvation. This theological and philosophical idea is formulated in prophetic texts as well as in Psalms; for example, "They have put their trust in abundance of chariots, in vast numbers of riders, and they have not turned to the Holy One of Israel" (Isa. xxxi 1; cf. Ps. xx 8, lxxvi 7); "When you take the field against your enemies, and see horses and chariots—forces larger than yours—have no fear of them, for the Lord your God, who brought you from the land of Egypt, is with you" (Deut. xx 1).

The folly of expecting to gain the upper hand in battle by means of horses and chariots is also mentioned in Psalm xxxiii: "Kings are not delivered by a large force; warriors are not saved by great strength; horses are a false hope for deliverance; for all their great power they provide no escape" (vv. 16–17). Proverbs interprets the human skills

[161] Note the same use of the prepositional *bêt* in the third-person pronoun *bô*: "where there is hate" (v. 17) "great wealth with confusion" (v. 16).

[162] On the horse, see §2.2.2.7.

applied to planning and waging battle as a heretical questioning of the Lord's might; consequently, human beings are called on to curb their mental prowess in the presence of the Lord. The saying is, in a sense, a statement of the importance of fearing the Lord as the sole source of security, as in "Fear of the Lord is a stronghold, a refuge for a man's children. Fear of the Lord is a fountain of life, enabling one to avoid deadly snares" (Prov. xiv 26–27).

The dismissal of wisdom, prudence, and counsel seems incompatible with the teacher's admonitions to internalize those very qualities, which are normally perceived as vital to a successful life. Von Rad interprets the seeming contradiction as a sign of the teacher's concern about the potentially dangerous implications of empirical human wisdom in opposition to faith, for this saying belongs to a group of maxims (Prov. xvi 9, xix 21, xxi 2, xx 24) that "combines two things—man's confidence in his ability to master life and at the same time, with all the wisdom in the world, an awareness of the frontiers and a preparedness to fail in the sight of God."[163] McKane explains the different approaches as expressing different stages in the development of wisdom literature. According to him, our anti-intellectual saying belongs with the practical maxims that were reworked and edited in the spirit of a religious faith and emphasize the fear of God.[164] However, noting the contradiction in the sayings does not prove that the text reflects different stages in the development of the wisdom literature. Instead, the inconsistency may be the product of different co-existing schools—the family, the royal court, the prophetic circle—each with its own ethos. In like manner, biblical literature is interspersed with folk proverbs that are not necessarily chronologically linked to an ancient wisdom tradition.[165] In any case, it is difficult to sketch a conceptual line in which empirical wisdom was rewritten or processed into religious-moral wisdom. Moreover, any division between secular and religious wisdom in the ancient period is problematic and unreliable.[166]

[163] Von Rad, *Old Testament Theology* I, p. 440.

[164] McKane, *Proverbs*, pp. 10–22, and Table on p. 12; R. N. Whybray, *The Composition of the Book of Proverbs* (JSOTSup 168; Sheffield, 1994), pp. 21–32.

[165] See Eissfeldt, *Der Maschal*, p. 33.

[166] See Frederick M. Wilson, "Sacred and Profane? The Yahwistic Redaction of Proverbs Reconsidered," *The Listening Heart: Essays in Wisdom and the Psalms in Honor of Roland E. Murphy* (JSOTSup 58; Sheffield, 1987), pp. 313–32.

2.2.3.3 *ʿŌrēb 'Crow, Raven' and Nešer 'Vulture' in a Metaphorical Saying*

> The eye that mocks a father and disdains the homage due a mother –
> The ravens of the brook will gouge it out, young vultures will devour it.
> (Prov. xxx 17)

The Animals

The noun *ʿōrēb* 'crow, raven' (*Corvus spp.*) is found in other Semitic languages: Akkadian *ā/ēribum*, Aramaic *ʿurbā,* and Arabic *ġurābun.* In English, *raven* is an inclusive term for several types of birds, including crows, rooks and jackdaws. Close observation of the raven in nature reveals its cunning behavior in seeking out food and in protecting its young. It is not uncommon to see ravens beating their wings over their nest while making sounds of rage when a stranger approaches.

The expression "all varieties of raven" (Lev. xi 15; cf. Deut. xiv 14) attests to the ancients' acquaintance with many members of the genus Corvus. Some features of the black type (*Corvus corax*) are supported by the description of the lover in the Song of Songs: "His locks are curled and black as a raven" (v 11).[167] The "ravens of the brook" (Prov. xxx 17) may be similar to the ravens of Wadi Cherith, who fed Elijah.[168]

The raven serves as a messenger in several episodes in the Bible: in the narrative of the Flood the raven is sent out to see if the waters have receded (cf. Gen. viii 7),[169] and in the story of Elijah mentioned above, the raven is commanded by God to supply bread and meat to the prophet: "You will drink from the wadi, and I have commanded the ravens to feed you there" (1 Kgs xvii 4).

[167] See Firmage, "Zoology," p. 1158, n. 45; Yair Aḥituv, "*ʿŌrēb,*" *EM* 6:362 [Hebrew].

[168] Tristram (*Natural History of the Bible*, pp. 198–201) identified eight types of ravens in Palestine, including the black raven (*Corvus corax*), the brown-neck raven (*C. corax ruficollis*), the grey raven (*C. corone*), the short-tail raven (*C. rhiphidurus*), the *qaʾq* (*C. monedula soemmeringii*), and the seeding raven (*C. frugilegus frugilegus*). See also Aḥituv, "*ʿŌrēb,*" *EM* 6:362–64 [Hebrew].

[169] The raven (along with the dove and swallow) appears as a messenger in the Flood Tablet (XI) in the Babylonian Epic of Gilgamesh (*ANET*, pp. 94–95).

Ravens appear along with other predatory birds, with their negative connotations, in several prophetic scenes of desolation; for example, "Jackdaws and owls shall possess it; Great owls and ravens shall dwell there. He shall measure it with a line of chaos and with weights of emptiness" (Isa. xxxiv 11).[170]

Among the ancients, the raven as scavenger produced flourishing myth and folklore. Its aggressive behavior[171] helped give it the erroneous image of a cruel parent, as exemplified in Job: "Who provides food for the raven when his young cry out to God and wander about without food?" (xxxviii 41; cf. Ps. cxlvii 9).[172] But this misperception is contradicted by the raven's devotion to its nestlings, which it feeds even in midflight, as described in ancient Greek accounts.[173]

Seeing or hearing a single crow (*Corvus cornix*) was regarded as an ill omen; the raven (*Corax corax*), on the other hand, was regarded as a messenger.[174] Its cunning and predatory qualities made it an easy target for the superstitious and inspired many fables about it.[175]

Aristotle described the raven's habit of assaulting its victims and pecking out the eyes of its prey (as in our verse) in his *Historia animalium*: "It does not confine its attacks solely to the smallest creatures, but assaults even the ass and the bull, alighting on their necks to kill them and peck out their eyes" (IX, 609b5). Aristophanes, too, writes of the threat that crows will peck out the eyes of the flocks and oxen of those who continue to worship the Olympian gods.[176] The same motif turns into a curse in the pseudepigraphic Psalms of Solomon: "Let crows peck out the eyes of hypocrites for they devastated without honor houses of many people and greedily scattered them" (iv 20). Apparently the raven's habit of plucking out the eyes of its victims is triggered by its attraction to glittering objects—a tropism that has contributed to the common negative perception of the raven as a thief.

[170] In the picture of the desolation of Nineveh (Zeph. ii 14), *ḥōreb* is a corruption of *ʿōrēb* 'raven'; the correct text is attested by LXX κόρακες and Vulgate *corvus*. See also Riede, *Im Spiegel der Tier*, pp. 50–51.

[171] Breeding ravens react aggressively to any bird of prey that invades their territory. See Smoʾli, *Birds in Israel*, p. 45. The Book of Jubilees (xi 11–25) speaks of the farmers' delivery from ravens that eat the seeds out of their sown fields.

[172] See: *Lev. Rab.* 19:1; *Pirqe R. El.* 21 (end).

[173] See Aristotle, *Historia animalium* VI, 563b11.

[174] John Pollard, *Birds in Greek Life and Myth* (Plymouth, 1977), pp. 127–28, 182.

[175] See, e.g., Aesop's Fables 204, 206, 212, 312.

[176] Aristophanes, *Birds* 582; cf. *Acharnians* 92.

The *nešer* 'vulture'[177] is mentioned as a bird that hastens to eat carrion (Hab. i 8) and provides food for its chicks from the carcasses (Job xxxix 27–30; cf. Matt. xxiv 28). The prophet Micah describes its bald neck: "Shear off your hair and make yourself bald for the children you once delighted in; make yourself as bald as a vulture, for they have been banished from you." (Mic. i 16).

The Text

This metaphorical saying[178] consists of two complementary clauses, each a synonymous parallelism.[179] The link between them is the "mocking eye," which is the subject of the first half and the object of the second half.

> *The eye* that mocks a father, and disdains the homage due a mother
> The ravens of the brook will gouge *it* out, young vultures will devour *it.*

The very same mocking eye is gouged out by the winged predators, the "ravens of the brook" and "young vultures."

The book of Proverbs contains numerous admonitions to honor one's parents in the spirit of the biblical precepts (cf. Exod. xx 12; Deut. v 15) and warns against scorning or cursing them: "One who reviles his father or mother, light will fail him when darkness comes" (Prov. xx 20); "There is a breed of men that brings a curse on its fathers and brings no blessing to its mothers" (xxx 11).[180]

Our saying uses figurative speech to drive home the importance of honoring one's parents. Here the son is represented by synecdoche as the mocking eye, recalling the wayward son who reviles his father and mother (Prov. xxx 11).[181]

In the Bible, the eye as a sensory organ, like the ear, is an organ of instruction, internalization, and obedience: "The ear that hears, the eye that sees—The Lord made them both" (Prov. xx 12). In our saying, however, the eye expresses the son's scorn for his parents.

[177] On *nešer* 'vulture', see §2.1.1.2.
[178] On the metaphorical saying, see §1.5.1.5.
[179] On different criteria for classifying parallelism, see Schökel, *A Manual of Hebrew Poetics*, pp. 52–57.
[180] See also Prov. xxiii 22; xxviii 24 compared with Exod. xxi 17; Deut. xxvii 16. On the educational role of the father and mother in Proverbs, see i 8; iv 3; vi 20; x 1; xv 20; xix 26; and Sir. iii 1–18. On the parental role in Deuteronomy, see Weinfeld, *Deuteronomy and Deuteronomic School*, pp. 309, 277–78.
[181] Kahana (*Sefer Mishley*, p. 142) comments that "the eye stands for the entire person, since it is the part of the body that is the window to the soul."

The collocation *yiqqăhat ʾēm*, used in parallel with *ʾāb* 'father', is interpreted in two different senses: (1) The ancient versions opted for "aged mother." The same idea appears in a similar admonition that uses the root *z-q-n:* "Do not disdain your mother when she is old" (Prov. xxiii 22b).[182] (2) *Yiqqăhat* combines two meanings in one—"gathering in" (KJV) and "obedience" (RSV), as in *yiqqᵉhat ʿamîm* (Gen. xlix 10)—interpreted as referring to being gathered together under the discipline and authority of someone. Here in Proverbs this would be the mother's authority.[183]

Both interpretations show a clear tendency to understand *yiqqăhat* as referring to a mother's authority and the son's obligation to honor his parents.

The grammatical switch from the nominative in the synonymous pairs of the opening line to the accusative in the synonymous pairs in the second line shapes the logical pattern of the deed-consequence nexus. This inversion fits with the perception of retribution in the saying: the eye that sinned in the opening strophe is the one being punished at the end. The image of the eye—mocking at first, gouged out and devoured in the end—shapes the circular principle of retribution.[184]

This paradigm of "cause and effect" or "deed-consequence nexus," found in many proverbs (see e.g., xxi 15, 21, 23, 25), argues in favor of complying with the moral principles of the social order.[185] A

[182] The LXX has γῆρας μητρός 'the old age of a mother'; cf. Tg. *qšîšutʾ* and Syr. *sybwtʾ*. Driver ("Some Hebrew Words," p. 394) compares the Ethiopic *lhq* 'old'. Thomas suggests the root *l-h-q* for the reading of *lᵉhāqā* or *lᵉhīqā* (D. Winton Thomas, "A Note on lyqat in Prov. xxx.17," *JTS* 42 [1941], 154–55). Greenfield holds that the ancient versions of 1 Sam. xix 20 and Prov. xxx 17 are based on traditions that recognized the existence of two homonymous roots *l-h-q* in BH, to be divided into **l-h-q* I 'adhere, join' (1 Sam. xix 20) and **l-h-q* II 'be hoary, old' (LXX of Prov. xxx 17). See Jonas C. Greenfield, "Lexicographical Notes I," *HUCA* 29 (1958), pp. 212–14.

[183] Ibn Ezra understands *yiqqăhat ʾēm* as the company of the mother, emphasizing her educational role (cf. Gersonides ad loc.). Rashi manages to merge the two senses by relating "gathering" to the wrinkles on an elderly mother's face (cf. Hameʾiri, *Proverbs*, p. 285). Ibn Janaḥ (*Sepher Haschoraschim,* s.v. *y-q-h*, pp. 202–203), invoking the Arabic root *yqhh,* meaning obedience and obeisance, understands *yiqqăhat ʾēm* as submission to the mother's educational authority.

[184] On the association between mockery and reviling, cf. "He who mocks the poor affronts his Maker" (Prov. xvii 5). On mockery associated with retribution, cf. "I will laugh at your calamity, and mock when terror comes upon you" (Prov. i 26).

[185] On the "deed-consequence nexus," see Koch, "Is there a Doctrine of Retribution in the Old Testament," pp. 57–87; Boström, *The God of the Sages,* pp. 90–96;

scornful and mocking attitude to one's social milieu is imprudent: "He who speaks contemptuously of his fellowman is devoid of sense; a prudent man keeps his peace" (Prov. xi 12). In contrast, he who behaves moderately, with patience and self-control, is to be praised for conducting himself wisely: "A hot-tempered man provokes a quarrel; a patient man calms strife" (xv 18). The topos of the foolish and disgraceful son (x 1, xv 20, xvii 21, xix 13a) includes offensive behavior towards parents as conduct to be condemned.

For the traditional medieval commentators (e.g., Rashi, Ibn Ezra), not only does the raven symbolize the son's punishment, it also stands for ethical and social values. In their readings, the mocking eye links up with the image of the raven and the vulture as associated with the theological notion that the Lord cares for and feeds all his creatures: "who gives the beasts their food, to the raven's brood what they cry for" (Ps. cxlvii 9; cf. Luke xii 24). The same concept, that the nestlings would starve were it not for Lord's help, is found when God speaks out of the whirlwind: "Who provides food for the raven when his young cry out to God and wander about without food?" (Job xxxviii 41). Here the motif of the ravens' cruelty toward their young is employed to illustrate the fate of the son who abuses his parents.

The application of the principle of divine retribution to the son who mocks his parents echoes the familiar curse motif of the desecration of the dead when carrion birds eat their flesh.

The insertion of this image within the sequence of numerical sayings in Prov. xxx 15–33 is problematic. Some scholars associate the son in this saying with the haughty and rebellious "breed of men … ready to devour the poor of the land" (v. 14), whose conduct suggests the insatiable appetite of the "rebellious son": "This son of ours is disloyal and defiant; he does not heed us. He is a glutton and a drunkard" (Deut. xxi 20). In like manner, the conjunction of drunkard and overeater with mocking scorn and disobedience to one's parents in Prov. xxiii 19–22 provides the thematic unity between our saying and the concise description of insatiable Sheol in the numerical proverb: "Three things are insatiable; four never say, 'Enough!' Sheol, a barren womb, Earth that cannot get enough water, and fire which never says, 'Enough!'" (Prov. xxx 15b–16). Other scholars cite the son's disdain for his parents and propose its thematic continuity with the series of

Whybray, *The Book of Proverbs*, pp. 119–122; Waltke, *Proverbs 1–15*, pp. 73–76.

statements about the generation's moral decline (Prov. xxx 11–14), which includes the denunciation of "the breed of men that brings a curse on its fathers and brings no blessing to its mothers" (v. 11).[186] It seems likely that the inclusion of our proverb in its present context derives from the mention of the vulture both in this saying and in the numerical saying that views the vulture as a wonder of nature: "How the vulture makes its way across the sky" (Prov. xxx 19).

In the book of Proverbs, a common theme or subject (e.g., sayings about the fool, the sluggard, and the evildoer) is frequently the organizing principle. But key words, imagery, language, and even tone also serve to organize it, as here.[187]

APPENDIX: HUNTING TECHNIQUES IN BIBLICAL POETRY

The various methods of hunting have inspired biblical poetry and prose. The psalmist employs terms borrowed from various forms of hunting to describe both the distress of the persecuted righteous and the retribution meted out to the evildoer. Thus any investigation of images or metaphors based on this semantic field requires technical analysis.[188]

There are at least four technical terms associated with trapping: *Paḥ yôqᵉšîm* 'fowler's trap', *rešet* 'net', *mōqᵉšîm* 'snares', and *ḥăbālîm* 'ropes'. There are also three associated methods: hiding traps, spreading cords, and setting nets.

> *Ps. cxxiv 7:* We are like a bird escaped from the fowler's trap; the trap broke and we escaped.
>
> *Ps. cxl 6:* The arrogant have hidden a trap for me, and with cords they have spread a net, along the road they have set snares for me. (NRSV)

[186] On thematic association with the rebellious generation, see Ibn Ezra ad loc.; among modern commentators, see: Tur-Sinai, *Mišley Šᵉlomoh* (Tel Aviv, 1947), p. 384; Toy, *Proverbs*, pp. 529–30; McKane, *Proverbs*, p. 636.

[187] On the organization and redaction principles of Proverbs, see Whybray, *The Composition of the Book of Proverbs*, pp. 62–129. On contiguous themes of the vulture in nearby literary units, see ibid., p. 152.

[188] For a detailed philological discussion of hunting terminology, see Dhorme, *The Book of Job*, pp. 261–62. For iconography of various methods of hunting in antiquity, see Keel, *The Symbolism of the Biblical World*, pp. 89–95.

Several hunting metaphors punctuate the speech of Bildad the Hushite (Job xviii 8–10) to convey the instability of the evildoer's prosperity.

> He is led by his feet into the net (*rešet*); he walks into the toils (*śᵉbākâ*).
>
> The trap (*paḥ*) seizes his heel; the noose (*ṣammîm*) tightens on him.
>
> The rope (*ḥebel*) for him lies hidden on the ground; his snare (*malkōdet*) on the path.

Here we encounter three more technical terms: *śᵉbākâ*, *ṣammîm,* and *malkōdet*, in synonymous parallelisms that link each with one of the terms we have already looked at: *śᵉbākâ* and *rešet*, *ṣammîm* and *paḥ, malkōdet* and *ḥebel.*[189]

The hunting terms in Job xviii 8–10 merit some attention. The terminology discussed below follows their order of occurrence as established by the pattern of poetic parallelism ($1^{a\text{-}b}$, $2^{a\text{-}b}$, $3^{a\text{-}b}$).

1^{a} *Rešet* 'net': The net seizes the victim by its legs (Ps. ix 16; xxv 15).

1^{b} *Śᵉbākâ* 'toils, latticework': This term denotes a net[190] stretched over a pit or trench, as described by Ben Sira: "walking over a net" (ix 13).

2^{a} *Paḥ* 'snare': The term *paḥ* denotes a snare for birds (cf. Jer. xlviii 44; Amos iii 5; Ps. cxxiv 7; Prov. vii 22; Qoh. ix 12). It is laid (cf. Jer. xviii 22; Amos iii 5; Ps. cxl 6, cxlii 4) on the path of the intended victim (cf. Hos. ix 8; Ps. cxlii 4; Prov. xxii 5).[191]

2^{b} *Ṣammîm* 'trap, noose': This hapax is usually rendered as "net" or "meshwork," but its nature and mode of operation are unclear. The root *ṣ-m-m*, from which *ṣammâ* 'veil' (see

[189] *Paḥ* is also associated with *ḥăbālîm* in Ps. cxl 6 [RSV 7].

[190] Cf. "nets of meshwork" in 1 Kgs vii 17 and 2 Kgs i 2. Dhorme (*The Book of Job*, p. 261) points to the Arabic *šabaka* 'be intertwined', from which are derived *šabakeh* 'net' and *šubbâk* 'net', in support of Hebrew *śᵉbākâ* = "network."

[191] Ehrlich provides the real background of Amos' metaphoric question, "Does a trap spring up from the ground unless it has caught something?" (iii 5), with a detailed description of the operation of the trap: "The *paḥ* is concealed in the earth, with its upper surface level with the earth. When the bird treads on the surface, two halves of a trap rise up on each side … and close in on the bird inside them" (A. B. Ehrlich, *Mikrâ ki-phschutô,* vol. 3 [Berlin, 1901; repr. New York, 1969], pp. 404–405 [Hebrew]).

Isa. xlvii 2; Song iv 1, 3; vi 7) is derived, suggests that this kind of trap, too, may have had the form of a net.[192]

3[a] *Ḥebel* 'rope': The rope is mentioned in connection with the *paḥ* (cf. Ps. cxl 6). Ropes were stretched out or hidden under the ground. The rope, which was apparently wound around the animal's neck and tightened by means of a special knot (like a lasso) after it was caught, was connected to the trap itself.

3[b] *Malkōdet* 'trap': The hapax *malkōdet* denotes a trap in general. The noun derives from the root *l-k-d* 'ensnare'. It could be spread both as a means of entrapment or as the lure. The trap is set on the path, much like the net spread near a path (cf. Job xviii 10b and Ps. cxl 6b).

This list of hunting terms reveals the difficulty of identifying some devices and defining how they worked. As we have seen, hunting terminology was frequently invoked in similes and metaphors or used in idioms, in ways that did not necessarily reflect their true use. Frequently a term was selected for its phonetic effects or through delight in word play, as with Jeremiah's repetition of the syllable *paḥ*: "Terror [***paḥ****ad*] and pit [*wāp****paḥ****at*], and trap [*wāp****pāḥ***]"(Jer. xlviii 43a); or, with added alliteration of the *pê,* in the following verse: "He who flees from [***mipp****^{e}nê*] the terror [*hap****paḥ****ad*] shall fall [*yi****ppō****l*] into the pit [*hap****paḥ****at*] and he who climbs out of the pit [*hap****paḥ****at*] shall be caught in the trap [***pāḥ***]" (Jer. xlviii 44).

In contrast to the lack of biblical evidence about methods of deer-hunting,[193] fowling with a *pāḥ* comes up in a wide variety of figurative expressions, such as the aforementioned "We are like a bird escaped from the fowler's trap; the trap broke and we escaped" (Ps. cxxiv 7), as well as in the image of the entrapment of the foolish lad: "He is like a bird rushing into a trap" (Prov. vii 23b) in the speech cautioning against the adulterous woman.

[192] Driver and Gray translate *ṣammîm* as "snare." See S. R. Driver and G. B. Gray, *The Book of Job* (ICC; Edinburgh, 1921), p. 159; see also M. H. Pope, *Job* (AB 15; New York, 1965), p. 134. On *ḥebel* 'rope' as a noose, see R. Gordis, *The Book of Job* (New York, 1978), p. 188. Ehrlich (*Psalmen, Sprüche und Hiob*, p. 252) derives *ṣammîm* from *ṣinnîm* 'thorns' (cf. Prov. xxii 5).

[193] The idiomatic expression *ṣebî muddāḥ* 'a gazelle that is chased' (Isa. xiii 14) may allude to deer hunting.

CHAPTER 3

PARADOXICAL JUXTAPOSITION OF ANIMAL IMAGERY AND SOCIAL CATEGORIES

3.1 Bear and Fool

Let a man encounter a bereaved she-bear rather than a fool in his folly. (Prov. xvii 12)

3.1.1 *The "Better-than" Saying*[1]

The image of the bereaved bear[2] is part of a structure that is logically, though not syntactically, related to the "better-than" saying. The formal pattern of that saying combines the initial adverb *ṭôb* 'better', which usually functions as a predicative, and the *mêm* of comparison prefixed to the second noun, creating an analogical relation—in this pattern, one of inequality—between the parts of the saying.

Here we have a variant of the "better-than" saying; The absolute infinitive *pāgôš* 'to meet, encounter', in the opening stich, and the negative particle *ʾal* 'do not' (rendered here, functionally, as "rather"), in the complementary stich give *pāgôš* a cohortative significance. The elliptical structure of the verbless clause "rather than a fool in his folly"[3] is completed in a contextual-logical relation between the two lines.

[1] On the "better-than" saying, see §1.5.1.3.

[2] On the bear, see §2.2.2.4. The passive participle *šakkûl* 'bereaved', i.e., deprived of her cubs, is in the masculine, even though the contextual meaning of she-bear requires the feminine. *Dōb,* like *keleb*, designates any individual of the species, regardless of sex, whereas the male and female of some other animals are indicated by distinct nouns (e.g., *tayiš* 'he-goat', *ʿēz* 'she-goat'). See GKC, §§37c, 122e; Joüon and Muraoka, *A Grammar of Biblical Hebrew* II, pp. 493–94, §134c.

[3] Cf. the same use of the adversative *wāw* conjoined with the negative particle *ʾal* to form what amounts to a "better-than" saying in Prov. viii 10a: "Accept my disci-

3.1.2 *Discussion of the Saying*[4]

The warning against the fool's folly employs an idiom found twice in the prophetic literature—the "bereaved she-bear." Hushai the Archite describes David and his men as being "as desperate as a bear in the wild robbed of her whelps" (2 Sam. xvii 8). The prophet Hosea, speaking for the Lord, threatens that "like a bear robbed of her young I attack them and rip open the casing of their hearts" (Hos. xiii 8a). In both passages, the image of the she-bear bereft of her cubs is intended to illustrate feelings of desperation, rage, and cruelty, as well as to arouse the listener's horror.

The combination of the infinitive absolute *pāgôš* 'meet', with the sense of the imperative, with the "bereaved bear" intensifies the impression that the listener is warned about encountering an animal perceived as the archetype of the dangerous beast, difficult to escape, as in "He is a lurking bear to me, a lion in hiding" (Lam. iii 10) and "As if a man should run from a lion and be attacked by a bear" (Amos v 19a).[5] The mention of the object of the encounter, *ʾîš* 'a man',[6] in the opening clause emphasizes the preference for meeting up with a bereaved bear (e.g., Prov. xii 8, 25, xv 23, xxiv 29) rather than with a fool and his folly.[7] The fool (*k^{e}sîl*) is the diametrical opposite of the

pline rather than silver." For the use of the absolute infinitive to govern a noun in the accusative, see, e.g. *ʾākōl d^{e}baš* "to eat honey" (Prov. xxv 27; cf. Prov. xiii 20). See GKC, §152g; Joüon and Muraoka, *A Grammar of Biblical Hebrew* II, §123.

[4] See Tova Forti, "Animal Images in the Book of Proverbs," *Bib* 77 (1996), pp. 56–57.

[5] The same paradigm of a "better-than" saying that offers a metaphoric choice between a dangerous animal and the fool is found in Egyptian didactic letters that prefer a known to an unknown evil: "Better is a serpent in the house than a fool who frequents it." See M. Lichtheim, *Ancient Egyptian Literature* III (Berkeley and Los Angeles, 1973), p. 195.

[6] *ʾÎš* appears as nomen regens in various construct states in Proverbs, denoting a wide range of human types within society; e.g.: "the angry man" (xv 18), "the wise man (xvi 14), "the lazy man" (xxiv 30), "the wicked man" (xvi 27), "the man who wanders from his place" (xxvii 8), "a man rapid in his work" (xxii 29).

[7] The LXX of Prov. xvii 12 leaves out the bear, replacing it with μέριμνα 'care, anxiety'. Lagarde brings Jäger's suggested reconstruction of its Hebrew *Vorlage*: *pāgôš dăʾabah b^{e}ʾîš śēkel* = "Care may befall a man of understanding"—a change in the word order. See P. A. de Lagarde, *Anmerkungen zur griechischen Übersetzung der Proverbien* (Leipzig, 1863), p. 56. On the root *d-ʾ-b* 'dismay' (similar in sound to *dōb* "bear"), cf. Ps. lxxxviii 10; Jer. xxxi 25; Deut. xxviii 65. McKane (*Proverbs*, 33)

wise man: "The tongue of the wise produces much knowledge, but the mouth of dullards pours out folly" (Prov. xv 2; cf. vv. 7, 14, xvii 16, 24). The rubric of foolishness also includes negative social behaviors such as quarrelsomeness, babbling, and haughtiness.[8]

The conjunction of a bear and a fool evokes surprise and amazement; the sense of fear and danger usually associated with a bereaved bear are replaced by mockery and sarcasm. The reference to the "fool in his folly" in the complementary clause forces the listener to reflect on the destructive potential of folly, which is made all the more vivid by the contrasting image of the bereaved she-bear. Here the sage manages to give new life to a hackneyed idiom by varying its application in content and form. The she-bear robbed of her whelps is usually related to a human referent; but according to the wisdom notion advanced here, the person is defined "a fool in his folly," the prime example of one who lacks reason and commonsense. The old image is given new life by changing the usual analogous pattern into a variant of the "better-than" proverb.[9]

3.2 Lion and Sluggard

> The sluggard says, "There is a lion outside! I shall be slain in the streets!" (Prov. xxii 13; RSV)
>
> The sluggard says, "There is a lion in the road! There is a lion in the streets!" (Prov. xxvi 13; RSV)

---

claims that the LXX deviation "may arise from a pietistic and moralizing tendency." Loewenstamm proposes an emendation based on the Vulgate's retrieved version of *y*ᵉʾ*ûš* 'despair' instead of *ʾîš* 'man', thereby creating an emotional fit with the image of the bear whose cubs have been killed. See Samuel E. Loewenstamm, "Remarks on Proverbs XVII 12 and XX 27," *VT* 37 (1987), pp. 221–22.

[8] See e.g., Prov. x 18; xii 16; xiv 16, 29; xviii 6–8; xx 3; xxvi 6; Qoh. vii 9. Several commentators attribute the fool's behavior to irresistible urges: Ibn Ezra; Delitzsch, *Proverbs of Solomon* I, p. 361; Hameʾiri, *Proverbs,* p. 173. Ehrlich (*Psalmen, Sprüche und Hiob*, p. 98) interprets it as stupidity, as in "a fool with his nonsense"(xvii 12b) or "so a dullard repeats his folly" (Prov. xxvi 11).

[9] On the processes of adaptation, assimilation, or integration of hackneyed idioms into new semantic contexts, see G. E. Bryce, *A Legacy of Wisdom* (Lewisburg, PA, 1979).

3.2.1 *Šaḥal 'Lion'*

Šaḥal is one of the biblical terms for lion: "The roar of the lion (*ʾaryēh*), the voice of the fierce lion (*šaḥal*), the teeth of the young lions (*kᵉpîr*), are broken. The strong lion (*layiš*) perishes for lack of prey, and the whelps of the lioness (*lābîʾ*) are scattered" (Job iv 10–11 [RSV]; cf. *b. Sanh.* 95a). The *šaḥal* appears in synonymous parallelism to *kĕpîr* (Hos. v 14; Ps. xci 13), *ʾărî* (Prov. xxvi 13), and *lābîʾ* (Hos. xiii 8b) and among other predators such as the leopard, bear, and "beasts of the field" (ibid. vv. 7–8).[10]

Šaḥal is used metaphorically for the foe and represents God's power to punish and destroy the impious who attack the righteous (see Job iv 10–11 and Ps. xci 13).[11]

3.2.2 *Discussion of the Saying*

These two sayings consist of an attribution—"the sluggard says"—followed by direct quotations: a consequential link (Prov. xxii 13), "There is a lion outside! I shall be slain in the streets!" or a synonymous parallelism (Prov. xxvi 13), "There is a lion in the road! There is a lion in the streets!"[12]

Each verse paints a miniature scene in which lions wander the streets and terrify pedestrians. If the sluggard leaves home he will be entering a dangerous zone where beasts of prey roam free. The lion is frequently evoked in the Bible as a symbol of the enemy, both in laments and in hymns of thanksgiving. For example, "They open their mouths at me like tearing, roaring lions" (Ps. xxii 14 [RSV 13]). The lion often poses mortal danger for the flock: "As a shepherd rescues

[10] The NJPS translates two out of seven occurrences of *šaḥal* in the Bible as "cub" (the case under discussion here, as well as Job iv 10). *Šaḥal* also appears twice in synonymous parallelism with *kᵉpîr* (Hos. v 14; Ps. xci 13). There is no decisive proof for this identification, however. On the lion, see §2.2.2.4.

[11] See Dhorme, *The Book of Job*, pp. 47–48; H. J. Kraus, *Psalms 1–59: A Commentary,* trans. H. C. Oswals (Minneapolis, 1988), pp. 95–99.

[12] In both Prov. xxii 13 and xxvi 13 the LXX has the noun φονευταί 'murderers', instead of the "I shall be slain" of xxii 13 (cf. 2 Kgs vi 32; Isa. i 21); the Peshitta has the same reading.

from the lion's jaws two shank bones or the tip of an ear, so shall the Israelites escape" (Amos iii 12).

In both aphorisms, the possible encounter between man and predatory beast represents a threat, similar to the encounter with the bereaved bear in the aphorism about the fool (Prov. xvii 12). But the fact that it is expounded by the sluggard minimizes the impact of the threat aroused by the thought of a lion wandering the streets and places it in a limited associative context applying only to the lazybones, thus rendering it not entirely believable. The author of the parable has deliberately created a logical gap between reality and its literary expression, thereby evoking a degree of incredulity, for the sluggard's pretext is ridiculous. In the end, readers cannot help wondering what relationship could exist between a sluggard and a lion roaming the streets.[13]

The stock image of the lazybones in Proverbs evokes a rich variety of humoristic descriptions: "The door turns on its hinge, and the lazy man on his bed" (xxvi 14). It is in this same spirit that he is rebuked: "How long will you lie there, lazybones; when will you wake from your sleep?" (vi 9; cf. xix 15). His laziness leads to hyperbole: "The lazy man buries his hand in the bowl; he will not even bring it to his mouth" (xxvi 15). He stays at home, lies in bed, and avoids all productive work.

In Prov. xxii 13a the adverb *baḥûṣ* 'outside' refers to the open spaces of the streets and the marketplace, an unprotected location beyond the four walls of the home. In this, it resembles Hosea's use of the word, "with thieves breaking in and bands raiding outside" (vii 1), as well as the plural noun *ḥûṣôt* in the prophet's description of destruction, "and its corpses lay like refuse in the streets" (Isa. v 25). The use of *baḥûṣ* here is intentional, because, alongside its primary meaning of "street," it also occurs in agricultural context: "Prepare your work outside, get everything ready for you in the field; and after that build your house" (Prov. xxiv 27 [RSV]), thereby suggesting the lazybones' typical conduct in another aphorism: "In winter the lazy man does not plow; at harvest time he seeks, and finds nothing" (Prov. xx 4). The scene of hustle and bustle in the street, repeated with slight variation in both of our sayings—"in the road," "in the streets"—is

[13] Clifford (*Proverbs,* p. 198) notes the play of sounds in xxii 13: *ʾărî* 'lion' in the first clause and the verb *ʾērāṣēaḥ* 'I shall be slain' in the second clause.

echoed in the verse, "The chariots race madly through the streets, they rush to and fro through the squares" (Nah. ii 5 [NRSV]).[14]

The dialogue style of the saying is reinforced by the sluggard's nonsensical hyperbole and lame excuses.[15] Direct speech is also used to characterize the trickster and illustrate his unreliable nature: "Like a madman scattering deadly firebrands, arrows, is one who cheats his fellow and says, 'I was only joking' " (Prov. xxvi 18–19).

It follows that our saying rests on a rhetorical echo that reflects the general consensus about the sluggard: the lazybones, known for his apathy and tendency to avoid any action (cf. Prov. vi 6–11, x 26, xix 15, 24, xxiv 30–34, xxvi 14–15), is described as afraid that he will encounter a wild beast if he goes outside. This statement, placed in his mouth, demonstrates one of the sluggard's infinite stock of excuses.[16]

3.3 Dog and Fool

As a dog returns to his vomit, so a fool repeats his folly. (Prov. xxvi 11)

3.3.1 *The Comparative Saying*

In this comparative saying,[17] the comparative *kāp* introduces the first clause, but the applicative particle *kēn* 'thus, so' is missing in the second clause. Here we have an analogy between the behavior of the fool and the dog. The fool, who constantly repeats his foolishness, is compared to the loathsome dog that returns to swallow its vomit.[18]

[14] For synonymous parallelism between *ḥûṣ* 'outside' and *rᵉḥōbôt* 'streets', see Prov. i 20; vii 12; between *ḥûṣôt* and *rᵉḥōbôt*, see Jer. v 1; and between *šᵉwāqîm* 'markets' and *rᵉḥōbôt*, see Song iii 2. The Tg. and Syr. translate *rᵉḥōbôt* in both sayings (xxii 13; xxvi 13) as "markets."

[15] On hyperbole as the comic and sarcastic element in both sayings, see: Hameʾiri, *Proverbs*, p. 116; Delitzsch, *The Proverbs of Solomon* II, p. 92; McKane, *Proverbs*, p. 596. On the element of surprise in shaping the comic atmosphere of the saying in Proverbs, see R. Alter, *The Art of Biblical Poetry* (New York, 1985), p. 172.

[16] Delitzsch (*The Proverbs of Solomon* I, pp. 24–26; II, p. 189) proposes that Prov. xxii 13 is the original and xxvi 13 secondary, based on the style. However, the phenomenon of repeated sayings with a variation in one of the clauses is frequent in Proverbs; e.g., xxi 9 and xxv 24; xviii 8 and xxvi 22; xix 24 and xxvi 15.

[17] On the comparative saying, see §1.5.1.1.

[18] The combination of the preposition *ʿal* 'on' with the verb *šāb* 'returns' instead of *ʾel* 'to(wards)' has led many commentators to understand that the dog returns to its

3.3.2 *Keleb 'Dog'*

The noun *keleb* is attested in other Semitic languages: Ugaritic *klb,* Akkadian *kalbum,* Aramaic and Syriac *kalbāʾ,* and Arabic *kalbun.*

In Ancient Near Eastern literature, the dog symbolizes a submissive, obedient animal, whose characteristic behavior is to grovel and humiliate itself in front of its master.[19]

The phrase *keleb mēt* 'dead dog' occurs several times in the historical books of the Bible as an idiom of self-abasement: "Against whom has the king of Israel come out? Whom are you pursuing? A dead dog? A single flea?" (1 Sam. xxiv 15; cf. 1 Sam. xvii 43; 2 Sam. ix 8, xvi 9; 2 Kgs viii 13).[20] On the one hand, the Bible depicts the dog as a wild animal prowling the streets (Ps. lix 7, 15; cf. xxii 21) or as a bloodthirsty beast rending its prey (Ps. lxviii 24), and as such is compared to the cruel enemy. On the other, it is a submissive creature that abases itself before its master—the faithful domestic dog (e.g., 1 Sam. xvii 43). Even though the unique epithet *kalᵉbê ṣōʾnî* 'sheepdogs' (Job xxx 1) attests to the existence of the domesticated dog, there are no descriptions of dogs that stay close to home and eat scraps under the table (cf. Matt. v 27). From the verse "you must not eat flesh torn by

---

own vomit and eats it. See, e.g., Arama, *Yad Avshalom*, p. 86; Kahana, *Sefer Mishley*, p. 124; McKane, *Proverbs*, p. 599; Murphy, *Proverbs*, p. 196.

[19] The image of the dog as a repulsive beast appears in the epic of Kirta, *CAT* 1.16, Tablet III, lines 2–3, 15–17 et passim. See: Parker, *Ugaritic Narrative Poetry*, pp. 30, 31, 34; Rimbach, *Animal Imagery,* pp. 76–77. For the use of dogs in curse formulas see: "The Vassal-Treaties of Esarhaddon," *ANET*, pp. 538b, 539a; Hillers, *Treaty-Curses*, pp. 61, 68; Marcus, "Animal Similes," p. 94 and n. 61. For the similarity between the Deuteronomic curse and the vassal treaties of Esarhaddon, see Weinfeld, *Deuteronomy and the Deuteronomic School*, p. 132. Sargon employs the image of the dog as an obsequious creature when he portrays the Manaean king and his nobles thus: *eli erbi rettīšunu iptaššilū kīma kalbī* 'grovelling on all fours in obeisance before him' (TCL 3, 12:58).

[20] The Akkadian parallel is *kalbu mītu*. See David W. Thomas, "*Kelebh*, 'Dog'; Its Origin and Some Usage of it in the Old Testament," *VT* 10 (1960), pp. 410–27 (esp. p. 417). On the link between *ʿebed* 'servant' and *keleb* 'dog' in a rhetorical question (cf. 2 Kgs viii 13) as a term of self-disparagement before a king, see Cogan and Tadmor, *II Kings*, p. 91. For *ardu, kalbu* in the Amarna letters, see W. L. Moran, *The Amarna Letters* (Baltimore and London), 1992, nos. 314–316, 319, 322–325, 378; *AHw*, p. 424b; *CAD* K 72. In the Lachish letters we find "Who is thy servant (but) a dog? (*my ʿbdk klb*)" (2.4, 5.4, 6.3); see *ANET*, p. 322; George W. Coats, "Self-abasement and Insult Formulas," *JBL* 89 (1970), pp. 14–24; Frank C. Fensham, "The Dog in Exodus XI: 7," *VT* 16 (1966), pp. 504–507.

beasts in the field; you shall cast it to the dogs" (Exod. xxii 30) we may infer that the dog did play a sanitary role in the household.[21] The dog, like the pig, is a scavenger,[22] which may explain why it is sometimes depicted as licking up blood on the battlefield. This motif appears frequently in curses (Jer. xv 3; 1 Kgs xiv 11, xvi 4, xxi 19, 23–24, xxii 38), in threats (Ps. lxviii 24), in the petition to the Lord for vengeance against one's enemy (Ps. ii 17, 21), and in the bold image of *lōʾ yeḥĕraṣ keleb lᵉšōnô* as a figurative expression for snarling (Exod. xi 7).[23]

3.3.3 *Discussion of the Saying*

The description of the dog that returns to its own pool of vomit and eats it arouses feelings of loathsomeness and disgust. In the Book of Proverbs, "vomit" stands for immoderate and unrestrained behavior, as in the warning against overindulgence: "If you find honey, eat only what you need, lest, surfeiting yourself, you throw it up" (Prov. xxv 16). It is also mentioned in the admonition against behavior driven by base appetites, such as overeating or excessive drinking (cf. xxiii 29–35), which utterly degrade a person (cf. Isa. xix 14, xxviii 8–9). Indeed, the *kᵉsîl* 'fool, dolt, dullard' in Proverbs "gains only contempt," as opposed to the wise man who "inherits honor" (iii 35). Because the archetypal *kᵉsîl* is brutish, ignorant, and emotionally dull, he can readily descend to moral depravity and wickedness.[24]

Yoking together the fool who repeats his folly with the dog who licks up its own vomit arouses the sort of revulsion we might feel in the presence of an overeater or drunkard.[25] The thematic pole of the

[21] For biblical allusions to dogs roaming outside human settlements and feeding off refuse, similar to pigs, see Ps. lix 7, 15; 1 Kgs xiv 11. See also: Firmage, "Zoology," p. 1143; Borowski, "Animals in the Literatures of Syria-Palestine," *HAWANE,* pp. 301–3. On temple rules in Babylonia barring dogs from the temple—"If a dog enters the house of God, the gods will not have mercy on the land" (quoted by Joann Scurlock, "Animals in Ancient Mesopotamian Religion," *HAWANE*, p. 369.

[22] On the pig, see §2.2.1.1.

[23] See BDB, *ḥāraṣ* I, p. 358, "sharpen"; and, figuratively, "decide, determine (a verdict)."

[24] The *kᵉsîl* 'fool' is mentioned in the Bible only in Proverbs (48 times), Qoheleth (17 times) and Psalms (3 times). On the *kᵉsîl*, see §2.2.2.7. See Shupak, *Where can Wisdom be Found*? pp. 201–204; Fox, *Proverbs 1–9*, pp. 41–42.

[25] Foolishness is perceived as a deviation from the human norm (cf. Prov. xiv 1, 8, xvi 22, xviii 13, xix 3). Consequently repeating foolishness leads to humiliation, as

saying deals with the repetition of something loathsome: the dog returns to its vomit, while the fool, the embodiment of worthless intellect, returns to his faulty way of thinking time and again.

The applicative clause, "so a fool repeats his folly," uses the verb *š-n-h*, which has the same meaning as the geminate verb *š-n-n* 'repeat'. Both are used to express the method of repetition used for learning (Deut. vi 6–7; cf. xi 19), but its application to the repetition of folly is ironic and mocking.[26] The fool's essential stupidity is elsewhere stated in an ironic image: "Even if you pound the fool in a mortar with a pestle along with grain, his folly will not leave him" (Prov. xxvii 22).

3.3.4 *The Expansion of Prov. xxvi 11 in the Septuagint and Ben Sira*[27]

> As when a dog goes to his own vomit and becomes abominable, so is a fool who returns in his wickedness to his own sin. [There is a shame that brings sin: and there is a shame that is glory and grace.]

The Septuagint version expands both clauses: the dog that returns to its vomit becomes loathsome; the fool is in fact wicked and his folly is redefined as "sin." Thus the scorn heaped on the fool in the Hebrew is replaced by contempt for the sinner in the Greek version.

The Greek translation presents a moral-religious evaluation of the *k^e^sîl* and considers him to be a sinner, and not merely a person lacking intellectual keenness (cf. LXX Prov. i 22, 32; iii 35; xiii 19). Here the Septuagint interpolates its own definition of two types of shame. At first glance this addition may seem to be irrelevant to the aphorism. But a close look at how the Septuagint views the *k^e^sîl* 'fool' clarifies the conceptual link between the biblical saying and the two types of shame.

Arama (*Yad Avshalom*, p. 86) explains: "The fool, whose original behavior is already spoilt, when he repeats it, such behavior becomes even more loathsome."

[26] For a possible semantic linkage between the geminate and the *tertiae yod š-n-n/ š-n-h*, see *z-k-k/ z-k-h*; *š-ḥ-ḥ/ š-ḥ-h*; *š-g-g/ š-g-h* and others in GKC, §§ 77d–e; G. Bergsträsser, *Hebräische Grammatik* (Hildesheim, 1962), 170, § 31; *HALOT* suggests *š-n-h* II as a secondary form of *š-n-h* II, meaning *wiederholen* 'repeat'; see 4: 1484.

[27] See Tova Forti, "Conceptual Stratification in LXX Prov. 26, 11: Toward Identifying the Tradents Behind the Aphorism," *ZAW* 119 (2007), pp. 241–58.

The Septuagint version of Prov. xxvi 11 occurs word for word (except for an added connective) in the Septuagint text of Ben Sira (Ecclesiasticus) iv 21. What is the link between the aphorism of dog and fool in Proverbs and the Septuagint's borrowing from Ben Sira, interpolated (apparently) to explain it?[28]

To answer this question we must clarify the nature of "shame," a key concept in the conceptual framework of Ben Sira.[29] He devotes an extended discourse to the subject, the *mûsar bōšet* 'Instruction on Shame' (xli 14–xlii 8).[30] His ambivalent use of "be ashamed"/"be not ashamed" is embedded within the structure of the maxim in iv 20–31: "My son, let your actions be timely; fear what is wrong, be not ashamed to be yourself. There is a sense of shame laden with guilt, and a shame that merits honor and respect." The word *bōšet,* which in the Bible means chiefly "something worthy of strong censure," underwent a semantic development in post-biblical literature and could also mean "consciousness of guilt"—a positive emotion, as it appears in Sirach: "Not every kind of shame is meet to retain, and not every kind of abashment is to be approved" (xli 16).[31] Ben Sira also applies *bōšet* to behavior that should be denounced: e.g., the poor person who, ashamed of his want, pretends to be wealthy (xx 21–23); a

[28] Baumgartner (*Etude critique*, pp. 225–26) noted that the addition of the two types of shame in Prov. xxvi 11 is simply a quotation from Sirach iv 21, but found it difficult to explain: "On ne se rend pas compte de la raison d'être de cette citation, dans un contexte qui traite de tout autre chose." Mezzacasa characterizes this phenomenon as a moral-theological gloss added by the translator; in some cases the inspired author quotes a saying without offering any reasonable explanation of his moral attitude; in other cases, along with the empirical truth of the biblical saying, we find a theological-dogmatic call to imitate an example, as in 2 Pet. ii 22; the concise character of the saying provides the reader with interpretive space. See G. Mezzacasa, *Il Libro dei Proverbi di Salomone: Studio Critico sulle aggiunte Greco-Alessandrine* (Rome, 1913), pp. 79–82.

[29] See Di Lella and Skehan, *The Wisdom of Ben Sira*, pp. 8–10.

[30] The text about "two kinds of shame" (Sir. iv 21), which is not preserved in the Masada Scroll, follows MS A from the Cairo Geniza, as translated by Skehan and Di Lella (*The Wisdom of Ben Sira*, p. 174); the section entitled "Instruction on Shame" (xli 14–xlii 8) follows Y. Yadin, *The Ben Sira Scroll from Masada* (Jerusalem, 1965), pp. 41–43.

[31] For a semantic development of *bōšet*, see, e.g., the *Mekilta de-Rabbi Yishmaʿel* to Exod. xx 17: "'And that his fear may be ever with you [*lit.* on your face]'—this is bashfulness. It is a good sign in a man if he is bashful. 'That you sin not'—this says that bashfulness leads one to piety [*lit.* to fear sin]." See Menahem Kister, "Some Notes on Biblical Expressions and Allusions and the Lexicography of Ben Sira," in T. Muraoka and J. F. Elwolde (eds.), *Sirach, Scrolls and Sages* (*STDJ* 33; Leiden, Boston, and Cologne, 1997), pp. 167–68.

father's shame at his son's stupidity (xxii 3, 5); the shame of a man whose wife supports him (xxv 22; xxvi 24–25).

In MS B of Sir. xli 14a, the heading *mûsar bōšet* 'Instruction on Shame' appears as an introductory formula to a list of actions of which should be ashamed (xli 14–xlii 1 [MS B from the Cairo Geniza]). One should be ashamed of involvement in immorality (adultery) or in a breach of justice and etiquette. Be ashamed of fornication in the presence of your parents (xli 17a), of perjury (xli 17b), of deceiving one's master and mistress (xli 18a), of a crime against the congregation and people (xli 18b), and more. The last item is the discourtesy of insulting a person who offers you a gift (xli 22c, d).

Ben Sira continues with a list of actions that should not be a source of shame (xlii 2–8). These examples are drawn from property and inheritance (xlii 3b) and fair business practices (xlii 4a–5a). How does this demand that one not be ashamed fit in with behaviors that are shameful? Apparently Ben Sira uses contrasting headings for each section as a rhetorical device. Although the formal stylistic variation may change the viewpoint, the moral standard remains firmly in place. The opening verse, "of the following things do not be ashamed, and do not sin to save face" (xlii 1; NRSV), formulates a moral rule that sins are to be denounced publicly, rather than concealed.

The "Instruction on Shame" sheds light on the declaration in iv 21 (MS A): *Yēš bōšet maśś^{e}ʾat ʿāwôn, w^{e}yēš bōšet ḥēn w^{e}kābôd,* "there is a sense of shame laden with guilt and a shame that merits honor and respect."[32] Some acts should be denounced and exposed, and concealing them is a sin. Ben Sira encourages the open recognition of sin and opposes its concealment, similar to the exposure of wisdom that is considered more advantageous than its concealment. On the other hand, it is better to hide stupidity than reveal it (iv 23; xli 15).

With these insights in hand, we return to the two types of shame in the expanded Septuagint version of Prov. xxvi 11. The fool's compulsive repetition of his foolishness is taken as a moral fault or sin and considered to be one of the expressions of shame and disgrace that should be exposed. Some would explicate the expanded Greek version by comparing it to the saying about the dog in 2 Peter ii 21–22: "For it had been better for them not to have known the way of righteousness,

[32] The Academy of the Hebrew Language, *The Book of Ben Sira, Text, Concordance and an Analysis of the Vocabulary* (Jerusalem, 1973) [Hebrew].

than, after they have known it, to turn from the holy command. But it happened unto them according to the true proverb, the dog is turned to his own vomit again; and the sow that was washed to her wallowing in the mire." Here, too, sinners who repeat their sin are compared to the loathsome behavior of the dog and the pig.[33] This comparison, however, leads us away from Ben Sira's conceptual world to a different theological framework, one that reflects another stage of development in the concept of sin.

The extended comparison between the Septuagint text of Proverbs xxvi 11 and Ben Sira helps explain the otherwise enigmatic deviation of the former from the Hebrew text. The difference between the concision of the biblical saying and the expanded gloss in the Septuagint demonstrates that the Greek translator interpreted the verse in the spirit and manner of Ben Sira's exhortations. The biblical saying contains no hint of the religious and moral ethos and mentions only the fool's stupidity, an intellectual limitation leading to failure.

We therefore suggest that the parallel between the Septuagint version and Ben Sira reflect a process of conceptual development. In other words, the Greek version adds a new and elaborated stratum of religious teaching in the spirit of the Law and Divine Covenant (cf. Sir. xlii 1–2a). The evidence from Ben Sira (iv 20–21; xli 16) helps solve the riddle of the Septuagint's interpolation in Proverbs xxvi 11. We have already recognized religious and moral admonitions in Proverbs, such as "The fear of the Lord is the beginning of knowledge" (i 7) and "The beginning of wisdom is the fear of the Lord, and knowledge of the Holy One is understanding" (ix 10). The Septuagint versions of Prov. i 7 and vii 1 sharpen the call to fear the Lord. The identification of the fool with the sinner in the discussion of principle of retribution, found only in the Septuagint version (i 22, 32, iii 35, xiii 19), reflects its stronger religious and moral bent. Ben Sira, too, places particular emphasis on the fear of God, equating the purpose of Wisdom with obedience to the Torah and Prophets. The Hebrew text of Ben Sira preserves the tradition of the *Bêt midrāš,* the "Study House," where the sages of Jerusalem gathered (li 23). The same hermeneutic approach can be traced in the Greek translation of Proverbs; here too

[33] See Mezzacasa, *Il Libro dei Proverbi di Salomone*, pp. 79–82; On the double gloss of the Greek expanded version, see d'Hamonville, *Les Proverbes*, p. 318.

we see the imprint of the school of sages who contributed to the conceptual stratification of the Book of Proverbs.

3.4 Dog and Provoker

> A passerby who provokes a fight is like one who takes a dog by the ears. (Prov. xxvi 17; free translation)
>
> *or:*
>
> He who meddles in a quarrel not his own is like one who takes a passing dog by the ears. (RSV)

This proverb[34] describes an episode of picking a quarrel: the picturesque image of someone who provokes a dog by pulling its ears (LXX: "tail")—considered to be a very sensitive organ—represents the quarrel-monger.

The Masoretic cantillation (*etnaḥ* under *keleb*) places the pause after "dog," attaching *ᶜōbēr* 'passing by' to the man of the comparandum (as in the first translation above). Moving the pause so that the participle is attached to the dog (as in the second version above) emphasizes the dog's chance presence and suggests that the man is smarting for a fight.[35] The asyndeton of the MT between the verbs *ᶜōbēr* and *mitᶜabbēr* can also be interpreted as indicating two different actions carried out simultaneously; one defines the man as a passerby (cf. the idiomatic use of *ᶜōbēr wāšāb* 'passerby' [Ezek. xxxv 7]), while the second relates to the provocateur's behavior.[36]

The negative nature of the image is reinforced by the verb *mitᶜabbēr* 'be infuriated', a denominative of *ᶜebrāh* 'rage, anger' (cf. Job xl 11). The same word appears in the warning against provoking a king: "The terror of a king is like the roar of a lion; He who provokes

[34] On the comparative saying and its variations, see §1.5.1.1.

[35] See, e.g., Gemser, *Sprüche Salomos*, p. 95; McKane, *Proverbs*, pp. 601–602. Toy (*Proverbs*, p. 478) considers that the adjective *ᶜōbēr* superfluous, because "the dog was not a domestic animal in Palestine, and to seize any dog was dangerous." *ᶜŌbēr* is probably a gloss or an erroneous repetition due to the adjacent *mitᶜabbēr*.

[36] The reading of the Aramaic translation, *nāṣê ûmitnᵉṣê* 'striving and struggling', intensifies the topic of strife by translating both verbs as derivatives of *ᶜ-b-r* 'infuriate'. The two meanings of *ᶜ-b-r*, "passing" and "becoming furious," appear in sequence in Deut. iii 25–26: "Let me, I pray, cross over and see the good land. … But the Lord was wrathful with me."

his anger (*mitʿabbēr*) risks his life" (Prov. xx 2).[37] The reflexive form (*hitpaʿel*) is also found in the antithetical comparison of the fool's vanity and overweening self-confidence with the prudence of the wise man, who behaves with caution: "A wise man is cautious and turns away from evil, but a fool throws off restraint (*mitʿabbēr*) and is careless" (Prov. xiv 16 [RSV]). The Vulgate and the Peshitta, reading by metathesis *mitʿārēb* 'get involved', point out the tendency of the hot-tempered person to get himself embroiled in a quarrel that has nothing to do with him. But the other occurrences of *mitʿabbēr* in Proverbs (see xiv 16, xx 2b) support the MT version. So do the frequent admonitions against being hot-tempered (see Prov. xiv 29, xv 18, xviii 8, xxii 8, xxvi 18), considered to be the typical behavior of the fool.

Our verse introduces a series of sayings (xxvi 17–22) that refer to the quarrelsome and querulous. They use fire imagery, because of the metaphoric fanning of the flames of anger and strife: "deadly firebrands" (v. 18), "charcoal for embers and wood for a fire" and "kindling strife" (v. 21). This is fitting, since *mitʿabbēr,* too, is associated with fire: "The Lord heard and He raged; fire broke out against Jacob, anger flared up at Israel" (Ps. lxxviii 21). This image is appropriate for a person who provokes quarrels and enflames others even as he himself becomes consumed with rage.[38]

Seizing a dog's ears exemplifies the dangerous situation that such a person can bring upon himself.

[37] On lion and king, see §2.2.2.3.

[38] Gersonides (ad loc.) interprets "someone else's quarrel" as stealing the dog's food in addition to grasping his ears; i.e., this is two-fold incitement to quarrel.

CHAPTER 4

ANIMALS AS MODELS FOR HUMAN SOCIETY

4.1 A Didactic Model within an Admonition: The Industrious Ant

> Go to the ant, O sluggard, Observe her ways and be wise, [Because] She has no arbitrator, She does without officer and ruler. She lays in her stocks in summer, and stores her food at harvest. How long, O sluggard, will you lie there? When will you rise from your sleep? A little sleep, a little slumber, A little folding of the hands to lie down, and poverty will come to you like a vagrant, and want like a beggar. (Prov. vi 6–11)[1]

4.1.1 *The Ant*

The noun *nᵉmālâ* 'ant' (*Formica spp.*) is attested in other Semitic languages, including Akkadian *namalu (namlu)*,[2] Syriac *nᵉmālā*, *nammālā*, and Arabic *naml*.

Ants are insects of the Formicidae family. Most ants feed off dead insects, but some eat plants, primarily seeds and grain. The harvester ant *(Messor semirufus)* collects grain from the territory near its anthill and stores it in upper chambers that serve as storehouses for the food before it is husked and cleaned. After the grain has been threshed it is stored in lower chambers. The chaff builds up near the anthill, where it serves as kind of protective barrier to rainfall seeping into the subterranean colony. The ant mentioned in Proverbs is identified with *M. semirufus* primarily because it is active throughout the year.[3]

[1] The translation follows McKane, *Proverbs*, p. 219.

[2] Akkadian *lammatu* 'ant' (*namalu, namlu*) is treated as a West-Semitic loanword (the standard Akkadian term for ant is *kulbābu*); see: *AHw* pp. 533, 725; *CAD* L p. 67; N/1 p. 208.

[3] See Tristram, *Natural History of the Bible*, pp. 319–21; Bodenheimer, *Animal*

The ants' social order consists of three classes: the fertile winged queen; winged males, whose sole function is to fertilize the queen; and a great number of sterile wingless female workers, who engage in numerous activities, such as foraging, carrying, threshing, sorting, and storing.

Ancient Near Eastern literature is full of observations of ants used to illuminate human behavior. The ant is mentioned twice in the Bible, both times in Proverbs. In both the sermon to the sluggard (vi 6–9) and the numerical saying (xxx 25) listeners and readers are enjoined to learn from the ant's diligence and efficient organization. Although Assyrian sources do not mention the industriousness of the ant, which stores food in summertime for the hard days of winter, a note of appreciation for it may be detected in Sargon's "Letter to the God" (TCL 3, 24:143), where his army's ability to traverse difficult terrain is compared with the ant's similar skill. Alongside this view of the ant as a model of diligence, hard work, perseverance, and navigational prowess, however, ant imagery in Assyrian royal inscriptions refers mainly to their limitless hordes, which are nevertheless insignificant and easily routed.

Another characteristic of the ant, its aggressive reaction to those who maltreat it, is mentioned in one of the Amarna Letters from Labʾayu, the governor of Shechem, in which he justifies his cruelty to prisoners by comparing his urge for revenge to the sting of a threatened ant: *kī namlu tumḫaṣu lā tikabbilu u tanšuku qāti amēli ša yimaḫḫaṣṣi*, "If one strikes an ant, does it not fight and sting the hand of the man who struck him?" (EA 252, lines 16–22).[4]

The ant is cast in a negative light in an idiomatic expression of self-abasement found in the Syriac version of the story of Aḥiqar, the wise counselor of Sennacherib and Esarhaddon. Ahiqar humbles himself before the king by describing his position "as one of the loathsome ants in the kingdom." The formula is repeated in the king's anger at the insult represented by the counselor's unimportance: "Have I become so light in the eyes of your master that he has sent me a loathsome ant in his kingdom?"[5]

Life in Biblical Lands II, p. 263.

[4] See William F. Albright, "An Archaic Hebrew Proverb in an Amarna Letter from Central Palestine," *BASOR* 89 (1943), p. 30; Moran, *The Amarna Letters*, pp. 305–306.

[5] See A. Yellin, *Sefer Aḥiqar he-Ḥakam* (Jerusalem, 1938), p. 44.

4.1.2 *The Parable*

The admonition[6] begins with an imperative addressed to the sluggard: "Go to the ant" (vi 6a). The imperative demands a dramatic change in his behavior,[7] recalling the urgency of the injunction to the man who has gone surety for his fellow: "Go grovel" (vi 3c) before the lender and appeal to his pity in any way, even the most humiliating.[8] Similarly, the image of the sluggard conveyed by "the door turns on its hinge and the lazy man on his bed" (Prov. xxvi 14; cf. v. 15), furnishes a suitable context for the command "go!" designed to rouse him from his slumber: "How long, O sluggard, will you lie there, when will you rise from your sleep? (vi 9)" The sluggard is urged to observe the ant's behavior and internalize its diligence.

The "ways" to be observed can be taken literally as the trail blazed by the harvest ants carrying their burdens, but it can also be understood as the path of moral rectitude. In Proverbs, *derek* and its synonyms *ʾōraḥ, nātîb, maʿăgāl,* and *mêšārîm* express a moral road that offers the choice between contrasting modes of life: one path leads to "righteousness, justice and equity" (ii 8); the other is the route taken by "men whose paths are crooked, and who are devious in their course" (ii 15).[9] Thus, the warning against laziness calls on the sluggard to imitate the ant's diligence in pursuit of an ordered and upright life.

The dependent clause, "[because] she has no arbitrator, she does without officer and ruler" (vi 7), provides the motive for the imperatives, "go," "observe" and "be wise": even without rulers, ant society is ordered and regulated. The teacher employs three terms of military

[6] On the admonition pattern, see §1.5.2.1.

[7] Hameʾiri (*Proverbs*, pp. 56–57) discusses the many uses of "go" in the Bible, from moving the body to stimulating the mind to reflect and act (Deut. xiii 7; Ps. xlvi 9; lxvi 5).

[8] See §2.1.3.1.

[9] The terms associated with wisdom—*ḥokmâ, daʿat, ʿormâ, t^ebûnâ, tûšiyyâ, m^ezimmâ,* and *taḥbûlâ*—denote cognitive abilities, competence, and intelligence, which are indispensable strategies for choosing the right path in life (see Prov. i 2–6). *Derek* is part of various compounds expressing contrasting moral behavior: *derek ḥayyîm* (vi 23) or *ʾōraḥ ḥayyîm* (xv 24) 'way of life', as opposed to *maʿăgal,* which is associated with *repāʿîm* and *š^eʾôl* (Prov. ii 18; v 5); i.e., the path leading to Sheol and to the shades. For the similar use of "way" in Egyptian Wisdom Literature, see B. Curoyer, "Le chemin de vie en Égypte et en Israël," *RB* 56 (1949), pp. 428–32.

and civil rank to contrast the human need for social organization with the self-sufficiency of the ant. Here *qāṣîn* 'arbitrator',[10] *šōṭēr* 'officer',[11] and *mōšēl* 'ruler'[12] are used synonymously for a figure of authority.[13] These terms of social hierarchy are not meant to reflect actual ranks in Israelite society, but to contrast the self-sufficiency exemplified by the ant with the defects of human behavior, despite the organization of human society.

Although the teacher is an astute observer of his surroundings and appreciates the inherent wisdom of nature, here he seems to be unaware of the highly regimented social order of the anthill, with the division of labor between the wingless female workers, the winged queen, and the winged males. He considers the human need for hierarchical order to be in some fashion inferior to what he perceives as the ant's autonomy and instinctive wisdom.

The ant also serves as a model for human behavior in its prudent preparations for winter: "She lays in her stocks in summer, and stores her food at harvest" (vi 8). Harvest ants are active during the daytime in winter and spring; in summer, they work during at night as well, storing up food during the harvest season to prepare for the winter. The same image of ants' gathering food in the summer is repeated in a numerical saying: "Ants are a folk without power, yet they prepare food for themselves in summer" (xxx 25).[14]

Here "summer" and "harvest" are synonyms, as also in x 5: "He who lays in stores during the summer is a capable son, but he who sleeps during the harvest is an incompetent."

[10] On the *qāṣîn* as a civil-legal authority, see Isa. iii 6–7, xxii 3; Prov. xxv 15; Mic. iii 1, 9; as a military leader, see Josh. x 24 and Judg. xi 6, 11. See Hameʾiri, *Proverbs*, p. 59; Toy, *Proverbs*, p. 134.

[11] The context of the occurrences of *šōṭēr* supports the meaning of "the executive enforcing the law" (cf. Exod. v 6; Num. xi 16; Deut. xx 5, xv 18). See: Alexander Rofé, "Judicial System," *Beit Miqraʾ* 21 (1976), p. 201 [Hebrew]; Moshe Weinfeld, "The Term *Šōṭēr* and his Duty," *Beit Miqraʾ* 22 (1977), pp. 418–19 [Hebrew].

[12] *Mōšēl* is applied to God (Ps. xxii 29; lix 14; lxxxix 10), Solomon (1 Kgs v 1), and to the administrator of a household (Gen. xxiv 2; xlv 8). Several passages in Proverbs deal with the appropriate relationship between ruler and subject (xxiii 1; xxviii 15; xxix 2, 12, 26; see also Qoh. ix 17; x 4).

[13] Hameʾiri (*Proverbs*, pp. 56–57) states that the appeal to the ant was intended "to show all present an example taken from the most worthless creature," similar to the moral lesson taken from the narrative of Jonadab the son of Rechab (Jeremiah 35).

[14] Delitzsch (*Proverbs of Solomon* I, pp. 140–41) discusses the different stages associated with the verbs *tākîn* and *ʾāgᵉrâ* in association with "summer" as a climatic season and "harvest" as an agricultural season.

Now the teacher turns from the objective description of the ant's positive qualities to rhetorical questions directed to the sluggard: "How long, O sluggard, will you lie there? When will you rise from your sleep?" (vi 9) The repetition of the interrogative *mātay*—"how long" and "when" (*ʿad mātay, mātay*)—and the use of the antithetical verbs "lie" and "rise" reflect the Teacher's emotional involvement.[15]

The end of the section, shaped as a moral exhortation, is repeated almost word for word in Prov. xxiv 33–34 in the Teacher's conclusions at the sight of the neglected field. His mocking tone is indicated by the threefold use of *meʿaṭ* 'a little [bit] of': "A little sleep, a little slumber, a little folding of the hands to lie down" (vi 10 and xxiv 33). The repetition sounds a repeated warning, but also serves as a grotesque imitation of the sluggard's desire for repose.

The consequence, "and poverty will come to you like a vagrant, and want like a beggar" (vi 11; cf. xxiv 34), indicates the disastrous outcome of the idler's misguided behavior and is similar to the metaphor of the fool's catastrophe in Qoheleth: "The fool folds his hands together and has to eat his own flesh" (Qoh. iv 5). Here, in Proverbs, the idler is warned that he risks becoming a wandering tramp (*ʾîš māgēn* is to be understood in light of the Ugaritic *mgn* 'beg, entreat') or *mehallēk* 'vagrant', who must beg his food from door to door.[16]

The structure of the passage orients the educational process. The introductory imperatives—"go," "observe," "be wise"—are sequential stages in the intellectual process. The exhortation "go" calls upon the sluggard to shake off his sloth and choose action instead of sinking further into inaction. Next, "observe" summons the sense faculties need to learn the lesson, which is then internalized and made habitual through the imperative "be wise."

The ant's perpetual activity is invoked by the Teacher as a counterweight to the stereotypical conduct of the lazy man: "In winter the

[15] For the rebuking tone of the rhetorical question "How long?" see also Prov. i 22; Exod. x 3; 1 Sam. i 14; xvi 1; 1 Kgs xviii 21; et passim. On the rhetorical question, see Claus Westermann, "Die Begriffe für Fragen und Suchen im Alten Testament," *FAT* 2 (1974), pp. 162–90; Moshe Held, "The Rhetorical Question in the Bible and in Ugaritic Poetry," *ErIsr* 9 (1969), pp. 72–79 [Hebrew].

[16] Most medieval commentators understood *ʾîš māgēn* to mean "shield bearer"; so do some moderns (e.g., Toy, *Proverbs*, p. 125). Another interpretation associates *māgēn* with the Ugaritic *mgn* 'beg, entreat', thus linking it to the parallel *mehallēk* 'vagrant, beggar'. See William F. Albright, "Some Canaanite-Phoenician Sources of Hebrew Wisdom," SVT 3 (1955), pp. 9–15. For other suggestions see: McKane, *Proverbs*, pp. 324–25; Fox, *Proverbs 1–9*, pp. 217–18.

lazy man does not plow; at harvest time he seeks, and finds nothing" (xx 4). It is paralleled by one of the definitions of the intelligent son: "An intelligent son stores up [food] in summer; the shameful son sleeps in harvest time" (x 5).[17] The ant and the wise son are privy to the secrets of nature and aware of the agricultural seasons; "storing up" (*ʾogēr*), "summer," and "harvest time" are key words both in the ant fable and in the adage about the intelligent son.

The ant that stores food in the summer for use in the winter is the model of foresight and industry.[18] It is mentioned in the warning against sloth (vi 6–11), which incorporates the parable of the ant as a model for emulation. The numerical saying (xxx 24–28) merely lists the main characteristic of the ant among various phenomena from the animal world.[19]

The same ideal represented by the ant underlies two other sayings that do not mention it explicitly: the wise son gathers his crops in summer, in contrast to the incompetent, or "shameful" son who sleeps through the harvest (x 5); the sluggard fails to plow in winter, and harvests nothing (xx 4). The anchoring of the figure of the idler in the social and material reality of an agricultural society is to be interpreted both literally and metaphorically. Drawing readers' attention to the seasonal tasks of agricultural life is a main element of the sage's moral teachings; however lofty its message, the book of Proverbs remains grounded in the daily fabric of life in biblical times and its models for human behavior are drawn from the Teacher's understanding of the order and balance of the natural world.[20]

4.1.3 *The Septuagint's Expanded Version of the Ant Parable*

Following the parable of the ant, the Septuagint text of Proverbs incorporates an addendum praising the bee.[21] Even though the admirable characteristics of insects are mentioned elsewhere in Proverbs

[17] The translation follows Fox, *Proverbs 1–9*, p. 216.

[18] See McKane, *Proverbs*, p. 661.

[19] See A. S. Herbert, "The Parable (*māšāl*) in the Old Testament," *SJT* 7 (1954), pp. 186–90; Johnson, "משל," pp. 162–69; Menachem Haran, "*māšāl*," *EM* 5:548–53 [Hebrew].

[20] See e.g., the warning against the evildoers (i 10–19); against giving surety (vi 1–5); against overly striving for wealth (xxiii 4–5); against intoxication (xxiii 29–35).

[21] The juxtaposition of ant and bee is also found in Aristotle, *Historia animalium*, 622b, 627a.

(xxx 25, 27), the bee, as a paragon of diligence and industry, does not appear in any of the wisdom books of the Bible. The addition (vi 8a–c) reads as follows:

> Or go to the bee, and learn how industrious she is, and how earnestly she performs work;
> Whose products kings and commoners use for health, and she is desired by all and respected.
> Though being weak physically, by having honored wisdom she has obtained distinction.

This praise for the diligent and productive bee, which contributes to the health of kings and commoners, is stated using stylistic and thematic elements typical of the admonitory pattern found in Proverbs 1–9. Just as he did with the ant, here the Teacher proposes that the lad model his behavior on the bee. By juxtaposing the bee's weakness with the recognition it has achieved he emphasizes the value of wisdom. A similar logic underlies the heading of the numerical saying, "Four are among the tiniest on earth, yet they are the wisest of the wise" (Prov. xxx 24).

The high esteem for the bee in the Greek version does not seem to be compatible with the bee's image as a pest and as a metaphor for enemies in the Hebrew Bible (Deut. i 44; Ps. cxviii 12; Isa. vii 18). But it fits in well with the evidence of Hellenistic sources on apiculture and the use of honey for food and medicinal purposes.[22]

Indeed, Septuagint scholars agree that this passage does not derive from a Hebrew *Vorlage* but should be ascribed to a translator located in the Alexandrian cultural milieu.[23] The structural and stylistic duplication of the ant parable in the praise of the bee reinforces the hypothesis that the latter is a secondary interpolation by the Greek translator.[24]

[22] The Bible mentions honey produced by wild bees (Deut. xxxii 13; Judg. xiv 8–9; 1 Sam. xiv 25–27; Ps. lxxxi 17), but there is no textual evidence of beekeeping in the Bible. For further discussion, see Tova Forti, "Bee's Honey: From Realia to Metaphor in Biblical Wisdom Literature," *VT* 56 (2006), pp. 327–41.

[23] See: de Lagarde, *Anmerkungen*, pp. 22–23; Baumgartner, *Étude critique*, p. 68; Mezzacasa, *Il Libro dei Proverbi di Salomone*, p. 127; G. Gerleman, *Studies in the Septuagint III. Proverbs* (Lunds universitets årsskrift 52/3; Lund, 1956), pp. 30–31; Roland L. Giese, "Strength through Wisdom and the Bee in LXX-Prov. 6, 8a–c," *Bib* 73 (1992), pp. 404–11; J. Cook, *The Septuagint of Proverbs*: *Jewish and/or Hellenistic Proverbs?* SVT 69 (1997), pp. 164–68; d'Hamonville, *La Bible d'Alexandrie*: *Les Proverbes*, p. 193.

[24] Ben Sira praises the bee in the spirit of the Greek addition: "Least is the bee

4.2 Animal Habits Worthy of Emulation, in Numerical Sayings

4.2.1 *Ant, Hyrax, Locust, Gecko*

> Four are among the tiniest on earth, yet they are the wisest of the wise: The ants are not a strong people, yet they prepare their food in the summer; the rock hyraxes are not a mighty people, yet they make their houses in the rocks; the locusts have no king, yet all of them go out in ranks; the house gecko grasps with its hands, yet it is in kings' palaces. (Prov. xxx 24–28)

The introductory clause of this numerical saying,[25] "Four are among the tiniest on earth, yet they are the wisest of the wise" (Prov. xxx 24), proposes a common denominator for the animals that follow: their intelligence provides ample compensation for their small size.[26] The sage is not listing the smallest creatures on earth, but rather a variety of tiny animals from different zoological categories that exemplify different aspects of life. Here, as elsewhere, he opts for effective rhetoric over scientific fact.[27] His juxtaposition of small size with practical wisdom inspires human reflection about animal modes of behavior worthy of emulation. The phrase *qᵉṭanê ʾāreṣ* 'tiniest of the earth' denotes not only physical size but also inferior social status and implicitly associates these creatures with aspects of organized human society such as *mōšēl ʾāreṣ* "the ruler of the land" (Isa. xvi 1) and *šōpᵉṭê ʾāreṣ* "rulers of the earth" (Isa. xl 23).[28] The antithetical

---

among winged things, but she reaps the choicest of all harvests" (xi 3). Instead of *qĕṭānā,* MSS A and B of the Geniza read *ʾĕlîl,* either "weak" (as in Syriac) or a diminutive of *ʾal* 'nothing' (cf. Zech. xi 17; Job xiii 4); see M. Z. Segal, *Sefer Ben Sîraʾ Hašālem* (Jerusalem, 1972), p. 67 [Hebrew].

[25] On the numerical saying, see §1.5.2.3.

[26] The MT *mᵉḥukkāmîm* is rendered by the LXX (followed by the Syr. and Vul.) as σοφώτερα τῶν σοφῶν "the wisest of/among the wise," the initial *mêm* being taken as a genitive instead of the prefix of the *puʿal* participle (cf. Exod. xii 9). See Delitzsch, *Proverbs of Solomon* II, p. 301; Murphy, *Proverbs*, p. 233.

[27] McKane (Proverbs, p. 661) puts it this way: "The author's activities as a naturalist are oriented by his search for 'parables' of human life."

[28] For *qṭn* with reference to inferior social status, see Gen. xxxii 11; 2 Sam. vii 19 (= 2 Chr. xvii 17); cf. *nikbaddê ʾāreṣ* 'the honored of the earth' (Isa. xxiii 8). *Qāṭōn* appears as a synonym for *bāzûy* 'despised' (Jer. xlix 15; 1 Sam. xv 17; Deut. i 17; 1 Kgs xxii 31). See: Delitzsch, *Proverbs of Solomon* II, p. 301; Y. Elizur, "The Wisdom of the Proverbs' Composer," *ʿOz Le-David* (Jerusalem, 1964), pp. 24–28 [Hebrew].

relationship between the two parts of the heading is also shaped by the repetition of the third person plural pronoun *hēm(â)* and the use of the consecutive *wāw* as an adversative conjunction.[29]

4.2.1.1 *Nᵉmālâ 'Ant'*[30]

> The ants are not a strong people, yet they prepare their food in the summer. (Prov. xxx 25)

The ant's outstanding traits are diligence and foresight. The verb "prepare" may be interpreted as the typical actions of gathering and storing food during times of plenty, as well as an exemplification of the abstract idea of being able to foresee difficult times and to prepare in advance.

The two verses in Proverbs (vi 8 and xxx 25) that refer to the ant present identical descriptions. But whereas the admonition (vi 8) is addressed to the sluggard and offers him the ant as a paragon to be emulated, the numerical saying (xxx 25) describes the ant impersonally as one example of natural phenomena that corroborate its opening declaration of wise animals. Here the sage portrays the ant in sociopolitical terms and invites readers to compare its traits and habits with an individual's integration into a social system. The description of the ants, *ʿam lōʾ ʿāz* 'not a strong people' (v. 25a), draws on a military idiom that echoes Num. xiii 28a: "However, the people who inhabit the country are powerful (*kî ʿaz hāʿām*)."

In the admonition to the sluggard (vi 6–8) the ant is praised for its hard work and efficiency and independence of rulers and leaders. In the numerical saying its behavior is invoked as exemplary because of the superiority of wisdom to physical strength.

4.2.1.2 *Šāpān 'Rock Hyrax'*

The *šāpān* is usually identified as the rock hyrax *(šāpān selaʿ)*, *Procavia capensis,* based largely on the Bible's description of its habitat (Prov. xxx 26; Ps. civ 18).[31] The hyrax lives in colonies in arid, rocky

[29] The forms *hēm* and *hēmâ* are used interchangeably in the headings of the numerical sequence sayings; for *hēmâ,* see Prov. xxx 18, 29.

[30] On the ant, see §4.1.

[31] The identification of *šāpān* with the coney (AV) is supported by the South Arabian *ṯafan;* see Bodenheimer, *Animal Life in Biblical Lands* I, p. 21. Onqelos and Ps.-

terrain, where it finds refuge in niches and crevices that protect it from predators and inclement weather.[32] It is roughly the size of a rabbit, tailless, with short ears and brownish-grey fur.

The *šāpān* is paired with the *ʾarnebet* ‘hare’ in the dietary laws in Lev. xi 5–6 and Deut. xiv 7, which describe both as nonungulate ruminants. Although hyraxes have a three-part digestive tract, they do not chew their cud.[33] The confusion between the *šāpān* and the hare can be traced back to the ancient versions, but the hyrax belongs to the order Hyracoidea, whereas the rabbit and hare belong to the order Lagomorpha and family Leporidae. Hyraxes are prevalent near the Dead Sea, in the hills of Upper Galilee, the Carmel, and the Negev highlands. The animal’s small size and footpads allow it to scale steep rocks and boulders to find shelter in crannies, as depicted in Psalms civ 18b: “the crags are a refuge for rock-hyraxes,” as well as in the saying under discussion, “they make their houses in the rocks” (Prov. xxx 26b).

The Text

> The rock hyraxes are not a mighty people, yet they make their houses in the rocks. (Prov. xxx 26)

The description of the hyraxes as *ʿam lōʾ ʿāṣûm* ‘not a mighty people’ again suggests military terminology, as in Balak’s appeal to Balaam, “Come then, put a curse upon this people for me, since they are too mighty [*or* numerous] (*ʿāṣûm*) for me” (Num. xxii 6).[34]

Jonathan on the Pentateuch render *šāpān* as *ṭapzāʾ*/*ṭapzayāʾ*, from the Aramaic root *ṭ-p-z* ‘jump’ (corresponds to Hebrew *q-p-ṣ*). The Septuagint (Prov. xxx 26 and Ps. civ 18) has χοιρογρύλλιος ‘rabbit’ (which the Vulgate transliterates in Lev. xi 5 and Deut. xiv 7). The Vulgate renderings of *šāpān* as *erinaciis* (dat. pl. of *erinacius*) in Ps. civ 18, and as *lepusculus* in Prov. xxx 26 demonstrate the confusion of hare and coney. See Tristram, *Natural History of the Bible*, pp. 75–77; I. Aharoni, *Torat Ha-Ḥay* (Tel Aviv, 1923), p. 68; Riede, *Im Spiegel der Tier*, p. 11. Most English translations have “badgers” or “rock badgers” (e.g., RSV, NJPS, NKJ), even though they live in holes, unlike the animal described here and in Ps. civ 18. See also Toy, *Proverbs*, p. 534.

[32] Gilbert, “The Native Fauna,” *HAWANE*, p. 21.

[33] See Firmage, “Zoology,” pp. 1143, 1157 n. 31.

[34] The adjective *ʿāṣûm* is often applied to ethnic collectives, such as *gôy* or *ʿam*, to indicate their military might (Num. xiv 12; Deut. ix 14; Joel i 6, ii 5), or as a quantitative expression to denote large numbers of people and possessions (Exod. i 7; Num. xxxii 1).

The *wāw* that links the two clauses functions as an adversative-emphatic *wāw,* drawing the reader's attention to how an innate sense of self-preservation may compensate for a creature's vulnerability.

In this context, the verbs (*yākînû* "prepare [food]" in v. 25b; *yāśîmû* "make [their home]" in v. 26b) denote a continuous action that signifies a habitual way of life. The wisdom of the hyrax is embodied in its inborn ability to find shelter and protect itself from external menaces, while the ant's wisdom lies in its ability to store up food despite its tiny size.

4.2.1.3 *ʾArbeh 'Locust'*

The Hebrew *ʾarbeh* 'locust' *(Schistocerca gregaria)*[35] has cognates in other Semitic language, such as Akkadian *a/eribu*, *erbūm,*[36] and Ugaritic *ʾirby*. The biblical term *ʾarbeh* 'locust' is commonly applied to the migratory phase of the insect in its fully developed winged stage, as described in the Eighth Plague on Egypt (Exod. x 4–5, 13, 19). Many other names appear in the Bible, however: *gôbay* (Amos vii 1; Nah. iii 17), *gēbîm* (Isa. xxxiii 4), *gāzām* (Amos iv 9; Joel i 4, ii 25), *ḥāgāb* (usually translated as grasshopper; see Lev. xi 22; Num. xiii 33; Isa. xl 22; 2 Chr. vii 13), *ḥāsîl* (1 Kgs viii 37; Isa. xxxiii 4; Joel i 4, ii 25; Ps. lxxviii 46; 2 Chr. vi 28), *ḥănāmal* (Ps. lxxviii 47), *ḥargol* (Lev. xi 22), *yeleq* (Jer. li 14, 27; Nah. iii 15, 16; Joel i 4, ii 25; Ps. cv 34), *solʿām* (Lev. xi 22), *ṣelāṣal* (Deut. xxviii 42), *ṣᵉpônî* (Joel ii 20).

The commentators tried to distinguish a precise meaning for each of these terms. Rashi says that *gāzām*, *ʾarbeh*, *yeleq*, and *ḥāsîl* are all variants of the generic term *gôbaʾy*. The term *yeleq* usually refers to the young hopper without wings, i.e., the larva (*Tg. Neb.* ad loc.) *Gāzām* is often associated with the verb meaning "to prune," and thus as designating the most advanced stage of molting. Similarly, *ḥāsîl* is derived from the root *ḥ-s-l* 'eliminate' and said to refer to the stage at which the insect eats even the seeds (Deut. xxviii 38; cf. *y. Taʿan.* 3:6).[37] The precise identification of each term is problematic, because

[35] See Forti, "Animal Images in the Book of Proverbs," p. 62.

[36] The Sumerian–Akkadian *ura=ḫubullu* lexicographical list presents about 20 kinds of locusts, denoted by compound terms with the first element *erib*. See Landsberger, *Die Fauna des alten Mesopotamien*, pp. 39–40, 121–125; Militarev and Kogan, *SED,* No. 11.

[37] See I. Aharoni, *The Locust* (Jaffa, 1920), pp. 5–39 [Hebrew]. Riede (*Im Spiegel der Tiere*, p. 293) defines *gāzām* as the penultimate stage of molting, and *ḥāsîl* as the

neither the contexts nor the etymologies are sufficient. The different nouns may indicate separate species, be collective terms (e.g., *gāzām* or *ḥāsîl*), or refer to different instars or stages of development, from larva to pupa to mature adult. But even the sequence in Joel i 4—*gāzām*, *ʾarbeh*, *yeleq*, and *ḥāsîl*—cannot help us identify the various names with the developmental stages of the locust.

Locusts, which are grasshoppers of the family Acrididae, go through a life-cycle that depends on climatic conditions, such as seasonal winds and moisture. Reproduction begins when the female finds appropriate soil conditions, i.e., moist ground in which to bury her eggs. The young hoppers (nymphs) that emerge pass through five molting stages. The adult, with wings that enable it to fly substantial distances, emerges after the fifth molt. In plague conditions, hundreds of millions of adults may take to the air. Young hoppers march off in search of vegetation and mature as they travel. Large swarms, guided by winds, devour every plant in sight and ravage the crops in the field, causing ruin and famine to farming societies (see Joel i 4; 1 Kgs viii 37; Amos iv 9).[38] The locust is described as a pest, destroying everything that grows, from the grass in the field to the fruit on the trees (cf. Exod. x 15). Carried by the east wind, during the hot season it lands like a heavy cloud; with the advent of the western wind and abatement of the heat it disappears suddenly (cf. Exod. x 13, 18; Nah. iii 17).

Locust in the Bible and Ancient Near Eastern Literature

The locust is mentioned among the insects that are permitted as food: "But these you may eat among all the winged swarming things that walk on fours: all that have, above their feet, jointed legs to leap with on the ground "(Lev. xi 22; cf. *b. Ḥul* 65b–66a; Damascus Document xii 14–15). The consumption of locust in the ancient Near East may be deduced from a relief in the palace of Sennacherib at Nineveh, which depicts locusts on skewers being served by servants at a banquet.[39]

---

second molting stage in the metamorphosis of the larva (p. 294). But the precise identity of each term in relation to the developmental stage of the locust continues to be a matter of speculation. See ibid., pp. 196–98.

[38] See: Bodenheimer, *Animal Life in Biblical Lands* II, pp. 320–27; Firmage, "Zoology," p. 1150; Gilbert, "The Native Fauna," pp. 40–41.

[39] R. D. Barnett, E. Bleibtreu, and G. E. Turner, *Sculptures from the Southwest Palace of Sennacherib at Nineveh* (London, 1998), pls. 436, 438–439. A report sent to Sargon II, describes the quantity and weight of locusts delivered for culinary purposes; see S. Parpola, *The Correspondence of Sargon II*, Part I (SAA 1; Helsinki 1987), No. 221.

A plague of locust is commonly understood as a figurative trope in threats of punishment for those who disobey God's covenant: "Though you take much seed out to the field, you shall gather in little, for the locust shall consume it" (Deut. xxviii 38). This is paralleled in the Vassal Treaties of Esarhaddon, as a sanction against those who violate them: "May Adad, the canal inspector of heaven and earth, put an end [to vegetation] in your land, may he avoid your meadows and hit your land with a severe destructive downpour, may locusts, which diminish the (produce) of the land, [devour] your crops" (47 lines 440–443a).[40] This imprecation has figurative and stylistic affinities with the Sefire treaty: "For seven years may the locust devour (Arpad), and for seven years may the worm eat, and ... may the grass not come forth that no green may be seen, (and may its) vegetation not be [seen]."[41]

In the Bible, swarming locusts are one of the afflictions, along with famine, pestilence, and blight, that may move the Israelites to utter special entreaties to the Lord in His Temple (1 Kgs viii 37; 2 Chr. vi 28). An invasion by locust was considered to be divine punishment, alongside other natural catastrophes (e.g., famine, blight, mildew, caterpillars). The ancients employed various oracular and mantic means to predict the arrival of locusts. Assyrian documents mention specific prayers and magical techniques employed against an onslaught of locusts, including the use of figurines, in supplications to the God Assur to rid the land of locusts.[42]

The menacing shadow that locusts cast over the inhabitants of Egypt is described in dramatic terms: "Locusts invaded all the land of Egypt and settled within all the territory of Egypt in a thick mass; never before had there been so many, nor will there ever be so many again" (Exod. x 14). A similar dramatic effect is ascribed to the hornet sent by God: "I will send my terror in front of you, and will throw into confusion all the people against whom you shall come, and I will make all your enemies turn their backs to you" (xxiii 27–28; NRSV).

[40] See *ANET*, p. 538 (cf. p. 540, lines 599–600). For a detailed comparison between the curses in the Deuteronomic covenant against those who violate God's treaty (Deut. xxviii 15–68) and those found in the vassal-treaties of Esarhaddon, see Weinfeld, *Deuteronomy and the Deuteronomic School*, pp. 116–29; idem, "The Vassal-Treaties of Esarhadon King of Assyria," *Shnaton* 1 (1976), pp. 109, 118 [Hebrew]; S. Parpola and K. Watanabe, *Neo-Assyrian Treaties and Loyalty Oaths* (SAA 2; Helsinki, 1988), 13:vi:1.

[41] *KAI* No. 222, A:27. See Weinfeld, *Deuteronomy and the Deuteronomic School*, p. 124.

[42] *ABL* 1214, rev. 13.

Swarming locusts darken the earth: "A day of darkness and gloom, a day of densest cloud spread like soot over the hills. A vast, enormous horde—Nothing like it has ever happened, and it shall never happen again through the years and ages" (Joel ii 2). The darkening of the sky is part of the apocalyptic battle between light and darkness, in which the locusts are messengers of the Lord and represent the primeval forces of nature (cf. Joel ii 10).

The frightening image of swarms of locusts swooping down on cultivated fields and denuding them of all vegetation is transformed into a similes for enemy armies: "Now Midian, Amalek, and all the other Kedemites were spread over the plain, as thick as locusts" (Judg. vii 12; cf. Isa. xxxiii 4; Jer. xlvi 23, li 27; Nah. iii 15). The prophet Joel makes more sophisticated use of the trope. He weaves a realistic picture of a plague of locusts into an eschatological prophecy of a military invasion: "For a nation has invaded my land, vast beyond counting" (i 6; cf. ii 5). The dramatic memory of the locust disaster and the regrowth of fields, proof of divine benevolence, is echoed in the salvation prophecy of the Day of the Lord; the image of a well-organized attack by swarms of locusts, despoiling everything in sight, is part of both the realistic and eschatological levels.[43]

In ancient Near Eastern literature, too, the image of the hosts of locusts marching inexorably forwards and devastating vast tracts of land is employed frequently. The annals of the Assyrian kings include descriptions of their enormous armies overwhelming enemy lands and cities. Sargon's army defeats the enemy "like locusts" (*aribiš*);[44] Sennacherib describes the advance of the coalition armies "like a springtime invasion of swarms of locusts" (*kīma tebût aribi maʾdi*).[45] The Ugaritic Kirta Epic applies the image of locust swarms to the armed hosts of the legendary king of Ugarit (1.14 IV 29): *km ʾirby tškn šd // kḥṣn pʾat mdbr*, "like locusts they spread over the field // like grasshoppers on the edge of the steppe."[46]

[43] For more on locusts, see: S. R. Driver, *The Books of Joel and Amos* (CBC; Cambridge, 1897), pp. 82–91; M. Cogan, *Joel* (Mikra Leyisrael; Tel Aviv and Jerusalem, 1994), pp. 25–28 [Hebrew].

[44] Winckler, *Sargon* 110:73.

[45] OIP 2, 43:56–57; J. A. Thompson, "Joel's Locusts in the Light of Near Eastern Parallels," *JNES* 14 (1955), pp. 52–55. For additional examples see: *CAD* E, pp. 257–58; Marcus, "Animal Similes in Assyrian Royal Inscriptions," pp. 98–99; Rimbach, *Animal Imagery in the Old Testament*, pp. 12–14.

[46] *CTA* 14:103–105; 192–194.

Returning to the book of Joel (i 4–12; ii 1–11), we observe that the sudden appearance of the locust is compared to the attack by an enemy (i 6) possessed of a well-trained and battle-ready cavalry (Joel ii 4–5). Joel uses four different names for the insects (i 4) to express the total annihilation of the crops at every stage of its development, from *gāzām* to *ʾarbeh* to *yeleq*, with whatever remains being eaten by the *ḥāsîl*: "What the cutter has left, the locust has devoured; What the locust has left, the grub has devoured; And what the grub has left, the hopper has devoured."

The Text

The locusts have no king, yet all of them go out in ranks. (Prov. xxx 27)

In Prov. xxx 27 the sage reflects on the locust's self-discipline—its ability to march in formation without a king—while ignoring its destructive aspects.[47] The roots *ḥ-ṣ-ṣ* and *ḥ-ṣ-h* (e.g., Gen. xxxii 8) mean "divide, fall into two parts" and would refer to the military tactic of dividing one's forces.[48] Thomas, alleging an etymological link between *ḥōṣēṣ* and the Arabic *ḥaṣṣa* 'cut', reads *ḥōṣēṣ* as an adverbial accusative: the locusts go out in 'divisions'. The Septuagint, too, opts for military terminology: ἐκστρατεύει ἀφ' ἑνὸς κελεύσματος εὐτάκτως, "they march orderly at one command."

The image of locusts marching in perfect order is also used by Joel: "They rush like warriors, They scale a wall like fighters. And each keeps to his own track. Their paths never cross; no one jostles another, each keeps to his own course. And should they fall through a loophole, they do not get hurt" (ii 7–8).[49]

Not unlike the self-discipline of the ants in the admonition to the sluggard (vi 6–7), the locusts are viewed from a societal perspective and are praised of their ability to act in a highly organized manner, despite the apparent lack of direct authority.

In Proverbs, in sharp contrast to other biblical passages that portray the locust in a negative light, the locust lifestyle—its organized society—is proposed as a model for human beings. Here the locust is a

[47] McKane, *Proverbs*, p. 662.

[48] Delitzsch, *Proverbs of Solomon* II, p. 302.

[49] See: David W. Thomas, "Notes on some Passages in the Book of Proverbs," *VT* 15 (1965), p. 276; McKane, *Proverbs,* p. 662. The Targum (followed by Ibn Ezra) interprets *ḥōṣēṣ* as an intransitive verb, "they all gather together as one."

wise creature that lives without formal rulers but has an organized social system worthy of emulation.

4.2.1.4 *Śᵉmāmît 'House Gecko'*

> The house gecko grasps with its hands, yet it is in kings' palaces. (Prov. xxx 28)

Although nothing in the Bible permits certain identification of the hapax *śᵉmāmît*, scholars generally rely on the tradition of the ancient versions. The Septuagint renders *śᵉmāmît* as καλαβώτη 'spotted lizard', the Vulgate as *stellio* 'spotted lizard', the Aramaic (based on the Syriac) as *ʾamqᵉtāʾ*/*ʾaqmᵉtāʾ* 'spider' or 'lizard'.[50] The variety of suggestions offered by commentators over the ages attests that this remains a crux. The Sages suggested writing *sᵉmāmît,* with a *sāmek* instead of *śîn,* and identified the animal with a type of poisonous spider (*b. Šabb.* 77b; *b. Sanh.* 103b; *y. Šabb.* 1:1 [3b]).[51] Medieval Jewish commentators accepted this identification and interpreted the phrase "grasps with its hands" (Prov. xxx 28a) as referring to the cunning legs of the spider, which spins a web to trap flies, mosquitoes, and other insects, even within royal palaces.[52] But the phrase seems particularly apt to the house gecko *(Hemidactylus turcicus),* with its remarkable hand-like feet equipped with adhesive pads that allow it to climb steep walls and cling to ceilings.

In fact, the meaning of the Masoretic vocalization *tᵉtappēś* is uncertain.[53] The vocalization *tittāpēś* (*nipʿal*)[54] offers several possibil-

[50] For the identification as lizard or house gecko, see: Löw, *Fauna und Mineralien der Juden,* pp. 265–66; Aharoni, *Torat Ha-Ḥay*, p. 62; Dor, *Zoological Lexicon* (Tel Aviv, 1965), pp. 192, 336–37; idem, *Animals in the Days of the Bible*, pp. 166–67; Elqanah Billiq, "*Śᵉmāmît,*" *EM* 8:321–22 [Hebrew]. Talshir, relying on etymology, identifies the Aramaic/Syriac *ʾamqᵉtāʾ* with the Hebrew *ʾănāqâ* 'lizard' (*Varanus griseus*) (Talshir, *The Nomenclature of the Fauna*, pp. 222–24). For the midrash in which the *śᵉmāmît*'s fear of the scorpion represents the weaker being's fear of the stronger, see *b. Šabb.* 77b. For a comprehensive survey of the hermeneutical tradition about *śᵉmāmît*, see Delitzsch, *Proverbs of Solomon* II, pp. 303–305.

[51] For the identification as spider by modern commentators, see Tristram, *Natural History of the Bible*, pp. 265–66; Tur-Sinai, *Mišley Šᵉlōmōh*, p. 153.

[52] Gersonides, ad loc; Arama, *Yad Avshalom*, p. 101. Other medieval commentators (R. Saʿadya Gaon; Ibn Janaḥ; and David Qimḥi) understood *śᵉmāmît* as *śᵉnûnît*, the swallow that nests in royal palaces. Ibn Ezra, focusing on *bᵉyādayim tᵉtappēś,* searched for an animal that resembles man in this way and suggested the ape, which grabs its food with its hands.

[53] The root *t-p-ś* 'seize, grasp, take possession of' is not found in the *piʿel.* For the

ities, however. The logical structure of the other verses, in which the opening clause refers to the animal's vulnerability, supports understanding *tittāpēś* as "can be grasped," thus emphasizing the animal's wisdom despite its frailty;[55] but equally likely is Rashi's notion that it alludes to the gecko's amazing ability to scale vertical walls. This interpretation fits with what we have seen of the sage as a close observer of the natural world.

In his focus on the unique qualities of the little reptile that climbs around in the king's palace the sage is expressing the same admiration and sense of wonder at natural phenomena as in the verses about the ant and the locust. The house gecko has a far greater ability to infiltrate the royal halls than do most human beings. In addition, the contrast between the lowly reptile and the grandness of palaces heightens the rhetorical effect of the saying.

4.2.1.5 *Summary*

The numerical saying of the tiny but wise introduces a group of animals whose physical slightness is offset by their perspicacity. This is not a random assembly of natural phenomena but rather a deliberate and systematic collection of animal habits that allude to human forms of behavior and social organization. The heading and body of the saying are mutually dependent: the heading defines the common denominator of the illustrations, which in turn demonstrate its veracity. Although each phenomenon occupies an independent syntactic and conceptual unit, the combination of all of them augments their rhetorical effect.

The fact that this numerical saying has no explicit moral has led scholars to characterize it as an encyclopedic rubric for classification of scientific phenomena. However, the very fact of selecting phenomena linked to the heading by a common concept points to the educational intent of the saying. The numerical saying is designed to stimulate the curiosity of readers and hearers and spur them to test the

---

idiomatic use of *t-p-ś bᵉyad* 'catch, seize', see Jer. xxxviii 23; for the variant *t-p-ś bakkāp*, see Ezek. xxi 16 and xxix 7.

[54] Cf. *tibbāʿēl* 'when she is married' (Prov. xxx 23a) and BHS ad. loc.

[55] Most modern scholars interpret *tittāpēś* as "can be grasped," emphasizing the animal's wisdom despite its frailty. See: Toy, *Proverbs*, p. 535; Gemser, *Sprüche Salomos*, p. 106; McKane, *Proverbs*, p. 662; Murphy, *Proverbs*, pp. 233, 236–237.

validity of the heading, "Four are among the tiniest on earth, yet they are the wisest of the wise."[56] The details initiate an educational process that begins with empathy for the tiny creatures, evokes admiration for the instinctual behavior that compensates for their handicap, and finally urges readers to adopt such modes of behavior. The numerical saying proposes that we look closely at the wonders of nature; but it calls, not for observation, but rather for applying the lessons learned to the human social order.[57]

4.2.2 Layiš 'Lion', Zarzīr Motnayim 'Rooster'(?), Tayiš 'He-goat': Fleet-footed Creatures

> There are three that are stately of stride, four that carry themselves well: The lion is mightiest among the beasts, and recoils before none; the *zarzīr motnayim,* the he-goat, the king whom none dares resist. (Prov. xxx 29–31)[58]

4.2.2.1 Layiš *'Lion'*

Layiš is a rare poetic term for lion.[59] It may apply specifically to the male, but its limited occurrence in the Bible (Isa. xxx 6; Job iv 11; Prov. xxx 30) allows no certain definition of type, age, or the like. Cognates of *layiš* are found in Aramaic, *laytāʾ/lētāʾ;* Arabic, *layṯ;* and Akkadian *nēšu* and *nēštu* (lioness).[60]

Layiš occurs only in the masculine form and with masculine verbs (Prov. xxx 30; Job iv 11). It is used in parallel with *b^e^nê lābîʾ* (Job iv 11) and paired with *lābîʾ* in the list of animals of the Negev (Isa. xxx 6).[61]

[56] On the saying's witty character and the surprise created by the antithetical headline, see Roth, *Numerical Sayings*, pp. 20–21. See also §1.5.2.3.

[57] Toy, *Proverbs*, p. 534.

[58] The translation follows NJPS except for the identification of *zarzīr motnayim.*

[59] On the various Hebrew terms for the lion, see §2.2.2.2.

[60] The l > n shift in initial position is uncommon in Akkadian, but does occur sporadically in dialects of Akkadian, Arabic, Aramaic and others. See Strawn, *What is Stronger than a Lion?* pp. 325–26.

[61] In Isa. xxx 6 and Prov. xxx 30, the Septuagint renders *layiš* as σκύμνος λέοντος 'lion's whelp' just as it does *k^e^pîr* (Judg. xiv 5) and *gûr* (Gen. xlix 9).

4.2.2.2 *Zarzīr Motnayim 'Rooster'(?)*

Although the noun *zarzīr* by itself appears in rabbinic literature as the name of a bird of the raven family—a starling, crow, or a magpie (*b. B. Qam.* 92b; *b. Ḥul. 65a; Gen. Rab.* 65:75), the identity of the hapax *zarzīr motnayim* in the Bible remains obscure.[62]

Commentators have interpreted *zarzīr motnayim* as referring to swiftness (*z-r-z*) and hence as an epithet for some swift creature, based on the heading of the saying: "There are three that are stately of stride" and the idea that the nomen rectum *motnayim* 'loins' may indicate swiftness of motion. The collocation of *z-r-z* and *motnayim* has also been understood on the basis of the Aramaic verb *z-r-z* 'gird' (cf. Tg. 1 Kgs xviii 46).[63] Modern commentators identify *zarzīr motnayim* with the rooster, based on early translations such as the paraphrastic version in the Septuagint (and the Targum), "a cock walking in boldly among the hens."[64]

The varied proposals for the identification of *zarzīr motnayim* prove the complexity of this issue. I prefer to second Rashi's frank admission: "I do know not what it is."[65]

[62] For a comprehensive discussion of the noun *zarzīr* and the construction *zarzīr motnayim*, see Delitzsch, *Proverbs of Solomon* II, pp. 305–309.

[63] Ibn Ezra makes the case for its being the "name of an animal based on the word *motnayim*, i.e., swift of loins." Gersonides opts for a "thin-hipped dog led by hunters" (thus modern translations "greyhound," such as KJV and NJPS; and cf. RSV Isa. lvi 11). David Qimḥi suggests "a leopard, which has thin flanks and strong legs, or a warhorse." See Kahana, *Sefer Mishley*, p. 144; Elqanah Billiq, "Zarzīr motnayim," *EM* 2:941 [Hebrew]. Bewer, followed by Gemser (*Sprüche Salomos*, p. 106), suggests emending *zarzīr motnayim* to *zarzīr mitnaśśēʾ* 'overweening *zarzīr* (for *mitnaśśēʾ*, cf. v. 32), on the basis of the LXX reading ἐμπεριπατῶν θηλείαις εὔψυξος 'walking in boldly among the hens'. See J. Bewer, "Two Suggestions on Prov. 30.31 and Zech. 9.16," *JBL* 67 (1948), p. 61.

[64] The Vg. reads *gallus succinctus lumbos* 'the cock whose loins are girded'. The Peshitta amplifies the text: "the rooster with a double comb who walks around proudly among the hens."

[65] Delitzsch (*Proverbs of Solomon* II, p. 309) follows the hypothesis, already raised by previous commentators, that the original reading *keleb* 'dog' was deliberately avoided "because it does not sound well in the Heb. collection of words." The expression *zarzīr motnayim* 'girt about the loins', i.e., "with strong loins" or "with slender limbs," should be considered a proper name of the hunting dog and not a descriptive attribute. Tur-Sinai (*Pᵉšuṭo šel Miqraʾ*, 386–87) agrees, noting the lack of correspondence between the lion and the good walkers promised by the heading. He cites the midrash about the three bold creatures that one cannot resist: "the dog among the animals, the rooster among the fowl, and others say even the goat among the small cattle" (*b. Beṣah*, 25b).

4.2.2.3 *Tayiš 'He-goat'*

The *tayiš* is one of the terms for a goat. The male is the *śᵉʿîr ʿizzîm* and the female is *śᵉʿîrat ʿizzîm*; the adult male is an *ʿattûd* or *tayiš* (Aramaic and Syriac *tᵉyāšāʾ*) or *ṣᵉpîr*, and the young is the *gᵉdî*. The ancestral wild goat (*Capra hircus*) is thought to have been first domesticated in Persia in the sixth millennium BCE. The goat has thick, outward curling horns, a dangling goatee, and strong legs, which facilitate its scrambling up and down steep hills.

4.2.2.4 *The Graded Numerical Sequence*

> There are three that are stately of stride, four that carry themselves well. (Prov. xxx 29)

The graded numerical sequence is not used unequivocally as a means of didactic admonition, but rather as a framework that joins several phenomena that share a common denominator based on values that are sometimes ambiguous. The educational message embodied in the saying is camouflaged by the empirical-scientific reporting style, forcing listeners to use their full critical faculties to decode the message.

Both of the parallel clauses in the heading of this graded numerical sequence contain the *hipʿil* present participle of the auxiliary verb *mêṭîb* 'make good, do well', linked to absolute infinitives of motion. In this construction the verb functions as an adverb, as in the phrase *mēṭib naggēn* 'plays skillfully' (Ezek. xxxiii 32; cf. 1 Sam. xvi 17).[66] Thus the reader/listener is called upon to search for the common feature of these phenomena.

> The lion is mightiest among the beasts, and recoils before no one. (Prov. xxx 30)

The lion is presented as the first among the good walkers, the mightiest beast that is afraid of no one. The proof that the *layiš* is the "mightiest among the beasts" is introduced by the *wāw* consecutive attached to an explicative clause: it "recoils before no one." That this is the meaning of *wᵉlōʾ yāšûb* 'does not return/turn back' can be

[66] On the auxiliary verb *hêṭîb* with the infinitive, see GKC, § 114n.

derived from another verse in which the phrase appears, "He scoffs at fear, he cannot be frightened, he does not recoil (*w^e^lōʾ yāšûb*) from the sword" (Job xxxix 22), as well as from the parallel image of the Lord as a lion that is not deterred by the shouts of the shepherds (Isa. xxxi 4). Thus, *w^e^lōʾ yāšûb* express the courage of one who never retreats. Even the dative phrase *mipp^e^nêy kōl* "before no one" emphasizes the perception of the lion as a paragon of courage.

> The *zarzīr motnayim,* the he-goat, the king whom none dares resist (*ʾalqûm ʿimmô*) … (Prov. xxx 31)

Verse 31 presents two animals, the *zarzīr motnayim* and the he-goat, linked in Hebrew by the disjunctive *ʾô* 'or', which translators tend to elide or render as a conjunctive *and.*[67] The reason for linking them is not explained by the syntax, but by the heading of the numerical saying: they are both "stately of stride" and "carry themselves well" (xxx 29). The inclusion of the he-goat as "stately of stride" is not a problem; Ibn Ezra on this verse explains that it walks in front of the flock, citing "like he-goats (*ʿattûdîm*) that lead the flock" (Jer. l 8).

The last clause (xxx 31b) seems to be out of place here, since it mentions a king rather than an animal. The enigmatic phrase *ʾalqûm ʿimmô* is generally rendered by taking *ʾalqûm* as two words—*ʾal qûm* or *ʾel qûm*—as found in certain textual traditions.[68] The Septuagint, followed by the Syriac and Aramaic, vocalize *ʿimmô* 'with him' as *ʿammô* 'his nation', to produce "a king publicly speaking before a nation."[69] Medieval commentators, too, favor a two-word construction, the negative particle *ʾal* plus the jussive *qûm* 'rise up', turning the clause into an injunction against rebelling against the king.[70]

[67] Thomas ("Textual and Philological Notes," p. 291) suggests that *ʾô tayiš* 'or he-goat' be read *w^e^tayiš* 'and he-goat', the *wāw* introducing an explanatory gloss on the obscure *zarzīr motnayim* (cf. McKane, *Proverbs*, p. 663).

[68] Eastern MSS divide *ʾalqûm* into two words, *ʾal* and *qûm*. See Ginzburg's note in his edition of the Bible.

[69] Toy (*Proverbs*, p. 537), assumes that the words *melek* and *ʾalqûm* are corrupted forms of kingly traits and movement of animals.

[70] See e.g. Rashi and Ibn Ezra, followed by modern translations like the NJPS: "The king whom none dares resist" (cf. Driver's slight change *ʿimmō lōʾ qām*, in "Problems in the Hebrew Text of Proverbs," p. 194). Others read "*qām ʿal* or *ʾel ʿammō* 'standing over his people' (cf. RSV "and a king striding before his people"). *Qūm* expresses rulership (Exod. i 8; Job xxv 3) as well as rebellion (see 2 Chr. xxi 4). *Qūm* as a term for government is borrowed for the animal kingdom: "Behold, a people! As a lioness it rises up (*yāqûm*) and as a lion it lifts itself" (RSV: Num. xxiii 24a).

According to the heading of the numerical saying, the lion, *zarzīr motnayim*, and he-goat are "good walkers." However, the lion is portrayed, not as "stately of stride," but as brave: it is his courage that is celebrated and not his gait. What, then, is the lion doing here?

We should recall that the enumeration of remarkable traits in the animal kingdom is aimed at enlightening and inspiring readers to adopt the right moral values in their own lives. It would seem, then, that the inclusion of the lion here derives from literary and editorial concerns rather than from observation. The multiple occurrences of *melek* 'king' in the adjacent units (see xxx 22, 27, 31; xxxi 1, 3, 4) suggest that the editor had a larger purpose in mind when he gathered and arranged them. As we have seen, the Book of Proverbs compares the lion to the ruler or the king (cf. *ʾărî* in xxviii 15 and *kᵉpîr* in xix 12). The association between lion and king is expressed clearly regarding proportionate and well-regulated behavior in the royal court. The king is also compared to the lion in the glory of his raiment and in his rage and cruelty to his subjects (xix 12, xx 2, xxviii 15).[71]

Although the identification of the *zarzīr motnayim*, the function of the disjunctive *or* before the he-goat, and the sense of *ʾalqûm* remain obscure, the evocation of lion and king in the same passage, under the rubric of those who are "stately of stride," hints at the royal aspect of the lion's self-confident gait.

This saying is one of five numerical sayings (xxx 16–33), four of them following the "three and four" sequence model (vv. 15b, 18, 21, 29) and one citing only "four" (v. 24). Some form of the word "king" occurs in three of them: "A slave who becomes king" (v. 22a); "the locusts have no king" (v. 27a), and "the house gecko … is in kings' palaces" (v. 28); "the king whom none dares resist" (v. 31). The superiority of the animals in these sayings—both the "tiniest on earth" and the "stately of stride"—is illuminated by the focus on kings: the locusts' self-discipline is an antithesis to human society, which needs a king to manage its affairs (v. 27); the gecko's wisdom is exemplified by its ability to penetrate royal palaces (v. 28); the epithet "stately of stride" applied to the *zarzīr motnayim* and the he-goat refers to the courtly manners appropriate in the presence of the king.

Describing animals in association with the king, against whom

[71] For a broader discussion of the lion in kingly sayings (xix 12, xx 2, xxviii 15), see §§2.2.2.2–2.2.2.4.

one should not rebel *(ʾal-qûm ʿimmô),* expresses praise for their natural wisdom, while at the same time alluding to the sage's critical attitude toward rulers' undue use of power.

The graded numerical sequence is not used unequivocally as a means of didactic admonition, but rather as a framework that joins several phenomena that share a common denominator based on values that are sometimes ambiguous. The educational message embodied in the saying is camouflaged by the empirical-scientific style, which forces listeners to use their full critical faculties to decode the message.

4.2.3 *Vulture and Serpent: Animal Conduct that Inspires Human Wonder*

> Three things are beyond my comprehension; four I do not understand: The way of a vulture in the sky,[72] the way of a serpent on a rock, the way of a ship on the high seas, and the way of a man with a maiden: Such is the way of an adulteress: She eats, wipes her mouth, and says, "I have done no wrong." (Prov. xxx 18–20)[73]

4.2.3.1 *Nāḥāš 'Snake, Serpent'*

Nāḥāš denotes any reptile of the suborder Ophidia. The onomatopoeic noun *nāḥāš* (Ugaritic *nḥš*, Arabic *ḥanašun*) is a generic term for a variety of snakes, including *śārāp*, *ṣepaʿ*, *ṣipʿônî*, *peten,*[74] *ʾepʿeh*, *šᵉpîpōn*, and *ʿakšûb.*[75]

The snake is one of the mythological beasts in the literature Syria-Palestine. Isaiah lists the enemies of Yahweh (the same as those of Baal in the epic of the rebellion of the sea): "In that day the Lord will punish, with His great, cruel, mighty sword Leviathan the Elusive Serpent (*naḥaš bariaḥ*), Leviathan the Twisting Serpent (*naḥaš*

[72] On the *nešer* in the Bible and its identification with the griffon vulture, see §2.1.1.2.
[73] Free translation.
[74] The noun *peten* is attested in Ug. *bṯn* (RS 24.244); Akk. *bašmu* (Landsberger, *Fauna*, pp. 55–60); Aram/Syr *pitnāʾ*; and Arab. *batanun* (Firmage, "Zoology," p. 1156). *Peten* is a poetical term in the Bible (see Isa. xi 8; Ps. lviii 5, xci 13; Job xx 14, 16).
[75] *ʿakšûb* is synonymous with *nāḥāš* in Ps. cxl 4; it is also one the six names (i.e., species) of serpent mentioned in *ʾAbot R. Nat.* xxxix 3 (ed. Schechter). On the various species of *nāḥāš* in the Bible, see §2.1.2.1.

ʿăqallātôn); He will slay the Dragon (*tannîn*) of the sea" (Isa. xxvii 1; cf. Amos ix 3; Ps. lxxiv 13–14, civ 26; Job xl 25). In the Canaanite epic, the same cosmic enemies are mentioned by his rival Mot as having been defeated by Baal: "When you killed Litan, the Fleeing Serpent, annihilated the Twisty Serpent, the Potentate with seven Heads."[76]

The *nāḥāš* is the first specific animal mentioned in the Bible (except for the *tannînim* of the Creation story); in the first two chapters, only broad categories (*b*ᵉ*hēmâ, ḥayyâ, ʿôp haššāmayim* [meaning *all* flying creatures and not just birds]) are mentioned. Its qualities are described at the outset: "Now the serpent was the shrewdest of all the wild beasts" (Gen. iii 1a). The personified serpent in the narrative of the Garden of Eden, who conducts a conversation with the woman and tempts her to eat the fruit of the Tree of Knowledge, has shaped all later perceptions of the snake as the archenemy of humankind (Gen. iii 15; cf. Gen. xlix 17; Ps. xci 13). The account of its punishment for provoking Eve into disobeying the divine prohibition (Gen. iii 1–5, 14–15) functions as an etiological fable to explain its form of locomotion (Gen. iii 14). This trait gave rise to the idea that snakes eat dust: "Let them lick dust like snakes, like crawling things on the ground!" (Mic. vii 17; cf. Isa. lxv 25).

The Bible mentions some snakes as living in arid regions (Deut. viii 15) or finding shelter among boulders, stone walls (Amos v 19; Qoh. x 8), and caves (Isa. xi 8).[77]

In the Bible, all snakes are considered to be poisonous (see Deut. xxxii 25, 33b; Jer. viii 17; Ps. lviii 5, c 4).[78] Their forked tongue, which snakes stick out toward their prey before they attack, gave rise to the belief that they kill with their tongue (Job xx 16b; Ps. cxl 4b), rather than their fangs.

[76] See Dennis Pardee, "The Baʿlu Myth," in W. W. Hallo and K. L. Younger (eds.), *The Context of Scripture, Volume 1: Canonical Compositions from the Biblical World* (Leiden, 1997), p. 265; Oded Borowski, "Animals in the Literature of Syria-Palestine," *HAWANE*, p. 305.

[77] See Yair Aḥituv and Samuel Loewenstamm, *"Naḥaš," EM* 5:821–22 [Hebrew]; Feliks, *Animals in the Bible*, p. 102; Firmage, "Zoology," pp. 1156, 1159, n. 77.

[78] Cf. Isa. xiv 29; Ps. lviii 5, cxl 4. A similar generalization is reflected in a rabbinic saying: "The best of snakes—crush its head" (*Mek.* Exod., *B*ᵉ*šallak* 1 (89).

4.2.3.2 *Discussion of the Saying*

The heading of this numerical sequence[79] saying employs synonymous parallelism between the numbers three and four and between the pattern set by the sequential numbers "three" and "four" and the copula complements, "[things] beyond my comprehension" and "[things] I do not understand." The sage's attitude toward the four wondrous phenomena that are beyond his ken—"Three things are beyond my comprehension (*nipl*ᵉ*ʾû*); four I do not understand"—is similar to Job's reactions to natural wonders: "Who is this who obscures counsel without knowledge? Indeed, I spoke without understanding of things beyond me (*niplāʾôt*) which I did not know" (xlii 3). It also recalls the psalmist's "It is beyond my knowledge [Qere: *p*ᵉ*lîʾâ*]; it is a mystery; I cannot fathom it" (Ps. cxxxix 6). The formula of astonishment arouses our curiosity and spurs us to investigate the sage's observation as he searches for the meaning of the marvels that are beyond his grasp. The first two are animal phenomena: the vulture, as an example of flight through the air; and the snake, as the earthbound movement of reptiles.

Elsewhere in the Bible, the ancients' admiration of the vulture's way of life is expressed with regard to three aspects of its behavior:[80] the high rocks in which it nests (e.g., Job xxxix 27–28; Jer. xlix 16; Obad. 4); its graceful gliding motion, despite the heaviness of its wings (e.g., Deut. xxviii 49; Isa. xl 31; Jer. iv 13, xlviii 40, xlix 22; Ezek. xvii 3, 7; Lam. iv 19), and its searching for prey on the battlefield to provide food for its young (Job xxxix 27–30; cf. Hab. i 8; Job ix 26).

The Assyrians' admiration of the *erû* 'eagle'—the emblematic bird of prey in Mesopotamia—for its bravery and prowess features prominently in royal inscriptions. Sargon's warriors are compared to brave eagles (*kīma erê qardūti*) flying beyond rivers and mountains.[81] Sargon himself compared his ability to capture the enemy in his net to the eagle's hunting its prey while flying (*kīma erê muttapriši abaršu ina šeti*).[82] Tiglath-Pileser I compared his protection of his lands to the eagle's spreading its wings (*ša nuballūšu kīma urinni eli mātāti šuparrurū*).[83] The eagle's nesting on mountain cliffs inspired

[79] On the numerical sequence saying, see §1.5.2.4.
[80] On the *nešer,* see §2.1.1.2.
[81] See: TCL 3, 6:25; Winckler, *Sargon* 56:329–30; 129:129.
[82] See *Iraq* 16 (1954), 186:45–46.
[83] See *AKA* 94:57–58.

Sennacherib's description of the enemy's encampment on the steep peaks of Mt. Nippur (*ša kīma erê ašared eṣṣūrē ṣēr zūqti Nippur šadî marṣi šubassun šitkunat*).[84]

The four wonders are described in a fixed pattern: *derek* 'way', as the nomen regens attached to the subject of four phenomena—the vulture, the snake, the ship, and a man—followed by a locative clause: "in the sky," "on a rock," "on the high seas," and "with a maiden."

The key word *derek* refers to the route of the vulture's flight and wonder at the riddle of the vulture's navigational abilities. Admiration of the mysterious movement of predatory birds is also mentioned the book of Job: "Is it by your wisdom that the hawk grows pinions, spreads his wings to the south?" (xxxix 26).

The same sense of wonder attaches to the earthbound, legless reptile that slithers along the ground without leaving a trace in its wake (cf. Gen. iii 14).[85]

At first it seems that the ship at sea does not fit in here, because the other items are natural creatures, whereas the ship is a product of human culture. But ships at sea made a profound impression on the ancients, who saw them as one of His marvels:

> How many are the things You have made, O Lord; You have made them all with wisdom; the earth is full of Your creations. There is the sea, vast and wide, with its creatures beyond number, living things, small and great, There go the ships, and Leviathan that You formed to sport with. (Ps. civ 24–26; cf. Wis. xiv 1–4)

In our verse, "the way of a ship on the high seas," it is the ship's movement that arouses astonishment, since it navigates without signposts or a marked route. Thus we may interpret the way of the ship in the high seas as the route that leaves no traces apart from the foam that subsides and vanishes in the ship's wake. In this fashion, the "way of a ship" resembles the ways of the vulture and the snake. The poet's astonishment is understandable, since the ancients considered the sailors

[84] See OIP 2, 36:77–79. On different versions of the same usage and on other occurrences of the same imagery, see Marcus, "Animal Similes in Assyrian Royal Inscriptions," pp. 94–96 and n. 72; Rimbach, *Animal Imagery in the O.T.*, pp. 50–54. On Assyrian imagery of winged creatures see Schott, *Die Vergleiche*, pp. 80–81, 91–92, 96–97; on the vulture/eagle, see ibid., Nos. 42, 74, 177, 286.

[85] Ibn Ezra emphasizes the wonder of the legless snake's "walking" on the rock; Gersonides stresses the mystery of his passing without a sign. Toy (*Proverbs*, p. 531) questions this, "since no trace is left on a rock by the passage of any animal," and says that the mystery is that it walks without feet.

to be wise people who were skilled in the highly valued art of navigation (see Ezek. xxvii 8–9).

Note that, in another context, vultures and ships are linked by Job: "My days fly swifter than a runner; they flee without seeing happiness, they pass like reed-boats, like a vulture swooping onto its prey" (ix 25–26).

In the fourth clause the sage shifts his focus to something quite different: the way of a man with a maiden (v. 19d); i.e., how man and woman can wondrously create new life (cf. Ps. cxxxix 13–16; Qoh. xi 5). Clearly the motif of wonder can also touch on male-female relations, the mystery of a woman's attraction to a man (see Gen. iii 16) and the secret of a man's attraction to a woman (see Song vii 10).[86] The fourth clause preserves the rhythm of the first three and fulfills the promise of the heading of four things beyond understanding. But now *derek* has a different sense—"manner" rather than "path."

The moral application follows: "Such is the way of an adulteress: She eats, wipes her mouth, and says, 'I have done no wrong' " (v. 20). The picture is of an adulterous woman who hides the evidence of her misdeeds; she is compared to the person who eats and then wipes her face, leaving no trace of her action.[87] Here eating is a metaphor for sexual intercourse; compare the *ʾēšet k^e^sîlût* 'woman of folly', who encourages the simpleton to taste the illegitimate pleasures she offers him, "stolen water" and "secret bread" (Prov. ix 17).[88] The "strange woman," too, offers the youth a festive meal (Prov. vii 13–23)—an invitation that no doubt evokes sexual implications. The image of the adulterous woman who conceals her actions is accompanied by her blatant declaration that "I have done no wrong."[89]

Although the use of the particle *kēn* is characteristic of the opening of the application clause in the comparative saying, the other characteristics of the pattern are missing. In the usual pattern, the first clause,

[86] Murphy (*Proverbs*, p. 235) interprets *derek* (v. 19d) as "the *course* of the attachment that has made the two one, the mystery of how this was accomplished."

[87] The LXX renders Heb. *māḥăṭâ pîhā* as ἀπονιψαμένη 'having washed herself'. The verb *m-ḥ-h* is used for wiping tears (Isa. xxv 8) and for wiping/cleaning a dish (2 Kgs xxi 13).

[88] See: Gemser, *Sprüche Salomos*, p. 106; R. B. Y. Scott, *Proverbs – Ecclesiastes* (AB 18; Garden City, N.Y., 1965), p. 181; Murphy, *Proverbs,* p. 236. "Stolen water" alludes to sexual intercourse in Prov. v 15–20. See Fox, *Proverbs 1–9*, pp. 199, 200, 302.

[89] For *ʾāwen* as 'sin, deceit, evil deed,' cf. Prov. xxii 8; Job xv 35. For "evil plots," cf. Prov. vi 18; Isa. lix 7; Jer. iv 14.

with one or two comparata, is introduced by the comparative *kap,* and the second clause by the particle *kēn;* e.g. "Like vinegar to the teeth, like smoke to the eyes, is a lazy man to those who send him on a mission"(Prov. x 26; cf. xxvi 1, 2, 8; xi 19; xxvi 19).[90] In our saying, no comparative *kap* linked to the four wonders prepares us for the *kēn* that introduces the adulterous woman. Without the asseverative *kēn*, we clearly have two separate literary units: a numerical saying composed of four nominative clauses with the same tempo (vv. 18–19); and a descriptive report punctuated by third-person feminine verbs: "She eats, wipes her mouth, and says …" (v. 20).

Some scholars, taking the *ᶜalmâ* to be a young woman betraying her husband, have interpreted the fourth wonder, "the way of a man with a maiden" (v. 19d) as the vehicle whose tenor is presented in the application clause (v. 20).[91]

The links that turn the graded numerical sequence and the application clause into a single conceptual unit are evidence of a secondary editorial process highlighting the warning against an immoral phenomenon. The particle *kēn* joins the adulteress clause with the graded numerical sequence, and specifically with "the way of a man with a maiden" (v. 19d). It also links the application clause to the heading of the graded numerical sequence, "Three things are beyond my comprehension; four I do not understand," offering an additional mystery: how an adulterous woman can avoid leaving any trace of her misdeeds. In addition, the ambiguity of the verb *y-d-ᶜ* 'know' in the heading, alluding to both intellectual and carnal knowledge, may foreshadow the physical intercourse between man and woman alluded to in the fourth example of the numerical saying (cf. Gen. iv 1, 17, 25; xix 8; Judg. xi 39).[92]

The key word *derek* 'way' functions as an anaphora in each line of the numerical saying. In the first three it refers to physical motion: the

[90] On the comparative saying, see §1.5.1.1.
[91] E.g., Ibn Ezra and Gersonides among medieval commentators. Delitzsch (*Proverbs of Solomon* II, pp. 296–98,) sees the use of *ᶜalmâ* as the key to understanding the saying; *ᶜalmâ* is a young woman ripe for marriage and pregnancy (cf. Gen. xxiv 43; Isa. vii 14), as opposed to *bᵉtûlâ* 'virgin' (Gen. xxiv 16). Hence "the way of a man with a maiden" indicates a sexual encounter with a young woman, and not a virgin, and links up with the adulterous woman in the application clause. Delitzsch glosses the prepositional *bêt* of *bᵉᶜalmâ* as *copula carnalis* (idem, p. 296); see also Toy, *Proverbs*, p. 531.
[92] See *ydᶜ* in *BDB*, p. 394.

flight of a vulture, the slithering of a snake over a rock, and the passage of a ship over the sea. In the fourth case, however, it is a metaphor for a sexual relationship, "the way of a man with a maiden" (19d).[93] The shift of meaning of *derek* paves the way for linking the four wonders to the adulterous woman and to moral reflection on human conduct.

The items of the numerical saying, taken from the sage's stock of empirical experiences, are free of moral coloring. The teacher's didactic messages are presented both in the headings and in the phenomena contained in the body of the saying. When he presents subjects that are worthy of emulation he spares no praise; but neither does he mince words when he wants to denounce certain forms of behaviors.[94] In the unit under discussion (xxx 18–20), he used the pattern of the numerical saying as a mold for casting his lesson.

The book of Proverbs includes many warnings against the adulterous woman.[95] Nevertheless, linking such an admonition to a numerical saying is unexpected. The rhetorical turning point is shaped by an encounter on two levels between different types of literary material: the structural linkage of the application clause of the comparative saying to the graded numerical sequence paradigm, and the conceptual encounter between empirical observation of natural phenomena and the application clause that focuses on moral behavior.[96]

[93] On *derek* as a way of life, parallel to the term *ʾōraḥ* 'menstrual period', see Gen. xxxi 35 and xviii 11. For the use of *derek* in a moral context, see Ps. cxxxix 3. Von Rad (*Old Testament Theology* I, p. 425) discusses the catchword *derek* in Prov. xxx 18–20 as the common feature of puzzling things that somehow must be mastered conceptually and will ultimately reveal analogies between natural phenomena and human life.

[94] For positive evaluations, see Prov. xxx 24, 29, in contrast to the negative ones in xxx 21 or vi 16.

[95] On the Strange Woman in Proverbs (ii 16–22, v 1–23, vi 20–35, vii 1–27), see Fox, *Proverbs 1–9*, pp. 134–41.

[96] See Toy's summarizing note in this regard (*Proverbs*, p. 531).

CONCLUSION

General Remarks

This study has focused on animal images in Proverbs as a lens through which the wise teacher's viewpoint can be discerned. The teacher's knowledge of the animal world derives from empirical observation, encyclopedic knowledge, and early wisdom traditions. Animal images are part and parcel of the teacher's appeal to the mystery of natural phenomena as a means for investigating the more obvious truths of human behavior.

The teacher of Proverbs never refers to the mythological animals and creatures found in the prophetic and poetic literature, such as the sea monsters *Leviathan* and *Tannin* (Isa. li 9; Ps. lxxxix 11); nor does he mention animals with human traits, such as the serpent of Eden (Gen. iii 1–4) or Balaam's ass (Num. xxii 21–30), that act as mediators between God and man. Generally speaking, the teacher draws on conventional animal images to present a universal point of reference. This tendency reflects his wider pragmatic approach to teaching.

The animal imagery in Proverbs draws on various zoological categories: birds, insects, and reptiles; wild animals and predators; and domesticated animals. Together they convey a variety of behavioral codes and habits. Wild animals are no less appreciated than domesticated ones, and even destructive insects win the sage's admiration. For example, the description of locust (in the numerical saying in Prov. xxx 24–28) as among the "tiniest on earth" yet exceedingly wise expresses a sober view free of emotional associations. Instead of being viewed as the ravenous insect that destroys crops, or the "swift messenger" (Isa. xviii 2) sent to strike the foe, the locust is taken as a wise creature that lives without formal rulers and whose organized system is worthy of human emulation: "The locusts have no king, yet all of them go out in ranks" (xxx 27). This perspective encapsulates the unique worldview of Proverbs.

This study has examined a representative sample of literary parallels to typological images of animals as found in ancient Near Eastern literature, such as the close association of royal power with the lion. Thus sayings about the king's conduct convey the ferocity evoked through the image of the lion: "The terror of a king is like the roar of a lion; he who provokes his anger risks his life" (Prov. xx 2).

Above all, the multi-level methodology followed here (see below) has revealed an impressive number of animal images presented in a broad range of literary patterns: concise paradigms such as the comparative saying, the antithetical saying, the "better-than" saying, the metaphorical saying, and first-person speech, as well as more complex structures such as the admonition and exhortation, the biographical confession, and numerical sayings. The contextual approach to interpreting the symbolic role of animals made it possible to illuminate the relationship between vehicle and tenor or comparatum and comparandum.

Philological Approach

Two remarks are in order here. First, inasmuch as an accurate philological understanding of each pericope is an indispensable first step toward literary and conceptual analysis, we strove to establish the philological basis of the various images, mindful of the various contexts from which their wording may have stemmed. To give one short example, the root *b-ṭ-ḥ,* used with reference to the confident lion in Prov. xxviii 1, conveys the motif of the righteous person's trust in divine grace. However, a full appreciation of the choice of this root here requires contrasting it with other occurrences of *b-ṭ-ḥ* and a more common term describing lions, namely *r-b-ṣ* (Gen. xlix 9b; Num. xxiv 9a, b). Although *b-ṭ-ḥ* can be traced from an original sense of "fall down" (Jer. xii 5), its dominant meaning is to "have confidence in somebody," which suits a righteous man but not a lion. Perhaps Prov. xxviii 1 purposely applies this term to the lion in order to make a tighter link between the image of the confidently sprawled lion (usually expressed by *r-b-ṣ*) and the theological domain of the righteous who place their trust in God.

Second, modern interpreters cannot always offer a definitive identification of an animal mentioned in the text. This problem is especially acute in cases of *hapax legomena* such as *zarzīr motnayim* (see §4.2.2.2) or in instances where the proposed identification does not suit the descriptive or semantic context of the passage in which it appears. In the latter, our study has paid special attention to other biblical occurrences of the problematic noun (e.g., *nešer* 'vulture' in §2.1.1.2)

LITERARY PARADIGMS WITH REFERENCE TO THE *GATTUNG*

Previous studies of animal imagery in the Bible have focused mainly on the role of the animal in representing ideas or codes of behavior, desirable or undesirable. The metaphoric intention and symbolic message of animal images have been analyzed only in terms of the link between the symbol (the animal) and what was symbolized. Our literary inquiry has taken account of the relations among three rhetorical elements: the vehicle/comparatum, tenor/comparandum, and the rhetorical pattern. The focus on the formal setting and literary paradigm of each animal image has revealed the dynamic hermeneutics between the animal image per se and its rhetorical uses. For example, as we saw in §2.1.2.1, with reference to the warning against drunkenness (Prov. xxiii 29–35), the viper's venomous bite is mentioned in conjunction with the picture of the drunkard's lurching movements after a riotous night of drinking. However, whereas the syntactical context of the snakebite in v. 32 refers to the drunkard's ultimate fate (his *ʾaḥărît*), the image of the lurching man in v. 35 is a concrete exemplification of his typical condition without reference to his end. That is to say, the hyperbole about the drunkard does not end with a moral lesson, but rather with the drunk's own pathetic confession when he sobers up: "They struck me but I was not hurt; they beat me but I did not feel it" (v. 35). This conclusion deviates from the typical form of the admonition speech, which usually offers its lesson in the final clause, as in i 19: "Such is the fate of all who pursue unjust gain; It takes the life of its possessor." We have accordingly assumed that the syntactic features of the direct warning (Prov. xxiii 31, 33–34) and the ultimate consequence (v. 32), regarded as stylistic components of the admonitory speech, were intentionally inserted into a poem mocking the drunk, such as that in Isa. v 21–22.

Literary Paradigms with Reference to Patterns and Clauses

Another literary dimension of our study focused on the various patterns into which animal images are embedded. The teacher of Proverbs cites observed traits of animals for didactic purposes in admonitions, backed up rhetorically by a variety of illustrative clauses, such as the causative clause, the situational clause, and the consequence clause. Thus the image of the vulture's swift flight in Prov. xxiii 5 ("You see it, then it is gone, it grows wings and flies away, like a vulture, heavenward"), employed as a situational clause to exemplify the speedy disappearance of riches, also functions as a consequence clause within the admonition against excessive effort in amassing wealth (ibid, v. 4). Similarly, the hunting scene in Prov. i 17 ("In the eyes of every winged creature the outspread net means nothing"), which is employed as a situational clause to exemplify the trap laid for the innocent lad by violent criminals, also functions as a consequence clause within the admonition against throwing in one's lot with such unsavory characters (ibid., vv. 10–19).

Our study has also emphasized the importance of sensitivity to the rhetorical significance of deviations from a common literary pattern. For example, the graded numerical saying in Prov. xxx 18–20 follows the general model of x followed by $x + 1$ items (in this case, 3 followed by 4). Verse 19 lists four phenomena that are enigmatic to the teacher: "The way of a vulture in the heavens, the way of a snake on a rock, the way of a ship on the seas, and the way of a man with a woman." But these four mysteries, which derive from the teacher's observations of natural phenomena, are supplemented in v. 20 by "the way of an adulteress, she eats, wipes her mouth and says, 'I have done no wrong.' " This fifth observation is juxtaposed to the preceding four and expresses a moralistic admonition against the adulteress. The rhetorical modification works on two different levels: on the thematic level the shift is from experience to moralizing; on the formal level, there is a stylistic shift from the declarative sentences of the numerical saying to the comparative clause of the admonition pattern.

Conceptual Aspect

The parameters of this study, in which wisdom literature is understood to function as a laboratory or workshop for the production of similes and related rhetorical forms, has enabled us to take a closer look at the conceptual aspect of the simile in its wider literary context, i.e., as part of the world-view and rhetorical intentions of the school that produced the simile or aphorism. For example, the image of the outspread net—"In the eyes of every winged creature the outspread net means nothing (Prov. i 17)—exemplifies the perils that attend the lad and is transformed into a figurative illustration of the perception of retribution. A full appreciation of the hunting scene can be achieved only if we recognize its contextual and educational setting. It follows that in order to interpret the specific figurative pattern one must pay attention to and elaborate upon the thematic contexts.

In a similar vein, the metaphorical encounters between animal images and unsavory social types society—such as bear and fool (xvii 12), lion and sluggard (xxii 13, xxvi 13), dog and fool (xxvi 11), dog and provoker (xxvi 17)—provide a window on the teacher's world-view. The encounter between man and animal stimulates the listener-reader to reflect on and assimilate the teacher's lesson.

In conclusion, the book of Proverbs is grounded in the daily fabric of life in biblical times. A variety of models of human behavior are drawn from the sage's understanding of the order and balance of the natural world. The wider perspective has enabled us to evaluate rhetorical emphases and conceptual tendencies expressed through animal imagery in wisdom teachings and to discern conceptions of and attitudes about certain animals. The methods employed illustrate an interpretive approach that may profitably be applied to the investigation of animal images in other parts of the Bible.

APPENDIX A

ANIMAL IMAGERY AS A HERMENEUTICAL TOOL FOR ANALYZING THE CONCEPTUAL POLARITY IN QOHELETH

The question of the Qoheleth's inclusion in the canon was debated by the rival schools of Hillel (for) and Shammai (against) (*m. Yad* 3:5, *ᶜEd.* 5:3; *b. Meg.* 7a). Rabbinic sources offer two main arguments against its inclusion among the canonical books: (1) the book contradicts itself (*b. Šabb.* 30b); (2) it expresses heretical views (*Qoh. Rab.* 1:3; 11:9; *Num. Rab.* 161b). Its eventual admission to the canon was evidently because of the ancient Jewish tradition that its author was King Solomon, "the son of David, king in Jerusalem (Qoh. i 1; cf. i 12; see also *Song Rab.* 1:1, 10), the archetypal wise man. Another explanation, no less important, may be the orthodoxy of its closing verses (xii 12–14; see *b. Šabb.* 30b).

The apparent lack of internal coherence, which was not lost on the ancient rabbis, is a recurring issue in modern scholarship about Qoheleth. Different voices are heard in the book: one in which the author refers to himself in the first person, and another that refers to Qoheleth in the third person. A more serious problem concerns the dissonance between conservative statements that relate to various phenomena of life, on the one hand, and skeptical observations that contradict traditional beliefs, on the other hand. The skeptical voice has been attributed to the original author—the *hākām* or sage—while the conservative views have been attributed to a pious glossator or editor (one or more).[1] Another approach attributes the contradictory

An earlier version of this appendix was published as "The Fly and the Dog: Observations on Ideational Polarity in the Book of Qoheleth, in *Seeking Out the Wisdom of the Ancients: Essays Offered to Honor Michael V. Fox on the Occasion of His Sixty-Fifth Birthday*, ed. R. L. Troxel et al. (Winona Lake, IN, 2005), pp. 235–255.

[1] See C. G. Siegfried, *Prediger und Hoheslied* (Göttingen, 1898), pp. 2–12. For surveys of theories about the identity of the alleged glossator(s), see: M. V. Fox, *Qohelet and his Contradictions* (JSOTSup 71; Sheffield, 1989), pp. 23–25; Roland E. Murphy, "The Sage in Ecclesiastes and Qoheleth the Sage," in *The Sage in Israel and the Ancient Near East,* ed. J. G. Gammie and L. G. Perdue (Winona Lake, IN, 1990), p. 263; C. L. Seow, *Ecclesiastes* (AB 18C; New York, 1997), pp. 38–43.

voices to the same author and offers two solutions for the inconsistencies: (1) The author is presenting a debate, with a genuine or fictional interlocutor, in which he quotes traditional views in order to contradict them.[2] (2) The author is expressing the changing perspectives of sequential stages in his life and the evolution of his own worldview.[3] In other words, the conflicting points of view represent a dialogue between Qoheleth and himself.

Qoheleth employs a wide variety of expressive modes for his observations and sketches a procedure for investigation. For example, he writes, "I set my mind to study and to probe with wisdom all that happens under the sun" (i 13); "and so I set my mind to appraise wisdom and to appraise madness and folly" (i 17); "for all this I noted and I ascertained all this" (ix 1). The style of Qoheleth's confessional monologue is characterized by strings of sentences connected by coordinating and subordinating conjunctions. For example, he uses the particle *še*-, along with *ăšer*, not only as a relative particle (as in classical biblical Hebrew) but also as a conjunction to introduce the subject of an object clause, a usage typical of late Biblical Hebrew.[4]

Although scholars have tried to analyze Qoheleth as a carefully planned composition divided into separate units,[5] it is difficult to demarcate the individual pericopes. Often there is a continuous flow of thought in the argument of a literary unit; elsewhere the thematic continuity seems to be forced. Given the complexity of this issue, it seems preferable to read the text in the order in which it has come down to us and to evaluate the content of each pericope in situ.

My main concern here is to evaluate the rhetorical impact of two aphorisms that involve animal imagery (first x 1 and then ix 4). An examination of their syntactic and thematic settings will shed light on two well-known scholarly problems:

[2] For different categories of quotations, see Robert Gordis, "Quotations in Wisdom Literature," *JQR* 30 (1939–40), pp. 123–47; H. W. Hertzberg, *Der Prediger* (KAT 17/4; Leipzig, 1963), p. 174; J. A. Loader, *Polar Structures in the Book of Qoheleth* (BZAW 152; Berlin, 1979); Michael V. Fox, "The Identification of Quotations in Biblical Literature," ZAW 92 (1980), pp. 416–31; Roger N. Whybray, "The Identification and Use of Quotations in Ecclesiastes," in *Congress Volume*: *Vienna, 1980,* ed. J. A. Emerton (SVT 32; Leiden, 1981), pp. 435–51.

[3] J. L. Crenshaw, *Ecclesiastes*: *A Commentary* (OTL; Philadelphia, 1987), p. 34.

[4] Seow, *Ecclesiastes*, p. 17.

[5] For various methodologies in delineating a planned structure of the book, see ibid., pp. 43–47.

a. *The conceptual aspect:* possible sources of and explanations for Qoheleth's contradictory statements;
b. *The literary aspect:* Identification of the boundaries or extent of each thematic unit in the book.

Demarcation of the borders of a literary unit can help us understand its meaning and assess the role of the imagery employed by it. In other words, identification of the thematic unit can help us understand the reciprocal relationship between the whole and its parts, so that the functions of the components contribute to understanding the form of the literary unit.[6]

For the division into thematic units, I will be guided by Qoheleth's own method of investigation: stating the thesis, moving on to the antithesis or a restrictive statement, and finally presenting the conclusion. The thematic development is followed by analysis of key terms and other literary features, including catchwords, repetitions, and juxtaposed and contrasted phrases and concepts (such as youth and old age, Qoh. xi 9–xii 7), all of which bind the unit together.

1. Perfumer's Ointment and Dead Flies: Wisdom and Folly

We turn first to ix 13–x 1, which questions whether wisdom has any advantages to foolishness. Despite its thematic unity, the passage employs a wide variety of literary means and stylistic features: a parable (ix 14–15), a proverbial metaphor (x 1), "better-than" proverbs (ix 16a; 18a), one "better-than" proverb without the word *ṭôb* 'better' (ix 17); and two formulas introducing the theoretical debate (ix 13 and 16aα).[7]

[6] I follow Meir Weiss, who applies the critical principles of the "Total Interpretation" method of the New Criticism to the biblical text. See Meir Weiss, "Die Methode der 'Total Interpretation': Von der Notwendigkeit der Struktur-Analyse für das Verständnis der biblischen Dichtung," in *Congress Volume: Uppsala, 1971,* ed. H. S. Nyberg (SVT 22; Leiden, 1972), pp. 88–112; idem, *The Bible From Within: The Method of Total Interpretation* (Jerusalem, 1984), pp. 1–46.

[7] On the delineation of the literary unit ix 13–x 1, see: R. Gordis, *Koheleth: The Man and his World* (New York, 1968), p. 309; R. B. Y. Scott, *Ecclesiastes* (AB 18; New York, 1965), p. 247; Fox includes the fool sayings in the literary unit (*Qohelet and his Contradictions*, pp. 261–62). Ogden compares the subunits ix 17–18 and x 1–4 and finds thematic parallels, such as wisdom versus folly and wisdom's superiority (ix 17; x 2–4) versus wisdom's vulnerability (ix 18b; x 1). He also calls attention to stylistic parallels, such as repeated words, chiastic structures, antitheses, and the keyword *leb* 'heart' (G. Ogden, *Qoheleth* [Readings; Sheffield, 1987], pp. 163–64). G. A.

"This thing too I observed under the sun about wisdom, and it affected me profoundly" (ix 13), states the author, introducing an instance of wisdom that astounds him. The illustration comes from the parable of the king and the poor wise man (ix 14–15), the amazing case of a poor man who saved (or might have saved) the entire city through his wisdom and overcame a great king and his warriors. Even more amazing, however, is the fact that no one remembers the poor man whose wisdom saved the city.[8]

Like Qoheleth here, the book of Proverbs praises wisdom over military might: "One wise man prevailed over a city of warriors and brought down its mighty stronghold" (Prov. xxi 22); "Plans laid in council will succeed; wage war with stratagems" (xx 18).[9] Proverbs also holds that overcoming evil impulses is more praiseworthy than bravery on the battlefield: "Better to be forbearing than mighty, to have self-control than to conquer a city" (xvi 32). The aphorisms in Qoh. ix 16–18 are thus an embedded cluster within a contemplative discussion of the value of wisdom in ix 13–x 1. These sayings share the idea that wisdom is superior to martial valor. The opening clauses of the first and last of these verses state the advantages of wisdom, while the closing clauses note a limitation to this truth. The structure of the pattern is "better-than" proverb + adversative *wāw* + restrictive saying. The *wāw* actually precedes a circumstantial clause that limits the main assertion of the "better-than" proverb of the opening clause:

> Qoh. ix 16: Wisdom *is better than* valor + *but* a poor man's wisdom is scorned, and his words are not heeded.
>
> Qoh. ix 18: Wisdom *is better than* weapons of war + *but* one sinner destroys much good.[10] (RSV)

The second of this trio of aphorisms (ix 17) expresses the logical paradigm of the "better-than" proverb without using the word *ṭôb* 'better'. Unlike the other two sayings, this saying is unqualified: "The

---

Barton includes x 1 in the literary unit x 1–20, which he entitles "Advice concerning one's attitude toward rulers": the genuine portions are x 4–7, 14b, 16, 17, 20; all the rest is interpolations (G. A. Barton, *The Book of Ecclesiastes* [ICC; Edinburgh, 1908], p. 169).

[8] S. Japhet and R. B. Salters, *The Commentary of R. Samuel Ben Meir (Rashbam) on Qoheleth* (Jerusalem, 1985), pp. 112–13 [Hebrew].

[9] See also Prov. xxiv 5–6; Qoh. vii 19.

[10] The *wāw* of *wᵉ-ḥôṭeʾ* function as an adversative: 'but one sinner'. See P. Joüon and T. Muraoka, *A Grammar of Biblical Hebrew* 2 (SubBi 14/1; Rome, 1996), §172a.

words of the wise spoken gently are heard more than the shout of a ruler among fools" (ix 17).[11]

The conceptual tension of the contradiction between the recommendation to be wise and the limited advantage that wisdom confers creates an extended dialectic. Let us take a closer look at the juxtaposed antonyms in the verses:[12]

The parable of the king (ix 14)

- Little city, few men ≠ great king, mighty siege works
- Poor wise man ≠ great king

The three aphorisms (vv. 16–18)

- Wisdom ≠ valor
- Poor man's wisdom ≠ scorned
- Wise men ≠ foolish ruler
- Spoken softly ≠ shouted
- Wisdom ≠ weapons of war
- Single ≠ much

The sayings in praise of wisdom (vv. 16a, 17, 18) can be interpreted as three independent aphorisms that follow one another because of free association. Their common feature—using the "better-than" proverb to contrast the relationship between wisdom and folly—echoes the same conceptual tension conveyed by the parable of the king's siege of the town and its rescue by the wise commoner. The arrogance of a ruler screaming among fools (v. 17) echoes the conceit of the great king who built great siege works against the city (v. 14).

The opening clause of v. 18 declares wisdom to be superior to "weapons of war." This statement, too, echoes the story of the poor wise man who overcame the mighty king. The second half of the verse—"but a single error destroys much of value"—however, challenges the categorical assertion that wisdom always prevails. Rashbam explains *ḥôṭeʾ ʾeḥād* 'one sinner' as a contrast to the lowly wise man of vv. 14–15: just as he alone saves the city through his wisdom, so can a single sinner destroy much good.[13] In the wisdom literature, a

[11] The translation follows Fox, *Qohelet and his Contradictions*, p. 261.

[12] On the polarity paradigm in Qoheleth, see Loader, *Polar Structures,* pp. 58–61.

[13] Rashbam (*Qoheleth*, pp. 112–113) also identifies the "fools" (v. 17b) in relation to the context of the "mighty siege works" of the ruler (v.17b) in the parable of the little city: "For they are fools since they have no wise counsel to overcome the strategy of this man, who is poor and wise."

*ḥôṭe*ʾ 'sinner' is often not a person who violates social or religious law, but rather one who exhibits negative traits and a lack of social concern, such as overweening pride and excessive self-confidence (Prov. xiv 21; xx 2) or haste and rashness (Prov. xix 2).[14]

The story of the wise man who saved the city has a retrospective appendix: "Yet no one remembered that poor man" (Qoh. ix 15c). Biblical commentators are divided as to whether this means that, because of his poverty, his wisdom was not heeded and the city fell; or that his wise stratagem was insufficiently appreciated and ultimately forgotten. The past tense *millaṭ* 'saved' seems to mean that the poor man did indeed save the city through his wisdom, which was subsequently forgotten by his fellow townspeople. Those who would take v. 16 ("a poor man's wisdom is scorned, and his words are not heeded") as a gloss on v. 15, however, understand that the townspeople did not heed the poor man's advice and his wisdom proved of no avail; they read *u-millaṭ hûʾ* as a hypothetical: if only they had listened to his words he could have saved the city.[15] This realistic appraisal of the poor man's social standing shows that there are limits to the benefits of wisdom. The lesson of the parable is then formulated as a "better-than" proverb stated in first person: "So I observed: Wisdom is better than valor; but ..." (16a). The qualifying phrase undermines the appreciation of wisdom, since "a poor man's wisdom is scorned, and his words are not heeded" (16b). No matter how we read the story, the wise man does not receive his well-deserved reward. Either the citizens forget him after the city is saved or they scorn his advice and do need heed his counsel (v. 15c).

The "better-than" proverb favors "words spoken gently by wise men" over the "the shout of a ruler among fools" (v. 17). On the surface, this does not seem to fit with the poor man's disappointment at not being rewarded for saving his city. In fact, the contradiction between the wisdom saying and the parable of the poor wise man expresses the dialectical tension between the ideal and the real.[16] There is an ideal of wisdom, but the forces of reality operate against it.

[14] *Ḥôṭe*ʾ 'sinner' (Prov. viii 36) derives its meaning from "missing the target," as in "Every one of them could sling a stone at a hair and not miss" (Judg. xx 16b).

[15] The translation follows Fox, *Qohelet and his Contradictions*, p. 261. See his discussion, pp. 263–64.

[16] Or as Seow puts it: "It is a contradiction between the principle and the reality, the rule and the exception" (*Ecclesiastes*, p. 322).

Although the poor man's wisdom should be heeded, despite his inferior social status, expecting a just reward may not meet the test of reality.[17]

The dialectical tension shared by the parable and the aphorisms that follow it establishes a thematic unity. The sayings present the conceptual association between a single error that destroys much of value (18b) and the "ruler among fools" (17b). The first halves of both verses support wisdom (v. 18a) and those who expound it (v. 17a), juxtaposed with the critical observation of the damage wrought by that "one sinner" and by the "ruler among fools."

All of this is relevant to our discussion because of the placement of the proverbial metaphor in ix 13–x 1: "Dead flies turn the perfumer's ointment fetid and putrid, weightier than wisdom is a bit of folly."[18]

Zᵉbûb 'fly', used for all members of the sub-order Brachycera, is an onomatopoetic noun that mimics the sound of the insects' flight.[19] There are only two explicit references to flies in the Bible: Qoh. x 1 and Isa. vii 18. In his prophecy to Ahaz (Isa. vii 10–25), Isaiah compares the onslaught of the Assyrian armies to the obnoxious hordes of flies and the bees that alight "in the rugged wadis, and in the clefts of the rocks, and in all the thornbrakes, and in all the watering places" (v. 19).[20]

Many biblical mentions of maggots and worms, however, refer to the larvae of flies.[21] The manna that was left over to the next day "became infested with maggots and stank" (Exod. xvi 20; cf. v. 24);

[17] To society's ingratitude to the wise advisor (ix 15b, 16b) we may compare Qoheleth's skeptical approach to the material gains of the wise: "nor wealth by the intelligent" (ix 11). On the Wise in Qoheleth, see Fox, *Qohelet and his Contradictions*, pp. 114, 207, 262.

[18] The translation follows M. V. Fox, *A Time to Tear Down, A Time to Build Up: A Rereading of Ecclesiastes* (Grand Rapids, MI, 1999), p. 297.

[19] For *zᵉbûb* 'fly' in Akkadian, cf. *zumbu* (*zunbu, zubbu*), CAD Z, 155. The Aramaic denominative verb *dbb* (from the noun *dîbābāʾ* 'fly') express the idea of moving and shaking.

[20] See Yaaqob Palmoni, "zĕbûb," *EM* 2: 893–94 [Hebrew]; M. Dor, *Animals in the Days of the Bible, the Mishnah and the Talmud* (Tel Aviv, 1997), p. 200 [Hebrew]. The gathering of the gods over the officiant at a sacrifice is compared to swarming hordes of flies in both Gilgamesh (XI, 161) and the *Iliad* (2.469–73).

[21] Evidence that ancient peoples were aware that flies develop from maggots is provided by a papyrus found in the mouth of an Egyptian mummy: "The worms will not become flies within you." See F. S. Bodenheimer, *Animal Life in Biblical Lands* (Jerusalem, 1965), 1: 116 [Hebrew]. See also Aristotle, *De generatione animalium* III, 9.758b. Aristotle states that the fly is created from garbage (*Historia animalium* V, 721).

this describes the rotting that can be attributed to the activity of fly larvae.[22] Other passages describe rotting meat: "My flesh is covered with maggots and clods of earth; my skin is broken and festering" (Job vii 5; cf. Isa. xiv 11; 2 Macc. ix 9).

The fly appears in many talmudic passages as a loathsome creature, a "disgusting fly" that spreads disease (*b. Ketub.* 77b). A fly that falls into a dish is sufficient pretext for divorce (*b. Giṭ.* 6b).

Our verse in Qoheleth refers to *z^e^bûbê māwet* 'flies of death', that is, flies that deserve or are fated to die. But the plural noun is not in agreement with the third-person singular verbs *yabʾîš* and *yabbîaʿ* (*lit.* "cause to stink and bubble"). This lack of concord is exacerbated by the comparison of the singular "a little folly" in the second clause of the verse to the plural "flies" in the opening clause.

The asyndeton *yabʾîš yabbîaʿ* creates syntactic and hermeneutic problems. Ibn Ezra says that *yabbîaʿ* is a transitive (causative) verb: the oil continues to stink because the dead flies make it bubble. Others, who dismiss *yabbîaʿ* as a dittography of *yabʾîš* or as an explanatory gloss that has been interpolated into the text, would omit the second verb. Still others emend *yabbîaʿ* to *g^e^bîaʿ* 'goblet', to eliminate the asyndetic string of verbs.[23]

S. D. Luzzatto, in his commentary on Qoheleth, proposed a redivision of the words: not זבובי מָוֶת but זבוב ימוּת 'a fly will die'; this division is more compatible with the idea of the damage caused by "a little folly."[24] Others propose זבוב מות 'mortal fly', designating someone who is destined to die, similar to the compound expression *ʾĕnôš yamût* 'a mortal man' (Isa. li 12).[25]

[22] The verse may be referring to larvae of *drosophila*, the fruit-fly found in overripe fruit. See Dor, *Animals in the Days of the Bible*, p. 202.

[23] The omission of *yabbîaʿ* as a dittography is supported by several ancient versions: Symmachus, the Aramaic Targum, and the Vulgate. BHS suggests emending *yabbîa* to *gābîaʿ* 'goblet' or 'vessel'. The LXX renders it as a noun, σκευασίαν 'preparation'; compare the Syriac *tûqnāʾ* 'vessel, container'. *Gābîaʿ* 'goblet' or 'vessel' is also interpreted as a metonym for its contents; R. Saadia Gaon translates it as "a container of oil." See H. L. Ginsberg, *Koheleth* (Tel Aviv, 1961), p. 119 [Hebrew]; Scott, *Ecclesiastes*, p. 248; Fox, *Qohelet and his Contradictions*, p. 265.

[24] S. D. Luzzatto, *Meḥqerey Ha-yahadut*, vol. 1: *Divrey Qohelet* (Warsaw, 1913), p. 100 [Hebrew]. Ginsberg follows Luzzatto and proposes *z^e^bûb yāmût* 'a fly about to die', similar to the pattern of *ʾĕnôš yāmût* 'a mortal man' (Isa. li 12). See: Ginsberg, *Koheleth*, p. 119. Fox, *Qohelet and his Contradictions*, 261. C. F. Whitley supports the reading *z^e^bûb* 'a fly', emphasizing its suitable counterbalance *siklût m^eʿ^āṭ* 'a little folly' (*Koheleth: His Language and Thought* [BZAW 148; Berlin, 1979], p. 83).

[25] The singular form is reflected by the Aramaic translation *kid^e^bûbāʾ* 'as a fly' (cf.

The saying conjures up a picture of dead flies falling into aromatic oil and turning it putrid. The term *šemen rôqēaḥ* indicates a compound of oils and fragrant spices (cf. Exod. xxx 25), which is spoiled by dead flies.[26] Because of the concise formulation of the statement, with its aphoristic quality, readers do not examine its empirical truth, but draw the appropriate analogy and absorb the moral.

The second half of the verse has a chiastic relationship to this image:

> Dead flies turn the perfumer's ointment fetid and putrid
> Weightier than wisdom is a bit of folly.

The adjective *yāqār* (normally "precious") modifying *šemen rôqēaḥ* here takes on the meaning of its Aramaic cognate *yaqqîr*—both "honorable" and "heavy." The Targum has *w^{e}-yaqqîr yattîr min ḥûkm^{e}tāʾ* 'and weightier than wisdom', thus rendering the verse as a "better-than" proverb.[27] The translation "dead flies turn the perfumer's ointment fetid and putrid, weightier than wisdom is a bit of folly"

---

y. Qidd. 1:10 and *Qoh. Rab.* Ibn Ezra accepts the reading of the MT, noting that in the Bible a singular verb plus a plural name is frequently used to denote each separate act of the singular. For example, *bānôt ṣaʿădâ ălê šûr* "its branches run over the wall" (Gen. xlix 22 [RSV]; cf. Exod. xxxi 14, Lev. xvii 14, Isa. ii 18, and Qoh. ii 7). Delitzsch prefers the reading *z^{e}bûbê māwet* 'death-flies, poisonous flies', corresponding to the LXX μυῖαι θανατοῦσαι 'pestilent flies', emphasizing the intentional dramatic effect of the simile in analogy to damage caused by a little folly. See F. Delitzsch, *Ecclesiastes,* trans. M. G. Easton (Grand Rapids, MI, 1960, pp. 370–71). K. Budde compares *z^{e}bûbê māwet* with other compound expressions, such as *k^{e}lê māwet* 'deadly weapons' (Ps. vii 14) and *ḥeblê māwet* 'snares of death' (Ps. xviii 5) (*Die Fünf Megillot* [Freiburg, 1898], p. 155); cf. C. H. H. Wright, *Book of Koheleth* (London, 1883), pp. 417–18. Fox argues against the reading *z^{e}bûb māwet* 'mortal fly': "But flies are not deadly ... nor is it relevant that they are doomed" (*Qohelet and his Contradictions*, p. 264).

[26] Ogden interprets *rôqēaḥ* as a participle "describing one who blends aromatic compounds, hence 'perfumer' (RSV)" (*Qoheleth,* p. 164). See *yayin hareqaḥ* 'spiced wine' (Song viii 2 [RSV]). The phrase *šemen rôqēaḥ* 'perfumer's oil' aided in the reconstruction of the Ugaritic lection *šmn rq[ḥ]* in UT, 3: 21 and *šm[n] rqḥ* in UT, 120: 5. That these readings are correct has been confirmed by the unpublished Ugaritic Tablet *RS* 24.43:21 with the phrase *lg šmn rqḥ,* 'a log of perfumers oil'. See Mitchell Dahood, "The Phoenician Background of Qoheleth," *Bib* 47 (1966), p. 278.

[27] On *yāqār* corresponding to *kābed* in Aramaic, see *yaqqirâ* (Dan. ii 11) as well as Aḥiqar and Aramaic papyri. See A. E. Cowley, *Aramaic Papyri of the Fifth Century B.C.* (Oxford, 1967 [1923[1]]), pp. 215–216, lines 93, 108, 111. Rashi and Rashbam compare *yāqār*, in the sense of a heavy property, to *y^{e}qārôt* 'choice [stones]' (1 Kgs v 31). For the association between *kābôd* and *kābed* as a property, cf. Gen. xxxi 1; Isa. x 3, lxi 6, lxvi 11, 12; Nah. ii 10; Ps. xlix 17, 18. The same antithesis between the borrowed meanings of *kābed* and *qal* is found between the antonyms *kābôd* 'honor' and *qālôn* 'disgrace' (Prov. iii 35) as well as *ăkabbed* and *yēqāllû* (1 Sam. ii 30).

follows Fox proposed emendation of *mkbwd* to *tkbd* 'to weight' and moving the caesura so that *yāqār* modifies "oil."[28]

Thus dead flies are compared to a little folly, and a fine ointment to wisdom. The damage caused by a tiny and worthless creature like a fly, to an expensive unguent is compared to the effect of a little folly, which can overcome wisdom.[29]

The proverbial dead fly is linked to the second half of the previous verse, "but one sinner destroys much good" (18b): the damage caused by a single misdemeanor is equated with that done by dead flies to fragrant oil. Hence, the proverb of the dead flies in the ointment is embedded as an illustrative device for the clauses that immediately precede and follow it

> One sinner destroys much good (ix 18b).
>
> Weightier than wisdom is a bit of folly (x 1b).[30]

Both analogies qualify the superior status of wisdom because they propose a sober examination of reality, in which sin and folly (the primary natural enemies of wisdom) are likely to prevail.

If small flies can ruin an entire vessel of fine oil—an illustration of the disproportionate relationship between size and negative effect—people should not underestimate the damage that "a single sinner" or "a little folly" can wreak.

The fable of the king and the poor wise man (ix 14–15) and the metaphorical saying about the fly (x 1) deal with precisely the same matter: the influence of wisdom on vital aspects of life. Both parables evoke the intensity of the confrontation between wisdom and its adversaries.[31]

[28] Fox's emendation breaks the asyndeton *mēḥokmâ mikkabôd* that turns the closing stich into a "better-than" proverb. See Fox, *Qohelet and his Contradictions*, p. 265; ibid., *A Time to Tear Down*, pp. 301–302

[29] On the variety of the analogy patterns of proverbial sayings see, for example, the comparative *wāw* (Prov. xxii 1, xxvi 3, 8, 14) or the comparative morphemes *k*^{e}- ... *kēn* (Prov. xxvi 1, 8; xxvii 18).

[30] On the role of the proverb in its context, see: J. L. Crenshaw, *Ecclesiastes*, p. 169; Fox, *Qohelet and his Contradictions*, pp. 264–65; Loader uses the term *tertium comparationis* to designate the third element, which compares and applies the image to its analogue (*Polar Structures*, p. 60).

[31] Rashbam (*Qoheleth*, 113) creates a hermeneutic link between the parable of the fly (x 1) and the fable of the king who besieges a small town with his army (ix 14–15), expressing the application of the principle of divine retribution. He claims that Qoheleth compares flies, "insects good for nothing," to a sinful ruler who is not worthy of his throne.

Like the parable of the king and city (ix 14) and the trio of aphorisms that follows it (vv. 16–18), the fly proverb employs antithesis:

fetid, putrid ≠ perfumer's ointment

little ≠ heavy and precious

wisdom, honor ≠ folly

In addition to Qoheleth's method of juxtaposing two contradictory statements to evoke a speculative debate, Qoheleth dresses his proverbs in a stimulating and challenging vocabulary:

yabʾîš: The root *b-ʾ-š* refers to the fetid odor caused by rotten food (Exod. xvi 20) or liquids (Exod. vii 21). Metaphorically it refers to disgraceful behavior: "A righteous man hates falsehood, but a wicked man acts shamefully (*yabʾîš*) and disgracefully" (Prov. xiii 5 [RSV]; cf. Gen. xxxiv 30 and 2 Sam. xvi 21). Here (Qoh. x 1) *b-ʾ-š* conveys both meanings at once, i.e., parable and lesson.

yabbîaʿ: Although the context would admit *b-w-ʿ* or *b-ʿ-ʿ* 'bubble up, froth', the *hipʿil* form of the root *n-b-ʿ* (as already suggested by Ibn Ezra) means 'flowing, bubbling'.[32] The first two roots would be appropriate for a description of foaming, that is, bubbles on the surface of the liquid caused by a fly's falling into it. The compound *mabbûêy* (*n-b-ʿ*) *māyim* in Isaiah expresses the bubbling of a spring: "torrid earth shall become a pool, parched land, fountains of water" (Isa. xxxv 7a; cf. xlix 10). The root *n-b-ʿ* is used with both meanings: "The words a man speaks are deep waters, A flowing stream, a fountain of wisdom" (Prov. xviii 4). The metaphoric use of *n-b-ʿ* is applied to fools and malicious people: "The tongue of the wise dispenses knowledge, but the mouths of fools pour out folly" (Prov. xv 2); "The mind of the righteous ponders how to answer, but the mouth of the wicked pours out evil things" (Prov. xv 28).

šemen rôqēaḥ: The precious oil is associated with the wise man's reputation, as in the famous "better-than" proverb: "A good name (*šem*) is better than precious oil (*šemen*)" (Qoh. vii 1a). Anointing the head with oil exemplifies the good life for

[32] Gordis, *Koheleth,* p. 315.

Qoheleth: "Let your clothes always be freshly washed, and your head never lack oil" (ix 8).[33] As the proverb states, "precious treasure and oil are in the house of the wise man, and a fool of a man will run through them" (Prov. xxi 20). That is, oil is a valuable item that the wise man deems precious, while his antithesis squanders it (cf. Prov. xxi 17). The use of the verb *n-b-ᶜ* in association with dead flies that pollute precious oil calls to mind the archetypal fool, evildoer, and slanderer of wisdom proverbs, including the 'one sinner' (Qoh. ix 18) and the fool, who are compared to the fly that putrefies the ointment.

The rhetorical use of words that are polar opposites, backed up by double meanings and opposition between adjacent proverbs in the unit, invigorates the dialectical discussion. Readers have to consider the contextual meaning of the key words and take a new look at the advantage of wisdom in light of the realities of human life.

2. Dog and Lion: The Living and the Dead

The end of chapter 8 (vv. 16–17) discusses the limitations of human intelligence in understanding divine deeds. The discussion continues in chapter 9, whose opening formula, "I set my heart" (ix 1a), gives voice to the inner reflections, ruminations, and experiences derived from life, from which Qoheleth draws his conclusions.[34]

Chapter 9 opens with the summarizing "for all this," using the opening *kî* as a causal particle to introduce specific explanations. The infinitive *lābûr* (ix 1b), evidently from the root *b-r-r*, expresses the process of his investigation.[35] Qoheleth declares that he has reached

[33] On the relation of oil and qualities that produce enjoyment of life, joyousness and a good name, see Ps. xxiii 5, xlv 8, xcii 11, cxxxiii 2; Prov. xxvii 9; Job xxix 6; Song i 3.

[34] On Qoheleth's procedure of discovery and argumentation, see Fox, *Qohelet and His Contradictions*, pp. 85–89.

[35] The verb *lābûr* (ix 1b) is not reflected in the LXX (which is followed by the Peshitta), whose Vorlage, reading by retroversion, must have been *wᵉ-libbî rāʾâ ʾet kōl* 'and my heart saw everything'—thus creating full parallelism between the two stichs. The principle of *lectio difficilior* supports the MT, however. For *b-r-r* with the meaning 'select' in late biblical Hebrew, see 1 Chr. vii 40; ix 22; xvi 41, and Neh. v 18. The root *b-w-r* is an ע"ו variant of the geminate *b-r-r* (cf. *g-d-d*, *g-w-d* [Gen. xlix 19]). See Gordis, *Koheleth,* p. 299; Ogden, *Qoheleth*, p. 144. Others emend *wᵉlābûr* to *wᵉlātûr* 'to search out for', as in Qoh. i 13; vii 25.

his conclusions after a process of investigation: "and all this I ascertained" (1b). The wise and righteous are no different from other human beings when it comes to knowledge of their final fate; hence, "their actions" (*ʿăbādêhem*) are in the hand of God.[36] Even love and hate are not revealed in advance: "Human beings know none of this in advance" (1d).[37]

He continues (v. 2) that "everything is like everything else" and "the same fate" awaits all human beings.[38] This affirmation raises the issue of the principle of reward and punishment and the unpredictable outcome of human actions and feelings. Events are under exclusively divine control. The view that death is the common fate of all human beings, without regard to their moral qualities, blurs the distinction between the antithetical poles of the righteous and the wicked, the good and the bad, the pure and the impure, those who bring sacrifices and those who do not, and those who swear and those who shun oaths.[39] Qoheleth's declaration that all share a common fate contradicts the accepted view that there is some sort of correlation between our deeds and our ultimate fate.

[36] The Targum, followed by Rashi, has *w^{e}talmîdêhôn* 'their students' in place of *ʿăbādêhem,* depicting an ideal picture of the disciples' submission to the Torah. Ibn Ezra understands it as *maʿăbādêhem* 'their works' (Job xxxiv 25). Ginsberg (*Koheleth*, p. 113) also understands *ʿăbādêhem* (from *ʿabdāʾ*) as an Aramaism and equivalent to Hebrew *maʿăśêhem* 'their deeds'. Whitley (*Koheleth,* p. 79) claims that the retention of the *qameṣ* under the second syllable in a plural noun with a heavy suffix indicates the word's Aramaic origin (cf. *k^{e}nāt, k^{e}nāwāt^{e}hôn* 'colleague', 'their colleagues', Ezra iv 17). Fox questions why an author composing in Hebrew would chose a rare Aramaism instead of the common *maʿăśeh* 'deed'; he assumes that the Hebrew translator from Aramaic (here following Ginsberg's hypothesis that the Hebrew of Qoheleth is a translation from Aramaic) misread it for *ʿabdêhôn* 'their slaves', misled by the conjunction with two nouns that refer to classes of people (*Qohelet and His Contradictions*, p. 256).

[37] The LXX (ματαιότης ἐν τοῖς πᾶσιν 'vanity is in all') reads the first word of v. 2, הכל 'everything', as הבל 'vanity' and attaches it to the end of v. 1, producing *hakkōl lipnêhem hebel;* that is, human beings cannot see the logical consequences of events. Another datum that indicates a deviation from the Masoretic verse division is Rashbam's division of the commentary units, in which the closing phrase of v. 1, *hakkōl lipnêhem,* appears as the opening phrase of v. 2, thus implying all the evils and punishments that may occur to human beings during their life (*Qoheleth,* p. 110).

[38] Gordis (*Koheleth*, p. 300) offers parallel idiomatic expressions of the idea that one thing is just like the other (e.g., *ʾehyeh ʾăšer ʾehyeh* 'I am whatever I am' [Exod. iii 14; cf. iv 14]).

[39] The antitype for *laṭṭôb* 'for the good one', missing in the MT, is attested in the LXX by the reading καὶ τῷ κακῷ 'and the bad', which is followed by the Syriac and the Vulgate.

In the series of antitheses, the positive type is always presented first, until the last pair, in which the order is inverted to mark the close of the literary unit. An additional stylistic variation in the unit may be seen in the use of the prepositional *kāp* in the last two couples instead of the prepositional *lamed* in the first three, and the use of the word *ḥôṭeʾ* 'sinner' as the opposite of *ṭôb* 'good.'[40]

Qoheleth links the *hôlēlôt* 'madness' of human behavior and wicked deeds "under the sun" with the perception of death as the expected end of all human beings; hence "afterwards they join the dead."[41] His deterministic worldview sees no correlation between moral behavior and death. A similar critical statement of the distortions and defects in God's handling of the world is conveyed even more sharply in Qoh. i 13b–15: "A twisted thing that cannot be made straight, a lack that cannot be made good" (v. 15).[42]

[40] The metathesis in the final hemistich and its lengthening form a "closing deviation" to the pericope. For this phenomenon as an intentional aesthetic structure, see M. Paran, *Forms of the Priestly Style in the Pentateuch* (Jerusalem, 1989), pp. 179–88 [Hebrew]. Gordis attributes the inverted order to an ethical tendency "to end on a favorable note, בכי טוב as in 3:8." He considers the change of the prepositional *lamed* of the first three pairs into the comparative *kāp* within the coordinate construction of two pairs to be a stylistic variation (Gordis, *Koheleth*, pp. 300–301). The term *hannišbāʿ* 'the one who swears' refers to one who does not take an oath seriously or even swears falsely (see Qoh. viii 2; Zech. v 3–4; Sir. xxiii 9–12). The participle *hannišbāʿ* 'the one who swears' presents another stylistic variant that is probably the MT original reading. See Crenshaw, *Koheleth*, p. 160. On the positive type of one "who shuns oaths" and denunciation of one "who swears," see Sir. xxiii 9–11 and Qoh. viii 2–3. The Akkadian semantic equivalent to the Hebrew idiom *yārēʾ šᵉbûʿâ* is *palāḫu māmīta* (see *AHw*, p. 1317) which is also contrasted with "the one who swears (falsely)" (e.g., *BWL*, 116, lines 2–4). See Seow, *Ecclesiastes*, p. 299.

[41] For a detailed discussion of the term *ʾaḥărāyw* and the peculiarity of the syntax *wᵉʾaḥărāyw ʾel hammētîm*, see Whitley, *Koheleth*, pp. 79–80. Fox offers three different ways of understanding *ʾaḥărāyw:* (1) "after him," referring to what will happen to an individual after death; (2) "after him," referring to what will happen on earth after his death; and (3) "afterward," referring to what will happen on earth while the individual is still alive. He opts for the third sense (*Qohelet and His Contradictions*, p. 199; cf. Barton, *Book of Ecclesiastes*, p. 160; Gordis, *Koheleth*, p. 301; Hertzberg, *Der Prediger*, p. 172. The LXX, Syriac, and Vulgate all render the Hebrew term *ʾaḥărāyw* in the plural ("their end"), to harmonize with the plural subject *bᵉnê hāʾādām*. Rashbam (*Qoheleth*, p. 111) reads *ʾaḥărāyw* as *ʾaḥărît*, "the end of each and every human being is to go with the dead, since death comes to all; this is why evildoers continue to do evil and do not repent." Ginsberg (*Qoheleth*, p. 113) renders *ʾaḥărāyw* 'his end', based on the parallel between *ʾaḥărāyw* and *ḥēleq* 'lot, share' (cf. Qoh. iii 22; vi 12).

[42] *Hôlēlôt* 'madness', spelled with a plene *ḥōlem* in the final syllable (see Qoh. i 17; ii 12; vii 25), appears with a *qibbûṣ* in Qoh. x 13, which is suspect. If the former vocalization is the authentic one, it may have arisen on analogy with the similar *ḥokmôt* 'wisdom' (Prov. i 20; ix 1) as the pluralis majestatis. See Joüon and Muraoka,

What interests us here is the placement of the figurative proverb "even a live dog is better than a dead lion" (ix 4b) within the literary unit ix 1–6, and the reasons given to support its statement:

> For he who is reckoned [Qere: is joined] among the living has something to look forward to (ix 4a)
>
> Since the living know they will die, but the dead know nothing; and they have no more recompense, for even the memory of them has died. (ix 5)

Qoheleth's gloomy observation of life is connected with the perception of ineluctable mortality. The aphorism "even a live dog is better than a dead lion" illuminates this dark reflection from a different perspective: It is better to be among the living than among the dead because "the living know they will die" (v. 5a), but those who have died "know nothing" (v. 5b). The deceased no longer have to deal with issues of reward and punishment; nor can they experience love, hate, or envy.

Qoheleth introduces his arguments with an independent relative clause that opens with the emphatic particle *kî mî ʾašer*: "For [he] who is."[43] The Kethib, *ybḥr,* is from the root *b-ḥ-r* 'choose',[44] making the clause is a rhetorical question: "Who is the one who chooses?" The implicit response is "no one": no mortal has free choice.[45]

The Qere is *yeḥubbar* 'be joined', the pu'al of *ḥ-b-r,* producing "for he who is reckoned among the living … ."[46] This fits better with what the following reference to *biṭṭāḥôn* 'confidence, trust', as in "What

---

A Grammar of Biblical Hebrew i 265–66. *Hôlēlôt* recurs in Qoheleth in association with *siklût*/*śiklût* 'folly' (i 17; ii 12; vii 25; x 13). It implies madness and unbridled behavior (see Jer. xxv 16) as well as arrogant, vain, boastful speech (see Ps. lxxv 5–6).

[43] *Mî ʾăšer* 'he who is' serves as the start of the nominal clause and not just of the relative clause. A similar usage of the particle *kî* is found in Num. xxiii 23; Isa. xv 1; Amos iii 7; Prov. xxx 2; Job v 2 and xxviii 1. The LXX translates *mî ʾăšer* as an interrogative, while the Vulgate reads it as a rhetorical question. The Syriac recognizes it as a relative equivalent to *kōl ʾăšer* 'he who is' (see Exod. xxxii 33; 2 Sam. xx 11; Qoh. v 9), and this seems correct. See Gordis, *Koheleth*, p. 304.

[44] Vocalized as *yibbāḥēr* (*nipʿal*, 3rd masc. imperfect) or as *yibḥar* (*qal,* 3rd masc. impf.) 'will choose', meaning the one who chooses.

[45] See Seow, *Ecclesiastes*, p. 300.

[46] The LXX, Vulgate, and Syriac reflect the Qere, as do medieval commentators, including Rashi and Rashbam. Crenshaw claims an ironic meaning in the Kethib juxtaposed to Qoheleth's denial of divine retribution in v. 3; thus the praise for life proposed by the Qere seems more plausible (*Qoheleth*, p. 161). Ogden opts for the root *b-ḥ-r* (Kethib), denoting choice, hence supporting the contrasting debate between the living and the dead (*Qoheleth*, pp. 147–48).

makes you so confident?" (2 Kgs xviii 19=Isa. xxxvi 4). Thus the argument of vv. 4–6 leads to the conclusion that full participation in all spheres of human activity expresses humans' confidence in life.[47]

The judgment that "even a live dog is better than a dead lion" is embedded among the argument clauses beginning with *kî* ("for he who is reckoned among the living [Qere] has something to look forward to"); the two additional motivational clauses provide further explanations: "since the living know they will die. But the dead know nothing; they have no more recompense, *for* even the memory of them has died" (v. 5). Skipping over v. 4b does not interrupt the thematic continuity of 4a–5. The reason for the hope and confidence of the living is that "the living know they will die," while the dog and lion proverb, when read in its context, undermines the credibility of the declaration regarding the benefit of living. The preference for life is expressed sardonically by alleging the superiority of the lowly dog, if alive, over the majestic lion, when dead.[48]

Here it is the lion that is dead and the dog that is alive. Elsewhere in the Bible we encounter the derogatory epithet 'dead dog' to express self-abasement, as in David's desperate protest to Saul: "Whom are you pursuing? A dead dog, a single flea?" (1 Sam. xxiv 15). Even when alive, the dog is a despised creature that evokes feelings of disgust: "As a dog returns to his vomit, so a fool repeats his folly" (Prov. xxvi 11).[49] The choice of the image of a "living dog" to illustrate the advantage of life over death, following the paradigm of the "better-than" proverb, gives the discussion a skeptical instead of the customary authoritative tone.[50]

This "better-than" proverb measures and then determines "what is best for a man to do in life" (Qoh. vi 12a). The anthropocentric orientation paradigm stems from its purpose of evaluating essential values and practical needs in the life of the individual.[51]

[47] Ibn Ezra understands *biṭṭāḥôn* as "hope" or "expectation": "While there is life there is hope" (so too Ginsberg, *Koheleth*, p. 114). Whitley follows the talmudic meaning of *biṭṭāḥôn* 'hope' in *y. Ber.* 9:13 (*Koheleth,* p. 80; cf. Wright, *Koheleth*, p. 408). For both meanings ("hope" and "confidence"), see Delitzsch, *Ecclesiastes,* p. 359. Fox argues for "hope": "knowing that one will die is not a 'hope' " (*Qohelet and His Contradictions*, p. 258).

[48] On the lion, see §2.2.2.2.

[49] See above, §3.3.2.

[50] On the "better-than" saying see §1.5.1.3.

[51] Walther Zimmerli, "Concerning the Structure of Old Testament Wisdom," in *Studies in Ancient Israelite Wisdom*, ed. J. L. Crenshaw (New York, 1976), pp. 175–

In another divergence from the usual pattern,[52] here the adjective *ṭôb* stands, not at the start of the saying, but in the second clause.[53] Thus the irony is heightened by means of the alternative form of the "better-than" paradigm: The (base) dog represents the living and the (glorious) lion the dead.

The proverb "even a live dog is better than a dead lion" is woven into the discussion in order to illustrate the superiority of life to death.[54] This passage contradicts another contemplative monologue that alleges precisely the opposite—"then I accounted those who died long since more fortunate than those who are still living" (iv 2). Furthermore, the speaker there advances the same argument for his praise of death—the evil deeds done under the sun (iv 3–5)—as in the enumeration of the advantages of life in Chapter 9.

The sage's pessimism about human conduct does not contradict his advice to partake as fully as possible of the pleasures of life. In the opposition of life and the netherworld, the balance is tipped toward life because there is "action, reasoning, learning, and wisdom" (ix 10) in life, but not in the netherworld.

The conceptual tension between life and death in Qoh. ix 1–6 is heightened by the use of contraries:

love ≠ hate
righteous ≠ wicked

207; H. J. Hermisson, *Studien zur israelitischen Spruchweisheit* (WMANT 28; Neukirchen and Vluyn, 1968), pp. 155–56; Glendon E. Bryce, "Better-Proverbs: An Historical and Structural Study," *SBLSP* 108/2 (Missoula, MT, 1972), pp. 343–54; Graham S. Ogden, "The 'Better' Proverb (Ṭôb-Spruch), Rhetorical Criticism and Qoheleth," *JBL* 96 (1977), pp. 489–505; Walter Baumgartner, "Die literarischen Gattungen in der Weisheit des Jesus Sirach," *ZAW* 4 (1914), pp. 165–98.

[52] For the use of the emphatic *lamed* elsewhere, see Isa. xxxii 1; Ps. xxxii 6. Fox argues that the prefix *lamed* in *lᵉkeleb* is not emphatic, because an emphatic particle would come before the predicate; see Qoh. ii 3; vi 12; viii 12 (*Qohelet and His Contradictions*, p. 258).

[53] Our saying resembles the ironic context of another "better-than" proverb: "I say, the stillbirth, is more fortunate than he" (Qoh. vi 3). In both sayings the undesirable states (the "live dog" and the "stillbirth") appear in the advantageous position within the aphorism.

[54] Another example of the way an idiomatic expression exemplifies a general truth within a debate is the laconic proverb: "skin for skin" (Job ii 4a). Here too the proverb is embedded in the series of arguments that test Job anew after his trials: "But lay a hand on his bones and his flesh, and he will surely blaspheme You to Your face" (Job ii 5). On the stylistic device of quoting popular sayings in debates with oneself, see Robert Gordis, "Quotations in Wisdom Literature," pp. 123–47; idem, "Quotations as a Literary Usage in Biblical, Rabbinic and Oriental Literature," *HUCA* 22 (1949), pp. 196–97.

good, pure ≠ impure
one who sacrifices ≠ one who does not bring sacrifices
one who swears ≠ one who shuns oaths
while they live ≠ the end
a live dog ≠ a dead lion

These polarities turn the perception of Divine providence and retribution on its head; the moral opposites become partners in a shared fate. Qoheleth depicts a chaotic universe that supports his skepticism about the common belief system.

The dog-and-lion proverb is embedded in a literary unit defined by an inclusio: the passage begins with the ignorance of their future loves and hates that is the lot even of the righteous and the wise (ix 1), and ends with the absence of all feeling and impulses, including as love, hate and jealousy, among the dead (ix 6).

> *Introduction*
>
> (1) For all this I noted and I ascertained all this: that the actions of even the righteous and the wise are determined by God. *Even love! Even hate!* Man knows none of these in advance. …
>
> *Proverb*
>
> (4–5) For he who is reckoned among the living has something to look forward to—even a live dog is better than a dead lion—since the livings know they will die. But the dead know nothing; they have no more recompense, for even the memory of them has died:
>
> *Close*
>
> (6) *Their loves, their hates,* their jealousies have long since perished; and they have no more share till the end of time in all that goes on under the sun.

All human beings, ranging from the wise poor to wealthy fools, share consciousness of their ultimate fate. This undermines the principle of reward and punishment, according to which God pays human beings according to their actions. Even the advice to live is exemplified through the superiority of a living dog over a dead lion, thus expressing an even more skeptical view of divine retribution.

Gordis includes the proverb within the unit that praises life (ix 4–12) and defines the theme of viii 10–ix 3 as the failure of the principle of divine retribution. It seems, however, that the proverb with its animal image (v. 4) is meant to serve as an exemplification of a theoretical discussion and is accordingly not the start of a new discussion. Rather, it is linked to the sage's continuing argument that human beings are not capable of speculating on their fate. Nevertheless, the advantage of the living over the dead emerges from the saying. The very fact of being alive renders people masters of their own consciousness.[55]

Qoheleth juxtaposes contradictory terms and values that are seen as equal forces in the cognitive process of making the right choices. This is how he chooses to express his ambivalence about life and to stimulate his audience to reflect about contradictory phenomena in human life. Within the dialectical discourse, the vividness and allusiveness of animal images helps illustrate the inherent polarities on both the conceptual and rhetorical levels.

[55] See Gordis, *Koheleth*, pp. 188–89; 304–308.

APPENDIX B

A NEW CRITERION FOR IDENTIFYING "WISDOM PSALMS"

Gunkel's systematic investigation of the literary types (*Gattungsforschung*) in the book of Psalms provided biblical scholars with a methodological introduction to the study of the "Wisdom Psalms." Gunkel employed the expressions *Gattung* and *Sitz im Leben*, which combine two planes of thought: the former defines and thus distinguishes among the various genres, while the latter determines the "situation," i.e., the life setting from the genre (in this case the psalm) developed.[1]

Gunkel's meticulous application of aesthetic laws to identify literary types left many psalms relegated to the category of "mixed psalms." Later scholars, though, have pointed out thematic parallels between Akkadian literature and the individual lament-prayer in Psalms. Both literary sources include descriptions of physical distress and pain, a sense of having been abandoned by the deity, and various hymnic elements that seek to placate the god. The common range of themes in both the Mesopotamian psalms of lamentation and the biblical mixed psalms call Gunkel's assumption into question.[2] His *a priori* assumption that short psalms and "pure" types are early compositions,

This appendix is a revised version of a lecture delivered in Berlin at the 2002 International Conference of the SBL and published in *Birkat Shalom: Studies in the Bible, Ancient Near Eastern Literature and Post-biblical Judaism presented to Shalom M. Paul on the Occasion of his Seventieth Birthday,* ed. Ch. Cohen et al. (Winona Lake, IN, in press).

[1] H. Gunkel and J. Begrich, *Introduction to Psalms: The Genres of the Religious Lyric of Israel,* trans. J. D. Nogalsky (Macon, GA, 1998). Buss discusses the problematic term coined by Gunkel in defining "situation" as "referred either to historical circumstances or to the condition expressly described by the text." See Martin J. Buss, "The Idea of *Sitz im Leben:* History and Critique," *ZAW* 90 (1978), pp. 158–9.

[2] See G. Widengren, *The Accadian and Hebrew Psalms of Lamentations as Religious Documents* (Stockholm, 1937); A. Falkenstein and W. von Soden, *Sumerische und akkadische Hymnen und Gebete* (Zurich, 1953); R. G. Castellino, *Le Lamentazioni individuali e gli inni in Babilonia e in Israele: raffrontati riguardo alla forma e al contenuto* (Turin, 1940).

while "mixed" and expanded types are "late," is now considered a dubious criterion in the reconstruction of form-critical history.[3]

The stylistic and thematic complexity of many psalms led to a subdivision of the main genres: e.g., the "song of prayer" was partitioned into the "individual prayer" and the "public prayer" and the former teased even further into the "prayer of the afflicted individual" and the "confessional prayer of the accused." But even such sub-subcategorization proves to be unable to identify the main theme of a psalm.

For cult psalms, one can easily identify the cultic ritual or festival background as their *Sitz im Leben*. The identification of the original context of the Wisdom psalm, though, is much more complex. There are no references to temple rituals or court ceremonies, or allusions to historical backgrounds or traditions that might facilitate identification of the cultural background. Moreover, as long as scholars cannot agree on criteria for identifying a "Wisdom psalm," there will be a methodological problem about its origin and message.

It was von Rad who asked who stands behind the intellectual activity that crystallized practical and empirical knowledge into a proverbial rule, wisdom saying, or poetry.[4] He examined the relationship between this literary activity and other biblical genres such as historiography and prophecy. It is precisely when we discuss the psalms as liturgical literature that von Rad's question takes on sharper focus. This is because of the difficulty in determining the *Sitz im Leben* of psalms that exhibit the ideas and language of Wisdom literature and their link to the creative workshop of the circles of the wise. Von Rad defused this difficulty by stating that we must not treat the copresence of prayer and didactic instruction as a dichotomy. His view was that texts originally composed as cultic psalms were reworked into didactic texts in the post-exilic period. Moreover, the Wisdom-literature features found in some psalms does not reflect a concrete picture of the *Sitz im Leben* but serves only to point out their literary link to the Wisdom milieu.

Murphy summed up the problem of defining the term "wisdom psalm" as follows: "The very idea is as broad as the wisdom literature."[5] In fact, the only criterion agreed upon by scholars is the

[3] For a critical approach to Gunkel's and Begrich's form-critical research, see Hans J. Kraus, *Psalms 1–59,* trans. H. C. Oswald (Minneapolis, 1998), pp. 39–41.

[4] G. von Rad, *Wisdom in Israel,* trans. J. D. Martin (New York, 1972), pp. 4–14.

[5] Roland E. Murphy, "A Consideration of the Classification 'Wisdom Psalms' "

conceptual linkage to wisdom thinking. But the place of speculative reflections in the prayer *Gattung* remains an unresolved question.[6]

The fluidity in the number of "Wisdom Psalms" counted by different scholars demonstrates the confusion and lack of consensus in defining the genre. Mowinckel, for example, initially classified three psalms (i, cxii, and cxxvii) as such. Later he added seven or eight more to the updated list (i, xix-b, xxxiv, xxxvii, xlix, lxxviii, cv, cvi, cxi, cxii, cxxvii).[7] Changes of this magnitude also appear in the different editions of Eissfeldt's *Introduction*. Seven psalms (i, xxxvii, xlix, lxxiii, lxxviii, xci, cxxviii) are mentioned in the 1934 edition, but the 1964 edition adds five more (xc, cv, cvi, cxxxiii, cxxxix).[8] The opposite tendency is exemplified in Murphy's studies: the number of "wisdom psalms" decreases from twelve in 1960 to seven in 1963. Luyten describes this situation as one of "chaos."[9] He refers not only to the increase or decrease in the number of "Wisdom Psalms" listed in various scholarly publications, but also to the fact that some scholars categorically deny the existence of any such genre.[10]

Notwithstanding the inadequacy of criteria for defining wisdom psalms, three aspects have been considered to be indispensable links to the Wisdom literature and the sages' circles: thematic and conceptual

---

(*SVT* 9; Leiden, 1963), p. 159.

[6] Mowinckel discusses the difficulty in distinguishing between the "learned" or "wise" men (*ḥăkāmîm*) or even the "scribes," who used to cultivate a special kind of literature, i.e., "the poetry of wisdom," from other social groups such as the priests, prophets, and Levites. "The psalm poets as a rule belonged to the temple singers" (p. 207), presumably the last collectors and even redactors of the psalms. "It is this learned, non-cultic psalmography which is followed up by the post-canonical, late Jewish psalmography" (pp. 216–17). See Sigmund Mowinckel, "Psalms and Wisdom," in *Wisdom in Israel and in Ancient East,* eds. M. Noth and D. Winton Thomas (*SVT* 3; Leiden, 1960), pp. 205–24.

[7] Mowinckel devotes chapter 16 to "The Learned Psalmography," which was cultivated in the circle of "learned" or "wise" scribes. The characteristic form of these "non-cultic" poems is the saying, the proverb and the exhortation, with moralizing and didactic contents." See S. Mowinckel, *The Psalms in Israel's Worship,* trans. D. R. Ap-Thomas (Oxford, 1962), vol. II, pp. 104–25.

[8] O. Eissfeldt, *The Old Testament: An Introduction,* trans. Peter R. Ackroyd (New York, 1965), pp. 124–27.

[9] J. Luyten, "Psalm 73 and Wisdom," *La Sagesse de L'Ancien Testament,* ed. M. Gilbert (Gembloux, Belgium, 1979), pp. 59–81.

[10] E.g., Castellino designates 19 psalms as "wisdom psalms" (R. G. Castellino, *Libro dei Salmi* [Turin and Rome, 1955], pp. 729–835), whereas Engnell believes that no psalm was originally composed as a didactic poem (I. Engnell, *The Book of Psalms, A Rigid Scrutiny: Critical Essays on the Old Testament,* trans. J. T. Willis [Nashville, 1969], p. 99).

features, linguistic and stylistic aspects, and the use of the wisdom vocabulary.[11]

I propose adding the use of animal imagery as a new criterion for identifying "Wisdom Psalms." The dynamic between animal images and their contextual implications provides another point of entry into the thematic and conceptual framework of each wisdom book. When applied to Psalms, this method shows that the use of animal imagery correlates with "wisdom psalms" and their conceptual background.

Examination of the syntactic and thematic setting of the image within its pericope enables us to clarify its rhetorical function. The combination of the zoological-behavioral and literary aspects allow us to evaluate the rhetorical impact of the Wisdom teaching through this particular aspect of animal imagery.

Here I focus on how the image of the moth in Psalm xxxix reveals its affinities with the Wisdom-psalm genre[12] and on the interpolation of a wisdom motif based on animal imagery—horse and mule—in Psalm xxxii (vv. 8–9).

1. The Moth: Destructiveness and Ephemerality

> You chastise a man in punishment for his sin, consuming like a moth his precious garment. (Ps. xxxix 12)

In this bold image the moth exemplifies Divine punishment of human beings for their transgressions.

The larvae of the cloth moth consume and destroy fabric in vast quantities, as described by Isaiah: "They shall all wear out like a garment, the moth shall consume them" (l 9).[13]

[11] A methodology for evaluating "Wisdom Psalms" is presented by Murphy, "Wisdom Psalms," pp. 156–67 (repr. in *SAIW*, pp. 456–67). Philological criteria for the identification of the "wisdom thesaurus" in the psalm are offered by Avi Hurvitz, "Wisdom Vocabulary in the Hebrew Psalter: A Contribution to the Study of 'Wisdom Psalms,'" *VT* 38 (1988), pp. 41–51; idem, *Wisdom Language in Biblical Psalmody* (Jerusalem, 1991) [Hebrew].

[12] For a previous version in which I presented a close examination of Psalm 39, see: Tova Forti, "The Moth Image: A Window on a Wisdom Psalm (39)," in *Homage to Shmuel: Studies in the World of the Bible,* ed. Z. Talshir, Sh. Yona, and D. Sivan (Jerusalem, 2001), pp. 319–31 [Hebrew].

[13] In the Bible the moth is *ʿāš*, which appears as a synonym for *rāqāb* (perhaps the tree worm) in Hos. v 12 and Job xiii 28. We also find *ʿāš* in relation to clothing in Sir. MS B (xlii 13) from the Cairo Geniza; the variant *sās* occurs in the scroll from

Scholars have classified Psalm xxxix as a "prayer of the individual," in which the poet appeals to God (v. 13) and reveals his intimate pain. The author perceives his suffering from the "plagues" as Divine punishment for his sins. Hence only God can remove these afflictions (vv. 9–12). Because of the many expressions of suffering and pain (vv. 3, 11), some scholars would define the psalm as one of "sickness and healing," a subcategory of the "prayer of the individual."[14]

Let us trace the rhetorical function of the moth in the structure of this psalm. The supplicant opens with a personal confession, but "bridles" or "muzzles" his mouth and refrains from complaining aloud about his sufferings, lest he sin by speaking against God. The refrain of his emotional storm changes into a polemic appeal to God and an argument for theological and philosophical explanations of human suffering. Meditations on the transience and vanity of human life and the uselessness of human possessions are presented as arguments that God should sympathize with human suffering.

The unexpected image, "consuming like a moth his precious garment" (v. 12), concludes an eight-verse unit (vv. 5–12) in which the supplicant goes from stifling his complaints to a meditative justification for God's intervention.

The image of the moth comes after the supplicant entreats God to heal his illness: "Take away your plague from me" (v. 11), thus providing a concrete illustration of the sufferer's collapse. The placement of the moth image (12b) between the theodicy of the first stich ("You chastise a man in punishment for his sin" [12a]) and the declaration of the existential nothingness of human beings in the third stich ("No man is more than a breath" [12c]) highlights the impact of the moth metaphor.

In various loci in the Wisdom Literature the moth exemplifies human transience, notably Job xiii 28–xiv 1: "Man wastes away like a rotten thing, like a garment eaten by moths; man born of woman is short-lived and is sated with trouble." In Job (xiv 2b), human life is a shadow that does not endure. So too in our psalm, "Man walks about

---

Masada: *kî mibbeged yēṣēʾ sās umēʾiššâ rāʿat ʾiššâ,* "For from the garment emerges the moth, and from a woman a woman's wickedness." For the biblical *hapax legomenon sās* (Isa. li 8), see H. R. (C.) Cohen, *Biblical Hapax Legomena in the Light of Akkadian and Ugaritic* (Missoula, MT, 1978), pp. 114 n. 21.

[14] Although Kraus states that the reflections in Psalm 39 place it in the form group of didactic poetry, he does not include it in the group of "wisdom psalms" in his introductory discussion of "Didactic Poetry" (Kraus, *Psalms 1–59*, pp. 58–60, 417).

as a mere shadow" (v. 7), where *ṣelem* cannot have its usual sense of image or likeness, but must mean a passing image or shadow (*ṣēl*), as in "Man is like a breath; his days are like a passing shadow" (Ps. cxliv 4).[15] Ironically, the double meaning of the word suggests a contradiction between the traditional perception of human beings as created in the "image (*ṣelem*) of God" (Gen. i 26, 27) and the Wisdom literature's perception of them as no more than a passing shadow (*ṣēl*).

Another characteristic term of the Wisdom literature found in this psalm is *hebel* 'breath', which recurs some forty times in Qoheleth and is also employed by Job to express the vanity of life: "I am sick of it. I shall not live forever; let me be, for my days are a breath" (vii 16). In Psalm xxxix, the word figures in a repeated (vv. 6 and 12) declaration of the vanity of human life—"no man is more than a breath" (cf. also v. 7)

Similarly, we find *tôḥelet* (v. 8) as a synonym of "hope" (cf. Prov. x 28) and *h*ᵃ*gîgî* 'thoughts' (v. 4b; cf. Ps. xlix 4), both of them drawn from the lexicon of Wisdom Literature. We also have *ḥeled* 'life expectancy'—"You have made my life just handbreadths long; its *span* is as nothing in Your sight" (v. 6a; cf. Ps. xlix 2; Job xi 17)—juxtaposed to *ḥādel* 'cease to exist' in the previous verse: the length of life granted to a person by God is terminated when God brings that life to an end. The metathetic interplay *ḥ-l-d* and *ḥ-d-l* emphasizes the contrast between "lifespan" and "cease to exist."

Note, finally, the idiomatic "before I pass away and am gone" (xxxix 14b), referring to the suddenness of death and the transient nature of human life, as lamented by Job: "The eye that gazes on me will not see me; Your eye will seek me, but I shall be gone" (Job vii 8).[16]

[15] See Ps. cii 12; Job viii 9; xvii 7; Qoh. vi 12. Note the conceptual linkage between *gēr* and *tôšāb* "sojourner" and "transient," and the image of "shadow" in 1 Chr. xxix 15 and in Ps. xxxix 7a, 13b. *HALOT* (צל"ם II, p. 1029) interprets "shadow" in comparison to the Akkadian *ṣalāmu* 'to be dark'. But the *mem* of the word *ṣelem* may be enclitic. For a detailed discussion, see Chaim Cohen, "The Meaning of צלמות 'Darkness': A Study in Philological Method," *Texts, Temples, and Traditions*: A Tribute to M. Haran, ed. M. V. Fox et al. (Winona Lake, IN, 1996), pp. 294–95, n. 28.

[16] *W*ᵉʾ*ênennî* 'I shall be gone' appears frequently in Job (e.g., iii 21, xxiii 8, xxiv 24, xxvii 19). For adverbial idioms of short time, transience of life, and their Akkadian counterparts, see Moshe Held, "Studies in Biblical Lexicography in the Light of Akkadian Parallels," *Studies in Bible Dedicated to the Memory of U. Cassuto on the 100*ᵗʰ *Anniversary of His Birth* (Jerusalem, 1987), pp. 104–14 [Hebrew].

Two stylistic devices characteristic of Wisdom literature are also worthy of mention:

1. The anaphora of the emphatic adversative *ʾak* (vv. 6c, 7a, 12c) emphasizes the themes of vanity, transience, and the futility of life (cf. Job xiii 15, 20; Ps. lxxiii 1–2);
2. The use of *ʾāmartî* 'I said' (v. 2) to introduce an inner monologue, sometimes based on statements of dogma (cf. Ps. liii 2; lxxxix 3–5; Job xxxii 7–8), or to introduce dialectical passages, as in Qoheleth (e.g., ii 1).[17]

In sum, the image of the moth provokes theological reflections about issues of Divine Providence and the essence of human existence and develops the contrast between human transience and God's omnipotent eternity. Its insertion between Divine chastisement and the reflection that "no man is more than a breath" creates a skeptical mood typical of speculative wisdom literature. Therefore, I would suggest that close examination of the moth image in Psalm xxxix constitutes an indispensable stage in the investigation of the formal-aesthetic and conceptual wisdom background of that psalm as a whole.

2. Curbing Animals and Guiding Human Beings

> Be not like a senseless horse or mule whose movement must be curbed by bit and bridle; far be it from you! (Ps. xxxii 9)

Here we are dealing with the interpolation of a didactic motif into an individual song of thanksgiving[18] or into a penitential psalm or confessional song—subcategories of the individual lament.[19]

The psalm opens with a double *ʾašrê* formula applied to the penitent (vv. 1, 2). The thanksgiving style changes into a personal lament

[17] For a detailed discussion of these stylistic devices, see Forti, "The Moth Image," 327–28. G. von Rad defines this literary genre as the *Hoffartsmonolog* or "insolence monologue" (G. von Rad, *Theologie des Alten Testament II* [Munich, 1962], p. 190, n.10; see also M. Dahood, *Psalms II* [AB; New York, 1968], p. 19).

[18] Kraus, *Psalms 1–59*, p. 367.

[19] Munch coined the term "Schulandachtspsalmen" for compositions used in devotions at school and in the synagogue (e.g., Psalms 19b, 25, 119); and "Unterrichtspsalmen" (e.g., Psalms 32, 34) as the *Sitz im Leben* for instruction in the wisdom schools. See P. A. Munch, "Die jüdischen 'Weisheitspsalmen' und ihr Platz im Leben," *AcOr* 15 (1937), pp. 112–40.

by the suffering sinner (vv. 3–4). This is followed by a dramatic transition in the petitioner's state, the result of his confession, which turns into a doctrine of faith: "Therefore let every faithful man pray to You" (vv. 5–6). God is described as providing sanctuary and refuge from "the rushing mighty waters" (vv. 6–7). Next the poet offers advice—an admonition that includes the proverb of the horse and mule (vv. 8–9). This is followed by a statement of the dogma of punishment for the wicked and reward for the righteous (v. 10). The psalm closes with an appeal to the righteous and the upright to rejoice in God (v. 11).

Psalm 32 is noteworthy for the variety of ideas and styles, which led scholars to classify it as a "mixed type." Gunkel categorized it as a song of thanksgiving with embedded wisdom elements, such as the importance of confession: "I did not cover up my guilt; I resolved, 'I will confess my transgressions to the Lord' " (v. 5). The same idea is presented in a similar way in Proverbs: "He who covers up his faults will not succeed; He who confesses and gives them up will find mercy" (xxviii 13). Nevertheless, Gunkel isolates the didactic admonition in vv. 8–9 and assigns it to wisdom thought: "the form of the beatitude, the expression 'teach the path of YHWH,' the image of the stubborn animal, characteristic forms of wisdom (admonition and instruction), and the content of wisdom (observing the essence of the fate of the godless)"—these, he says, are thoughts and forms of wisdom literature, so that "the thanksgiving song thereby approaches wisdom teaching."[20] Mowinckel, who originally classified Psalm xxxii as a didactic psalm and regarded it as part of the "learned psalmography" intended to "reinforce the faith of the young" by means of moral instruction, does not include Psalm xxxii among the "non-cultic" poems and claims that in spite of the didactic character of the "learned psalmography" these psalms must be considered "prayers."[21] Kuntz includes Psalm xxxii among the mixed wisdom psalms, a subcategory of the wisdom psalm.[22] Murphy emphasizes the difficulty in locating

[20] Gunkel, *Introduction to Psalms*, §10, pp. 297–98.

[21] Mowinckel considers even the admonition to the congregation to be the worshiper's personal experience. For his earlier evaluation, see Mowinckel, "Psalms and Wisdom," pp. 213–14; for the later one, in which he considers Psalm xxxii to be a "personal thanksgiving psalm" along with Psalms xxx, xxxiv, xl 2–11, lxxiii, xcii, ciii, and cxvi, see Mowinckel, *The Psalms in Israel's Worship II*, pp. 31–43, 137.

[22] Kenneth J. Kuntz, "The Canonical Wisdom Psalms of Ancient Israel; Their Rhetorical, Thematic and Formal Dimensions," in *Rhetorical Criticism-Essays in Honor of James Muilenburg,* ed. J. J. Jackson and M. Kessler (PTMS 1; Pittsburgh,

the entire cluster of wisdom characteristics in any psalm assigned to the category of the Wisdom psalms (i.e., Ps i, xxxii, xxxiv, xxxvii, xlix, cxii, cxxviii). He distinguishes between the "wisdom environment" as the background from which the psalm emerged and the wisdom influence, and the "life setting" (*Sitz im Leben*) of its use in worship and prayer. The use of the psalm as a "song of thanksgiving" provides an opportunity to incorporate wisdom elements as a teaching.[23]

Craigie outlines the overall structure of the psalm, demonstrating the chiastic relationship between its two main parts:

Part I	(1) Wisdom (vv. 1–2)	A
	(2) Thanksgiving (vv. 3–5)	B
Part II	(1) Thanksgiving (vv. 6–8)	B′
	(2) Wisdom (vv. 9–10)	A′

The inclusio formed by the wisdom elements reflects the process of its composition. The individual's thanksgiving psalm "has been given literary adaptation according to the wisdom tradition."[24]

As the history of the proposed genre classifications of Psalm xxxii shows, there is no consensus about the definition of the "wisdom psalm." Even among those scholars who have attempted to define a specific "wisdom psalm" genre there is a clear tendency to classify Psalm xxxii as a "mixed psalm."

The *ʾašrê* formula is a frequent didactic "overture" to a psalm.[25] But the only other accumulation of wisdom terminology here is in vv. 8–9: "Let me instruct you and teach you which way to go; let me offer counsel; my eye is on you. Be not like a senseless horse or mule whose movement must be curbed by bit and bridle; far be it from you!"

1974), p. 210. The literary unit Ps. xxxii 8–10 (11) is defined as an independent wisdom paragraph by O. S. Rankin, *Israel's Wisdom Literature* (New York, 1969) p. 1 n. 1.

[23] Murphy ("Wisdom Psalms," pp. 162, 167) identifies Psalm xxxii as a "wisdom psalm," but omits it in R. E. Murphy, *In Seven Books of Wisdom* (Milwaukee, 1960).

[24] See P. C. Craigie, *Psalms 1–50* (WBC 19; Nashville, 1983) p. 265.

[25] *ʾašrê* 'blessed' (vv. 1b; 2a) appears 26 times as an introduction to a psalm, eight times in Proverbs, once in Job, once in Qoheleth, and nine times in other books. See: Waldemar Janzen, "*Ašrê* in the Old Testament," *HTR* 58 (1965), pp. 215–26; Murphy, *Wisdom Psalms*, p. 159 (bibliography on *ʾašrê* in n. 2); R. N. Whybray, *The Intellectual Tradition in the Old Testament* (BZAW 135; Berlin and New York, 1974), p. 154; Leo G. Perdue, "Didactic Poems and Wisdom Psalms," in *Wisdom and Cult: A Critical Analysis of the Views of Cult in the Wisdom Literatures of Israel and the Ancient Near-East* (SBLDS 30; Missoula, 1977), p. 323; Kenneth J. Kuntz, "The Retribution Motif in Psalmic Wisdom," *ZAW* 89 (1977), pp. 224–25.

"The way you should go" (v. 8b): Here *bᵉderek zû tēlēk* expresses the idea of guidance in choosing the correct path in life. *Derek* 'path, way' occurs frequently in the Wisdom literature (65 times in Proverbs, 16 times in Job, and twice in Qoheleth), along with its synonyms *maʿgal* 'course'[26] and *ʾoraḥ* 'path'. The physical condition of the path and its straightness are metaphors for honesty (ethical straightness) or dishonesty (ethical crookedness).[27]

"I will counsel you with my eye upon you" (8c): This idiomatic expression, referring to the eye of the wise counselor, is employed for the choice of the right path, similar to what is said of God in Proverbs: "For a man's ways are before the eyes of God; He surveys his entire course" (Prov. v 21; cf. xv 3, xxix 13). In Psalm xxxii, however, it is linked to the root *y-ʿ-ṣ,* which is associated with wise counsel.[28]

The lesson is phrased using an image taken from the world of domestic animals: "Be not like a senseless horse or mule whose movement must be curbed by bit and bridle; far be it from you!" (vv. 8–9).

These verses are full of the scholastic vocabulary: *ʾaśkîlᵉka* ("I will instruct or conduct you") and *ʾôrᵉka* ("I will teach you"). The root *y-r-h*, followed by the prepositional *beth* denotes a teaching model, as in "I will teach you what is in God's power" (Job xxvii 11a); "I instruct you in the ways of wisdom, I guide you in straight courses" (Prov. iv 11). The last wisdom lexeme here is the negative infinitive *ʾêyn habîn* 'senseless, without understanding', derived from the noun *bînah*, a wisdom term indicating the cognitive capacity to understand and discern.

Although the speaker of vv. 8–9 is not identified, the intellectual qualities mentioned clearly relate to the wise man, as personified by the wise teacher in Proverbs.[29] But the didactic vocabulary of vv. 8–9

[26] Held offers another synonym for *maʿgal*, reading *śādôt* 'fields' for *šᵉnat* (Ps. lxv 12), suggesting the pair *maʿgal/śādeh* as the analogous parallelism *śādeh/derek* "field/path" (Jer. vi 25). See Moshe Held, "Hebrew ma'gāl: A Study in Lexical Parallelism," *JANESCU* 6 (1974), pp. 107–109.

[27] On *derek* in the Bible, see B. Curoyer, "Le chemin de vie en Egypte et en Israël," *RB* 56 (1949), pp. 412–32. For *derek* in wisdom literature, see: Whybray, *Intellectual Tradition*, 124–34; M. V. Fox, *Proverbs 1–9* (AB 18A; New York, 2000), pp. 115, 117.

[28] For the wisdom term *ʾîʿăṣâ* "offering counsel" in other books, see Exod. xviii 19; Num. xxiv 14; 1 Kgs i 12; Jer. xxxviii 15. For *ʾîʿăṣâ ʿāleykā ʿênî* the LXX has ἐπιστηριῶ ἐπὶ σὲ τοὺς ὀφθαλμούς μου, i.e., "fixing the eyes upon" or "strengthening the eyes."

[29] Gunkel identifies the speaker as the psalmist, who like the sage addresses the inexperienced (H. Gunkel, *Die Psalmen*⁵ [Göttingen, 1968], p. 135). Kraus (*Psalms 1–*

follows a series of ethical terms—transgression, sin, guilt and confession (vv. 1–5). Consequently, the identity of the author of the whole psalm is unclear: is it the *ḥākām* 'wise man' or the *ḥāsîd* 'pious and faithful man'?[30]

A direct appeal by the teacher produces an admonition shaped as a proverb: "Be not like a senseless horse or mule, whose movement must be curbed by bit and bridle; far be it from you!" (xxxii 9).[31] The mention of accessories for curbing animals indicates that we are dealing with beasts of burden or transportation. The *resen* 'bridle' (cf. Isa. xxx 28) fits onto the head of the animal and is tied around its cheeks, while the *meteg* 'bit' fits into the animal's mouth (see 2 Kgs xix 28; Isa. xxxvii 29) and is fastened to the rings on the bridle so that the head can be turned to the sides and be reined in.

The *pered* 'mule' is the offspring of a male donkey and a mare. Mule and horse are described as steered with the bit and curbed with the bridle. These devices, used to control animals, illustrate the different didactic approaches for human beings and animals.[32] The devices used to control such animals are also mentioned in Proverbs: "A whip for a horse and a bridle for a donkey, and a rod for the back of dullards" (xxvi 3).[33] In our psalm the image of the harnessed animals indicates the animals' lack of understanding, in contrast with the human capacity to choose the right way: "Let me offer counsel; my eye is upon you" (xxxii 8).

This image illuminates the moral-religious principle of confessing one's sins. Human beings are given the choice of repenting and

---

59, p. 371) claims that the individual statements in vv. 8–9 are divine utterances quoted in a song of thanksgiving: "עליך עיני, 'on you is my eye' assured the petitioner of the healing presence of God."

[30] Among the impressive variety of epithets applied to supplicants (*ṣaddîq, ʿebed, ʿāni, ʿānāw, ʾebyôn, dal*), *ḥāsîd* (xxx 4, xxxi 24, xxxvii 28) designates the conditions of loving and devotion. See Kraus, *Psalms 1–59,* pp. 76–77.

[31] The compound *ʿedyô liblôm* has raised difficulties. *ʿedyô* could be rendered as *ʿādāyw*, i.e., prepositional *ʿad* plus the 3rd per. acc. suffix, with the sense of *baʿadô* 'against him'. For a summary of the different readings of עדיו, see Giorgio Castellino, "Psalm XXXII 9," *VT* 2 (1952), pp. 37–42; as a third homonym of *ʿ-d-h* 'gallop', based on the Arabic verb *ġada̱ā*, see A. A. Macintosh, "A Third Root עדה in Biblical Hebrew?" *VT* 24 (1974), pp. 454–73. The hapax verb *b-l-m* occurs in later Aramaic and rabbinic Hebrew with the sense of "block" or "hinder" (see *b. Ḥul.* 89a). The Syriac employs *b-l-m* to render *ḥ-s-m* in 'you shall not muzzle' (Deut. xxv 4).

[32] The principle use of the horse was for pulling chariots. On horses and asses, see Edwin B. Firmage, "Zoology," pp. 1135–37.

[33] The rod serves as a means of instruction and chastisement in the book of Proverbs: x 13, xiii 24, xix 18, xxii 15, xxiii 13–14.

choosing the right way, whereas animals, controlled by bit and bridle, do not have freedom of choice.

A closer examination of the lexical and conceptual aspects of these two verses in their literary context shows that this unit is probably a secondary interpolation. Removing the image does not damage the conceptual integrity of the psalm, which begins with a description of the suffering of the supplicant, as punishment for his sin (vv. 3–4), continues with his confession and prayer, and concludes with a total reversal—"many are the torments of the wicked, but he who trusts in the Lord shall be surrounded with favor" (v. 10). Within this framework, the uniqueness of human understanding is contrasted to the senseless of animals.

The didactic illustration of the horse and the mule (v. 9) does not fit with the doctrine of retribution (v. 10) that brings the psalm to a conclusion in harmony with its beginning. Thus, verse 8, which introduces the image of the horse and the mule in v. 9, may also be a secondary interpolation, the work of a later redactor (from the social milieu of the *sôp^{e}rîm-ḥ^{a}kāmîm*), who drew on a reservoir of aphorisms and didactic rhetoric associated with Wisdom literature.

Summing up, in the attempts to determine criteria for the "Wisdom Psalm" genre, various criteria have been proposed that combine linguistic and conceptual tests for identifying the degree to which Wisdom Literature has influenced the literary character of the psalms. The two cases discussed here prove the presence of different degrees of wisdom influence on individual psalms. Although both psalms contain features of the individual prayer, i.e., repentance and confession, descriptions of distress and trust in God's delivery, only Psalm xxxix reflects the overall structure of the Wisdom tradition. Reflection, meditation, and didactic terminology can be found throughout. Classification of Psalm xxxii as a wisdom psalm is less certain, because its wisdom affinities are limited to two verses (vv. 8–9) that are reminiscent of the animal imagery of the Wisdom literature. It seems likely, than, that they are a secondary didactic elaboration within a thanksgiving psalm, whether an original (though non-essential) part of the psalm or added by a later editor.

A careful evaluation of animal imagery thus provides an additional criterion for identifying a "wisdom psalm" or a wisdom dimension in a psalm of another type.

BIBLIOGRAPHY

Academy of the Hebrew Language. *The Book of Ben Sira. Text, Concordance and an Analysis of the Vocabulary.* Jerusalem, 1973 [Hebrew].

Aharoni, I. *The Locust.* Jaffa, 1920 [Hebrew].

——. *Torat Ha-Ḥay.* Tel Aviv, 1923 [Hebrew].

Aḥituv, Yair. "*Ōrēb.*" Cols. 821–22 in *Encyclopedia Miqraʾit* 6. Jerusalem, 1971 [Hebrew].

—— and Shmuel Loewenstamm. "*Nāḥāš.*" Cols. 821–22 in *Encyclopedia Miqraʾit* 5. Jerusalem, 1978 [Hebrew].

Albright, William F. "An Archaic Hebrew Proverb in an Amarna Letter from Central Palestine," *Bulletin of the American Schools of Oriental Research* 89 (1943), pp. 29–32.

——. "Some Canaanite-Phoenician Sources of Hebrew Wisdom," Supplements to Vetus Testamentum 3 (1955), pp. 1–15.

Alonso Schökel, Luis "Hermeneutical Problems of a Literary Study of the Bible." Pp. 1–15 in *Congress Volume Edinburgh 1974.* Supplements to Vetus Testamentum 28. Leiden, 1975.

——. *A Manual of Hebrew Poetics.* Subsidia biblica 11. Rome, 1988.

Alt, Albrecht. "Solomonic Wisdom." Pp. 102–12 in *Studies in Ancient Israelite Wisdom.* Edited by J. L. Crenshaw, translated by D. A. Knight. New York, 1976 [= "Die Weisheit Salomos," *Theologische Literaturzeitung* 76 (1951), pp. 139–44].

Alter, R. *The Art of Biblical Poetry.* New York, 1985.

Arama, Isaac, *Yad Avshalom.* Edited by I. Freimann. Leipzig, 1858–59.

Aristotle. *Historia Animalium.* Translated by A. L. Peck. Loeb Classical Library. Cambridge, MA, 1970.

Barnett, R. D., E. Bleibtreu, and G. E. Turner. *Sculptures from the Southwest Palace of Sennacherib at Nineveh.* London, 1998.

Barton, G. A. *The Book of Ecclesiastes.* International Critical Commentary. Edinburgh, 1908.

Baumgartner, A. J. *Etude critique sur l'état du texte du Livre des Proverbes d'après les principales traductions anciennes.* Leipzig, 1890.

Baumgartner, Walter. "Die literarischen Gattungen in der Weisheit des Jesus Sirach." *Zeitschrift für die alttestamentliche Wissenschaft* 4 (1914), pp. 165–98.

Bergsträsser, G. *Hebräische Grammatik.* Hildesheim, 1962.

Berlin, A. *The Dynamics of Biblical Parallelism.* Bloomington, 1985.

Bewer, J. "Two Suggestions on Prov. 30.31 and Zech. 9.16." *Journal of Biblical Literature* 67 (1948), pp. 61–62.

Billiq, Elqanah. "Zarzīr motnayim." Col. 941 in *Encyclopedia Miqraʾit* 2. Jerusalem, 1965 [Hebrew].

——. "*Śĕmāmît.*" Cols. 321–22 in *Encyclopedia Miqraʾit* 8. Jerusalem, 1982 [Hebrew].

—— and Shmuel E. Loewenstamm. "*Ṣĕbī.*" Cols. 661–63 in *Encyclopedia Miqraʾit* 6. Jerusalem, 1971 [Hebrew].

Black, Jeremy. "The Imagery of Birds in Sumerian Poetry." Pp. 23–46 in *Mesopotamian Poetic Language: Sumerian and Akkadian* 2. Edited by M. E. Vogelzang and H. L. J. Vanstiphout. Cuneiform Monographs 6. Groningen, 1996.
Bodenheimer, F. S. *Animal Life in Palestine*. Jerusalem, 1935.
——. *Animal Life in Biblical Lands*. 2 vols. Jerusalem, 1949–1956 [Hebrew].
Borowsky, Oded. "Animals in the Literatures of Syria-Palestine." Pp. 289–306 in *A History of Animal World in the Ancient Near East*. Handbuch der Orientalistik 64. Edited by B. J. Collins. Leiden, Boston, and Cologne, 2002.
——. "Animals in the Religions of Syria-Palestine." pp. 405–24 in *A History of Animal World in the Ancient Near East*. Handbuch der Orientalistik 64. Edited by B. J. Collins. Leiden, Boston, and Cologne, 2002.
Boström, Lennart. *The God of the Sages: The Portrayal of God in the Book of Proverbs*. Coniectanea Biblica; Old Testament Series 29. Stockholm, 1990.
Breniquet, Catherine, "Animals in Mesopotamian Art." Pp. 145–68 in *A History of Animal World in the Ancient Near East*. Handbuch der Orientalistik 64. Edited by B. J. Collins. Leiden, Boston and Cologne, 2002.
Briggs, Charles A. and Emilie G. Briggs. *The Book of Psalms*. International Critical Commentary. 2 Vols. Edinburgh, 1976 (1907[1]).
Bright, John. "The Apodictic Prohibition: Some Observations." *Journal of Biblical Literature* 92 (1973), pp. 185–204.
Bronowski, Jacob. *The Origins of Knowledge and Imagination*. New Haven and London, 1978.
Brown, Stephen J. *Image and Truth: Studies in the Imagery of the Bible*. Rome, 1955.
Bryce, Glendon E. "Better-Proverbs: An Historical and Structural Study." *Society of Biblical Literature Seminar Papers* 108, 2 (1972), pp. 343–54.
——. *A Legacy of Wisdom*. Lewisburg, PA, 1979.
Budde, K., *Die Fünf Megillot*. Freiburg, 1898.
Buss, M. J. "The Idea of *Sitz im Leben*: History and Critique," *Zeitschrift für die alttestamentliche Wissenschaft* 90 (1978), pp. 157–190. .
Cassuto, Umberto. "Biblical and Canaanite Literature." In *Biblical and Oriental Studies* II. Translated by I. Abrahams. Jerusalem, 1975, pp. 16–59.
Castellino, Giorgio R. *Le Lamentazioni individuali e gli inni in Babylonia e in Israele: raffrontati riguardo alla forma e al contenuto*. Turin, 1940.
——. "Psalm XXXII 9," *Vetus Testamentum* 2 (1952), pp. 37–42.
——. *Libro dei Salmi*. Turin and Rome, 1955.
Clifford, Richard J. *Proverbs*. The Old Testament Library. London and Leiden, 1999.
Coats, George W. "Self-Abasement and Insult Formulas." *Journal of Biblical Literature* 89 (1970), pp. 14–26.
Cogan, Mordechai. *Joel*. Mikra Leyisrael. Tel Aviv and Jerusalem, 1994.
—— and Hayim Tadmor. *II Kings*. Anchor Bible 11. New York, 1988.
Cohen, Chaim (H. R.). *Biblical Hapax Legomena in the Light of Akkadian and Ugaritic*. Missoula MT, 1978.
—— "The Phenomenon of Negative Parallelism and its Ramifications for the Study of Biblical Poetry." *Beer-Sheva* 3 (1988), pp. 69–107 [Hebrew].
——. "The Meaning of צלמות 'Darkness': A Study in Philological Method." Pp. 287–308 in *Texts, Temples, and Traditions: A Tribute to M. Haran*. Edited by M. V. Fox et al.; Winona Lake, IN, 1996.
Collins, Billie J. "Animals in the Religions of Ancient Anatolia." Pp. 309–334 in *A History of Animal World in the Ancient Near East*. Handbuch der Orientalistik 64. Edited by B. J. Collins. Leiden, Boston, and Cologne, 2002.

——, editor. *A History of Animal World in the Ancient Near East.* Handbuch der Orientalistik 64. Leiden, Boston, and Cologne, 2002.
Cook, Johann. *The Septuagint of Proverbs: Jewish and/or Hellenistic Proverbs?* Supplements to Vetus Testamentum 69. Leiden, 1997.
Cowley, Arthur E. *Aramaic Papyri of the Fifth Century B.C.* Oxford, 1967.
Craigie, Peter C. *Psalms 1–50.* Word Biblical Commentary 19. Nashville, 1983.
Crenshaw, James L. "Prolegomenon." Pp. 1–60 in *Studies in Ancient Israelite Wisdom.* Edited by J. L. Crenshaw. New York, 1976.
——. "Wisdom." Pp. 225–64 in *Old Testament Form Criticism.* Edited by J. H. Hayes. San Antonio, 1977.
——. *Ecclesiastes: A Commentary.* Old Testament Library. Philadelphia, 1987.
——. "The Sage in Proverbs." Pp. 204–16 in *The Sage in Israel and Ancient Near East.* Edited by John G. Gammie and Leo G. Perdue. Winona Lake, IN, 1990.
Curoyer, B. "Le chemin de vie en Égypte et en Israël." *Revue biblique* 56 (1949), pp. 412–32.
Dahood, M. "The Phoenician Background of Qoheleth," *Biblica* 47 (1966), pp. 264–82.
——. *Psalms* Vols. I–III. Anchor Bible. New York, 1968.
Day, John. "Foreign Semitic Influence on the Wisdom of Israel and its Appropriation in the Book of Proverbs." Pp. 55–70 in *Wisdom in Ancient Israel: Essays in honor of J. A. Emerton.* Edited by J. Day et al. Cambridge 1995.
Delitzsch, Franz. *Biblical Commentary on the Proverbs of Solomon* I, II. Translated by M. G. Easton. Grand Rapids, MI, 1960.
Delitzsch, F., *Ecclesiastes.* Translated by M. G. Easton. Grand Rapids, MI, 1960.
d'Hamonville, David M. *La Bible d'Alexandrie: Les Proverbes.* Paris, 2000.
Dhorm, E. *A Commentary on the Book of Job.* Translated by H. Knight. Leiden, 1967.
Di Lella, Alexander A., and Patrick Skehan. *The Wisdom of Ben Sira.* Anchor Bible 39. New York, 1987.
Dor, Menahem. *Lešonénu* 27–28 (1963–4), pp. 290–92 [Hebrew].
——. *Zoological Lexicon.* Tel Aviv, 1965 [Hebrew].
——. "Hannešer w^{e}hāᶜayit." *Animals in the Days of the Bible, the Mishnah and the Talmud.* Tel Aviv, 1997 [Hebrew].
Driver, Godfrey R. "Some Hebrew Words." *Journal of Theological Studies* 29 (1928), pp. 390–96.
——. "Problems in Proverbs." *Zeitschrift für die alttestamentliche Wissenschaft* 50 (1932), pp. 141–48.
——. "Hebrew Notes." *Vetus Testamentum* 1 (1951), pp. 241–50.
——. "Problems in the Hebrew Text of Proverbs." *Biblica* 32 (1951), pp. 173–97.
——. "Birds in the Old Testament." *Palestine Exploration Quarterly* 86 (1955), pp. 5–20; 87 (1955), pp. 129–140; 90 (1958), pp. 56–58.
Driver, Samuel R. *The Book of Joel and Amos.* Cambridge Bible Commentary. Cambridge, 1897.
—— and George B. Gray. *The Book of Job.* International Critical Commentary. Edinburgh, 1921.
Ehrlich, Arnold B. *Prophecy, Miqrâ ki-Pheschutô,* vol. 3. Berlin, 1901. Repr. New York, 1969 [Hebrew].
——. *Psalmen, Sprüche und Hiob.* Randglossen zur hebräischen Bibel, vol. 6. Leipzig, 1913. Repr. Berlin, 1968.
Eissfeldt, Otto. *Der Maschal im Alten Testament.* Beihefte zur Zeitschrift für die alttestamentliche Wissenschaft 24. Berlin and New York, 1913.

——. *The Old Testament: An Introduction*. Translated by Peter R. Ackroyd. New York, 1965.
Elizur, Y. "The Wisdom of the Proverbs' Composer." Pp. 24–28 in *ʿOz Le-David*. Jerusalem, 1964 [Hebrew].
Emerton, John. A. "Wisdom." Pp. 214–37 in *Tradition and Interpretation: Essays by Members of the Society for Old Testament Study*. Edited by G. W. Anderson. Oxford, 1979.
Engnell I. *The Book of Psalms, A Rigid Scrutiny: Critical Essays on the Old Testament*. Translated by J. T. Willis. Nashville, 1969.
Erman, Adolf. *The Literature of the Ancient Egyptians: Poems, Narratives and Manuals of Instruction from the Third and Second Millennia B.C.* Translated by A. M. Blackman. New York, 1927.
Falkenstein A. and W. von Soden. *Sumerische und akkadische Hymnen und Gebete*. Zurich, 1953.
Feliks, Yehudah. *Animals in the Bible*. Tel Aviv, 1954 [Hebrew].
Fensham, Frank C. "The Dog in Exodus XI, 7." *Vetus Testamentum* 16 (1966), pp. 504–507.
Firmage, Edwin B. "Zoology (Fauna)." Pp. 1109–1167 in *Anchor Bible Dictionary* 6. New York, 1992.
Fontaine, Carole R. *The Use of Traditional Sayings in the Old Testament*. Sheffield, 1982.
Forti, Tova. "Animal Images in the Book of Proverbs." *Biblica* 77 (1996), pp. 48–63.
——. "The Moth Image: A Window on a Wisdom Psalm (39)." Pp. 319–31 in *Homage to Shmuel: Studies in the World of the Bible*. Edited by Z. Talshir, Sh. Yona and D. Sivan. Jerusalem, 2001 [Hebrew].
——. "The Fly and the Dog: Observations on the Ideational Polarity in the Book of Qoheleth." Pp. 235–55 in *Seeking Out the Wisdom of the Ancients: Essays Offered to Honor Michael V. Fox*. Edited by R. L. Troxel et al. Winona Lake, IN, 2005.
——. "Bee's Honey: From Realia to Metaphor in Biblical Wisdom Literature," *Vetus Testamentum* 56 (2006), pp. 327–341.
——. "Conceptual Stratification in LXX Prov 26,11: Toward Identifying the Tradents Behind the Aphorism." *Zeitschrift für die Alttestamentliche Wissenschaft* 119 (2007), pp. 241–58.
—— and Zipora Talshir. "Proverbs 7 in MT and LXX: Form and Content," *Textus* 22 (2005), pp. 129–67.
Foster, Benjamin R. "Animals in Mesopotamian Literature," Pp. 271–88 in *A History of Animal World in the Ancient Near East*. Handbuch der Orientalistik 64. Edited by B. J. Collins. Leiden, Boston, and Cologne, 2002.
Fox, Michael V. "The Identification of Quotations in Biblical Literature," *Zeitschrift für die alttestamentliche Wissenschaft* 92 (1980), pp. 416–31.
——. *Qohelet and his Contradictions*. JSOT Supplement Series 71. Sheffield, 1989.
——. "The Social Location of the Book of Proverbs." Pp. 227–39 in *Texts, Temples, and Traditions: A Tribute to Menahem Haran*. Edited by M. V. Fox, V. A. Hurowitz et al. Winona Lake, IN, 1996.
——. *A Time to Tear Down: A Reading of Ecclesiastes*. Grand Rapids, Michigan, 1999.
——. *Proverbs 1–9*. Anchor Bible 18A. New York, 2000.
——. "LXX-Proverbs as a Text-Critical Resource." *Textus* 22 (2005), pp. 95–128.
Gemser, Berend. *Sprüche Salomos*. Handbuch zum Alten Testament 16. Tübingen, 1963.

Gerleman, Gillis. *Studies in the Septuagint. III: Proverbs*. Lunds universitets årsskrift 52/3. Lund, 1956.
Gersonides (Levi ben Gershom, Ralbag). Commentary. In *Mikraᶜot gedolot.*
Gesenius' Hebrew Grammar. Edited by E. Kautzsch. Translated by A. E. Cowley. 2nd edition. Oxford, 1910.
Gevirtz, Stanley. *Patterns in the Early Poetry of Israel*. Studies in Ancient Oriental Civilizations 32. Chicago, 1963.
Giese, Roland L. "Strength through Wisdom and the Bee in LXX-Prov 6, 8a–c." *Biblica* 73 (1992), pp. 404–11.
Gilbert, Allen S. "The Native Fauna of the Ancient Near East," Pp. 3–75 in *A History of Animal World in the Ancient Near East*. Handbuch der Orientalistik 64. Edited by B. J. Collins. Leiden, Boston, and Cologne, 2002.
Ginsberg, H. Louis. *Koheleth*. Tel Aviv, 1961.
Gordis, Robert. "Quotations in Wisdom Literature," *Jewish Quarterly Review* 30 (1939–40), pp. 123–47.
——. "ᶜal Mibneh Hashirah Haᶜibrit Hakedumah." Pp. 136–59 in *Sefer Hashanah Lihude Amerikah* 5693. New York, 1944 [Hebrew].
——. "Quotations as a Literary Usage in Biblical, Rabbinic and Oriental Literature." *Hebrew Union College Annual* 22 (1949), pp. 196–97.
——. *Koheleth, The Man and his World.* New York, 1968.
——. *The Book of Job*. New York, 1978.
Gordon, Edmund I. *Sumerian Proverbs*: *Glimpses of Everyday Life in Ancient Mesopotamia*. Museum Monographs. Philadelphia, 1959.
Greenberg, Moshe. "Noisy and Yearning: The Semantics of שק"ק and its Congeners." Pp. 339–44 in *Texts, Temples, and Traditions: A Tribute to Menahem Haran.* Edited by M. V. Fox et al. Winona Lake, IN, 1996.
Greenfield, Jonas C. "Lexicographical Notes I." *Hebrew Union College Annual* 29 (1958), pp. 203–28.
Greenstein, Edward L. "Two Variations of Grammatical Parallelism in Canaanite Poetry and their Psycho-Linguistic Background." *Journal of Near Eastern Studies* 6 (1974), pp. 96–105.
Gunkel H. *Die Psalmen.* Göttingen, 1968.
—— and J. Begrich. *Introduction to Psalms*: *The Genres of the Religious Lyric of Israel.* Translated by J. D. Nogalsky. Macon, GA, 1998.
Hameʾiri, R. Menachem ben Shelomo. *Pêrûš Hameʾiri ᶜal Seper Mišley*. Edited by Menachem Mendel Meshi-Zahav. Jerusalem,. 1969
Haran, Menachem. "Biblical Categories, the Pattern of the Numerical Sequence, its Forms and Relations to the Formal Types of Parallelism." *Tarbiz* 29 (1970), pp. 109–136 [Hebrew].
——. "The Graded Numerical Sequence and the Phenomenon of 'Automatism' in Biblical Poetry." Supplements to Vetus Testamentum 69 (1972), pp. 238–67.
——. "*Māšāl*." Cols. 548–53 in *Encyclopedia Miqraʾit* 5. Jerusalem, 1978 [Hebrew].
Heimpel, Wolfgang. *Tierbilder in der Sumerischen Literatur*. Studia Pohl 2. Rome, 1968.
Held, Moshe. "The Action-Result (Factitive-Passive) Sequence of Identical Verbs in Biblical Hebrew and Ugaritic." *Journal of Biblical Literature* 84 (1965), pp. 272–82.
——. "The Rhetorical Question in the Bible and in Ugaritic Poetry." *Eretz-Israel* 9 (1969), pp. 71–79 [Hebrew].
——. "Hebrew *maᶜgāl*, pp. A Study in Lexical Parallelism," *Journal of the Ancient Near Eastern Society of Columbia* 6 (1974), pp. 107–109.

——. "Studies in Biblical Lexicography in the Light of Akkadian Parallels." Pp. 104–14 in *Studies in Bible Dedicated to the Memory of U. Cassuto on the 100th Anniversary of His Birth.* Edited by H. Beinart. Jerusalem, 1987 [Hebrew].

Herbert, A. S. "The Parable *(māšāl)* in the Old Testament." *Scottish Journal of Theology* 7 (1954), pp. 180–96.

Hermisson, Hans-Jürgen. *Studien zur israelitischen Spruchweisheit.* Wissenschaftliche Monographien zum Alten und Neuen Testament 28. Neukirchen and Vluyn, 1968.

Herodotus. *The Histories.* Translated by A. D. Godley. Loeb Classical Library. Cambridge, MA, 1920.

Hertzberg, H. W. *Der Prediger.* Kommentar zum Alten Testament 17/4. Leipzig, 1963.

Hesse, Brian, and Paula Wapnish. "An Archaeological Perspective on the Cultural Use of Mammals in the Levant." Pp. 457–91 in *A History of Animal World in the Ancient Near East.* Handbuch der Orientalistik 64. Edited by B. J. Collins. Leiden, Boston, and Cologne, 2002.

Hillers, Delbert. R. *Treaty-curses and the Old Testament Prophets.* Biblica et orientalia 16. Rome, 1964.

Houlihan, Patrick F. "Animals in Egyptian Art and Hieroglyphs," Pp. 97–143 in *A History of Animal World in the Ancient Near East.* Handbuch der Orientalistik 64 Handbuch der Orientalistik 64. Edited by B. J. Collins. Leiden, Boston, and Cologne, 2002.

Hrushovski, Benjamin. "Poetic Metaphor and Frames of Reference," *Poetics Today* 5 (1984), pp. 5–43.

Hurvitz, Avi. "Studies in the Language of the Book of Proverbs: Concerning the use of the Construct Pattern *baʾal* x." *Tarbiz* 55 (1986), pp. 1–17 [Hebrew] .

——. "Wisdom Vocabulary in the Hebrew Psalter: A Contribution to the Study of 'Wisdom Psalms,' " *Vetus Testamentum* 38 (1988), pp. 41–51.

——. *Wisdom Language in Biblical Psalmody.* Jerusalem, 1991 [Hebrew].

Japhet, S. and R. B. Salters. *The Commentary of R. Samuel Ben Meir (Rashbam) on Qoheleth.* Jerusalem, 1985 [Hebrew].

Ibn Janah, Jonah. *Sepher Haschoraschim; Wurzelworterbuch der hebraischen Sprache.* Edited by W. Bacher. Berlin, 1896. Repr. Amsterdam, 1968.

Ibn Kaspi, Yosef. *Ḥăṣoṣᵉrot Kesep* (Trumpets of Silver), in *ʿĂśārâ Kᵉlê Kesep* (Ten Instruments of Silver). Edited by Isaac Last. Pressburg, 1903; repr. Jerusalem, 1969/70.

Janzen, Waldemar. "*Ašrê* in the Old Testament." *Harvard Theological Review* 58 (1965), pp. 215–26.

Johnson, A. R. "משל." Supplements to Vetus Testamentum 3 (1955), pp. 162–69.

Joines, Karen R. "The Serpent in the Old Testament." Ph.D. dissertation, Southern Baptist Theological Seminary, 1966.

Joüon, Paul, and Takamitsu Muraoka. *A Grammar of Biblical Hebrew.* 2 vols. *Subsidia biblica* 14/1. Rome, 1996.

Kahana, Avraham. *Sefer Mishley.* Miqraʾ Meforash. Tel Aviv, 1939 [Hebrew].

Kampinski, Aaron. "Hunting and Fishing." Cols. 716–17 in *Encyclopedia Miqraʾit* 6. Jerusalem, 1971 [Hebrew].

Kayatz, Crista. *Studien zu Proverbien 1–9.* Wissenschaftliche Monographien zum Alten und Neuen Testament 22. Neukirchen and Vluyn, 1966.

Keel, Othmar. *The Symbolism of the Biblical World: Ancient Near Eastern Iconography and the Book of Psalms.* Translated by T. J. Hallett. Winona Lake, IN, 1997.

Kister, Menahem. “Some Notes on Biblical Expressions and Allusions and the Lexicography of Ben Sira.” Pp. 160–87 in *Sirach, Scrolls and Sages*. Edited by T. Muraoka and J. F. Elwolde. *Studies on the Texts of the Desert of Judah* 33. Leiden, Boston, and Cologne, 1997.

Koch, Klaus. “Is There a Doctrine of Retribution in the Old Testament?” Pp. 57–87 in *Theology in the Old Testament*. Edited by J. L. Crenshaw. Translated by T. H. Trapp. Philadelphia, 1983 [= *Zeitschrift für Theologie und Kirche* 52 (1955), pp. 1–42].

Kraus, Hans J. *Psalms*: *A Commentary*. 2 vols. Translated by H. C. Oswald. Minneapolis, 1998.

Kugel, James L. *The Idea of Biblical Poetry*. New Haven and London, 1981.

Kuntz, Kenneth J. “The Canonical Wisdom Psalms of Ancient Israel: Their Rhetorical, Thematic and Formal Dimensions.” in Pp. 186–222 in *Rhetorical Criticism*: *Essays in Honor of James Muilenburg*. Edited by J. J. Jackson and M. Kessler. Pittsburgh Theological Monograph Series 1. Pittsburgh, 1974.

——. “The Retribution Motif in Psalmic Wisdom.” *Zeitschrift für die alttestamentliche Wissenschaft* 89 (1977), pp. 224–25.

Lagarde, Paul de. A. *Anmerkungen zur griechischen Übersetzung der Proverbien*. Leipzig, 1863.

Lambert, Maurice. “Le signe <u>bur</u>$_5$ et sa signification ‘moineau.’” *Revue d’assyriologie et d’archéologie orientale* 48 (1954), pp. 29–32.

Lambert, Wilfred G. *Babylonian Wisdom Literature*. Oxford, 1960.

Landsberger, Benno. *Die Fauna des alten Mesopotamien nach der 14. tafel der Serie ḪAR-RA=ḪUBULLU*. Abhandlungen der Sächsischen Akademie der Wissenschaften 42:6. Leipzig 1934.

——. *The Fauna of Ancient Mesopotamia*, Tablets XIII, XIV, XVIII. *Materialien zum sumerischen Lexicon* 8: I-II. Rome, 1960–1962.

Lane, Edward W. *An Arabic–English Lexicon*. London, 1863–1893. Repr. Beirut, 1968.

Lemaire, André. “The Sage in School and Temple.” Pp. 165–81 in *The Sage in Israel and the Ancient Near East*. Edited by J. G. Gammie and L. G. Perdue. Winona Lake, IN, 1990.

Lichtheim, Miriam. *Ancient Egyptian Literature* III. Berkeley and Los Angeles, 1973.

Lindblom, Johannes. “Wisdom in the Old Testament Prophets.” Supplements to Vetus Testamentum 3 (1960), pp. 192–203.

Loader, J. A. *Polar Structures in the Book of Qoheleth*. Beihefte zur Zeitschrift für die alttestamentliche Wissenschaft 152. Berlin, 1979.

Loewenstamm, Samuel E. “Remarks on Proverbs XVII 12 and XX 27.” *Vetus Testamentum* 37 (1987), pp. 221–24.

—— and Joshua Blau, *Otsar Leshon HaMiqraʾ: Concordance and Dictionary*. 3 vols. Jerusalem, 1957–1968 [Hebrew].

Löw, Immanuel. *Fauna und Mineralien der Juden*. Hildesheim, 1969.

Luyten, J. “Psalm 73 and Wisdom.” Pp. 59–81 in *La Sagesse de L’Ancien Testament*. Edited by M. Gilbert. Bibliotheca ephemeridum theologicarum lovaniensium 51. Gembloux, Belgium.

Luzzatto, Samuel David. *Meḥqerey Ha-yahadut*, vol. 1: *Divrey Qohelet*. Warsaw, 1913 [Hebrew].

Macintosh, A. A. “A Third Root עדה in Biblical Hebrew?” *Vetus Testamentum* 24 (1974), pp. 454–73.

Marcus, David. “Animal Similes in Assyrian Royal Inscriptions,” *Orientalia* 46 (1977), pp. 86–106.

McKane, William. *Proverbs, A New Approach.* Old Testament Library. London, 1970.
McMahon, G. "Instructions to Priests and Temple Officials." Pp. 217–21 in *The Context of Scripture*, Volume 1: *Canonical Compositions from the Biblical World.* Edited by W. W. Hallo. Leiden, 1997.
Meier, Gerhard. *Die Assyrische Beschwörungssammlung Maqlû.* Archiv für Orientforschung: Beiheft 2. Osnabrück, 1937.
Mezzacasa, Giacomo. *Il Libro dei Proverbi di Salomone: Studio Critico sulle aggiunte Greco-Alessandrine.* Rome, 1913.
Militarev, Alexander and Leonid Kogan. *Semitic Etymological Dictionary, Vol. II; Animal Names.* Alter Orient und Altes Testament 278/2. Münster, 2005.
Moran, William L., editor and translator. *The Amarna Letters.* Baltimore, 1992.
Mowinckel Sigmund. "Psalms and Wisdom." Pp. 205–224 in *Wisdom in Israel and in the Ancient Near East.* Edited by M. Noth and D. Winton Thomas. Supplements to Vetus Testamentum 3. Leiden, 1960.
——. *The Psalms in Israel's Worship.* Translated by D. R. Ap-Thomas. Oxford, 1962.
Munch, P. A. "Die jüdischen 'Weisheitspsalmen' und ihr Platz im Leben." *Acta Orientalia* 15 (1937), pp. 112–40.
Murison, R. G. "The Serpent in the Old Testament." *American Journal of Semitic Languages and Literature* 21 (1905), pp. 115–130.
Murphy, Roland E. *Seven Books of Wisdom.* Milwaukee, 1960.
——. "A Consideration of the Classification 'Wisdom Psalms.' " Supplements to Vetus Testamentum 9 (1963), pp. 156–167.
——. "Form Criticism and Wisdom literature." *Catholic Biblical Quarterly* 31 (1969), pp. 475–83.
——. "Wisdom: Theses and Hypotheses." Pp. 35–42 in *Israelite Wisdom: Theological and Literary Essays in Honor of Samuel Terrien.* Edited by J. G. Gammie et al. New York, 1978.
——. "The Sage in Ecclesiastes and Qoheleth the Sage." Pp. 263–71 in *The Sage in Israel and the Ancient Near East.* Edited by J. G. Gammie and L. G. Perdue. Winona Lake, IN, 1990.
——. *Proverbs.* Word Biblical Commentary 22. Nashville, 1998.
Nel, Philip J. *The Structure and Ethos of the Wisdom Admonitions in Proverbs.* Beihefte zur Zeitschrift für die alttestamentliche Wissenschaft 158. Berlin and New York, 1982.
Ogden, Graham S. "The 'Better' Proverb (Ṭôb-Spruch), Rhetorical Criticism and Qoheleth." *Journal of Biblical Literature* 96 (1977), pp. 489–505.
——. *Qoheleth.* Readings. Sheffield, 1987.
Palmoni, Yaaqob. "Zĕbûb." Cols. 893-94 in *Encyclopedia Miqraʾit 2.* Jerusalem, 1981.
Paran, Meir. *Forms of the Priestly Style in the Pentateuch.* Jerusalem, 1989 [Hebrew].
Pardee, Dennis. "The *Baʿlu* Myth." Pp. 241–74 in *The Context of Scripture, Volume 1: Canonical Compositions from the Biblical World.* Edited by W. W. Hallo and K. L. Younger. Leiden, 1997.
Parker, Simon B., editor. *Ugaritic Narrative Poetry.* Society of Biblical Literature Writings from the Ancient World 9. Atlanta, 1997.
Parpola, S. *The Correspondence of Sargon II*, Part I. State Archives of Assyria 1. Helsinki 1987.
—— and K. Watanabe. *Neo-Assyrian Treaties and Loyalty Oaths.* State Archives of Assyria 2. Helsinki, 1988.

Perdue, Leo G. *Wisdom and Cult: A Critical Analysis of the Views of Cult in the Wisdom Literatures of Israel and the Ancient Near-East.* Society of Biblical Literature Dissertation Series 30. Missoula, MT, 1977.
——. "Liminality as a Social Setting for Wisdom Instructions." *Zeitschrift für die alttestamentliche Wissenschaft* 93 (1981), pp. 114–26.
Perelman, Chaim. *L'empire rhétorique: rhétorique et argumentation*. Paris, 1977.
Perles, Felix. *Analekten zur Textkritik des Alten Testaments*. Leipzig, 1922.
Pollard, John. *Birds in Greek Life and Myth*. Plymouth, 1977.
Pope, Marvin H. *Job*. Anchor Bible 15. New York, 1965.
Porten, Bezalel, and Ada Yardeni. *Textbook and Aramaic Documents from Ancient Egypt,* Vol. III: *Literature, Accounts, Lists*. Jerusalem and Winona Lake IN, 1993.
Qimḥi, David (Radaq). *Sefer Hashorashim*. Edited by J. H. R. Biesenthal and F. Lebrecht. Berlin, 1847 (repr. Jerusalem, 1967).
Rad, Gerhard von. *Theologie des Alten Testament II.* Munich, 1962.
——. *Old Testament Theology*. Translated by D. M. G. Stalker. 2 vols. Edinburgh, 1962.
——. *Wisdom in Israel*. Translated by J. D. Martin. New York, 1972.
Rankin, Oliver S. *Israel's Wisdom Literature.* New York, 1969.
Richter, Wolfgang. *Recht und Ethos*: *Versuch einer Ortung des Weisheitlichen Mahnspruches*. Studien zum Alten und Neuen Testament 15. Munich, 1966.
Riede, Peter. *Im Spiegel der Tier*. Orbis biblicus et orientalis 187. Fribourg and Göttingen, 2002.
Rimbach, James A. "Animal Imagery in the O.T.: Some Aspects of Hebrew Poetics." Ph.D. dissertation, Johns Hopkins University, 1972.
Rofé, Alexander. "The Numerical Sequence X/X+1 in the Old Testament." *Vetus Testamentum* 12 (1962), pp. 301–307.
——. "Judicial System." *Beit Miqra*ʾ 21 (1976), pp. 199–210 [Hebrew].
——. "The Valiant Woman, γυνὴ συνετὴ, and the Redaction of the Book of Proverbs." Pp. 145–55 in *Vergegenwärtigung des Alten Testaments*: *Beiträge zur biblischen Hermeneutik; Festschrift für Rudolf Smend zum 70. Geburtstag.* Edited by C. Bultmann, Walter Dietrich, and Christoph Levin. Göttingen, 2002.
Roth, Wolfgang M. W. "The Numerical Sequence X/X+1 in the Old Testament." *VT* 12 (1962), pp. 301–307.
——. *Numerical Sayings in the Old Testament.* Supplements to Vetus Testamentum 13. Leiden, 1965.
Schmid, Hans H. *Wesen und Geschichte der Weisheit.* Beihefte zur Zeitschrift für die alttestamentliche Wissenschaft 101. Berlin, 1966.
Schott, Albert. *Die Vergleiche in den akkadischen Königsinschriften.* Mitteilungen der Vorderasiatisch-ägyptischen Gesellschaft 30. Leipzig, 1926.
Scott, Robert B. Y. "Folk Proverbs in the Ancient Near East." Pp. 417–26 in *Studies in Ancient Israelite Wisdom.* Edited by J. L. Crenshaw. New York, 1976 [= *Transactions of the Royal Society of Canada* 15 (1961), pp. 47–56].
——. *Proverbs–Ecclesiastes*. Anchor Bible 18. Garden City, NY, 1965.
Scurlock, Joann. "Animals in Ancient Mesopotamian Religion." Pp. 361–87 in *A History of Animal World in the Ancient Near East.* Handbuch der Orientalistik 64. Edited by B. J. Collins. Leiden, Boston, and Cologne, 2002.
Segal, Moshe Z. *Sefer Ben Sira Hašalem*. Jerusalem, 1972 [Hebrew].
Semoʾli, Eliezer. *Birds in Israel*. Tel Aviv, 1957.
Seow, Choon L. *Ecclesiastes*. Anchor Bible 18c. New York, 1997.

Shupak, Nili. "The Sitz im Leben of the Book of Proverbs in the Light of a Comparison of Biblical and Egyptian Wisdom Literature." *Revue biblique* 94 (1987), pp. 98–119.

——. *Where Can Wisdom Be Found? The Sage's Language in the Bible and in Ancient Egyptian Literature.* Orbis biblicus et orientalis 130. Fribourg and Göttingen, 1993.

Siegfried, C. G., *Prediger und Hoheslied.* Göttingen, 1898.

Snell, Daniel C. *Twice-Told Proverbs and the Composition of the Book of Proverbs.* Winona Lake, IN, 1993.

Snijders, Lambertus A. "The Meaning of 'zar' in the Old Testament: An Exegetical Study." *Oudtestamentische Studiën* 10 (1954), pp. 1–154.

Stevenson, William B. "A Mnemonic Use of Numbers in Proverbs and Ben Sira." *Transactions of the Glasgow University Oriental Society* 9 (1938/39), pp. 26–38.

Strawn, Brent A. *What is Stronger than a Lion?* Orbis biblicus et orientalis 212. Fribourg and Göttingen, 2005.

Talshir, David. "The Nomenclature of the Fauna in the Samaritan Targum." Ph.D. dissertation, The Hebrew University of Jerusalem, 1981 [Hebrew].

——. "The Semantic Shift of the *Nesher ʿayit and Dayah* in Hebrew," *Lešonénu* 62 (1999), pp. 107–27 [Hebrew].

——. "Haṣṣab, Ḥahardon Vehaqarpadah." *Lešonénu* 65 (2003), pp. 351–73 [Hebrew].

Teeter, Emily. "Animals in Egyptian Literature." Pp. 251–70 in *A History of Animal World in the Ancient Near East.* Handbuch der Orientalistik 64. Edited by B. J. Collins. Leiden, Boston, and Cologne, 2002.

Thomas, David W. "A Note on lyqat in Prov. xxx 17." *Journal of Theological Studies* 42 (1941), pp. 154–55

——. "Textual and Philological Notes on Some Passages in the Book of Proverbs." Supplements to Vetus Testamentum 3 (1955), pp. 280–92.

——. "Kelebh, 'Dog'; Its Origin and some Usage of it in the Old Testament." *Vetus Testamentum* 10 (1960), pp. 410–27.

——. "Notes of some Passages in the Book of Proverbs." *Vetus Testamentum* 15 (1965), pp. 271–79.

Thompson, John A. "Joel's Locusts in the Light of Near Eastern Parallels." *Journal of Near Eastern Studies* 14 (1955), pp. 52–55.

Toy, Crawford H. *The Book of Proverbs.* International Critical Commentary. Edinburgh, 1959.

Tristram, Henry B. *Natural History of the Bible.* London, 1867.

——. *The Fauna and Flora of Palestine: The Survey of Western Palestine.* London, 1884.

Tur-Sinai, Naphtali Herz. *Mišley Šᵉlōmōh.* Tel Aviv, 1947.

——. *Halašon vehasefer.* Vol. 1, Jerusalem, 1948.

——. *Pᵉšuṭo šel Miqraʾ* 4/1. Jerusalem, 1967 [Hebrew].

Van Leeuwen, Raymond C. *Context and Meaning in Proverbs 25–27.* Society of Biblical Literature Dissertation Series 96; Atlanta, GA, 1984.

——. "Wealth and Poverty: System and Contradiction in Proverbs." *Hebrew Studies* 33 (1992), pp. 25–36.

Waltke, Bruce K. *The Book of Proverbs Chapters 1–15.* The New International Commentary on the Old Testament. Grand Rapids, MI and Cambridge, 2004.

—— and Michael O'Connor. *An Introduction to Biblical Hebrew Syntax.* Winona Lake, IN, 1990.

Watanabe, Chikako E. *Animal Symbolism in Mesopotamia: A Contextual Approach*. Wiener Offene Orientalistik, vol. 1. Vienna, 2002.
Watson, Wilfred G. E. *Classical Hebrew Poetry: A Guide to its Techniques*. JSOT Supplement Series 26. Sheffield, 1984.
Weinfeld, Moshe. *Deuteronomy and the Deuteronomic School*. Oxford, 1972.
——. "The Vassal-Treaties of Esarhadon King of Assyria." in *Shnaton: An Annual for Biblical and Ancient Near Eastern Studies* 1 (1976), pp. 89–122 [Hebrew].
——. "The Term *Šōṭēr* and his Duty." *Beit Miqra*ʾ 22 (1977), pp. 417–20 [Hebrew].
Weiss, Meir. "Die Methode der 'Total Interpretation': Von der Notwendigkeit der Struktur-Analyse für das Verständnis der biblischen Dichtung." Supplements to Vetus Testamentum 22 (1972), pp. 88–112.
——. *The Bible from Within: The Method of Total Interpretation*. Jerusalem, 1984.
——. "On Three ... and on Four." Pp. 13–26 in *Scriptures in their own Light: Collected Essays*. Jerusalem, 1987 [Hebrew].
——. *The Book of Amos: Commentary and Notes*. Jerusalem, 1992 [Hebrew].
Westermann, Claus. "Die Begriffe für Fragen und Suchen im Alten Testament." *Forschungen zum Alten Testament* 2 (1974), pp. 162–90.
Whitley F. *Koheleth: His Language and Thought.* Beihefte zur Zeitschrift für die alttestamentliche Wissenschaft 148. Berlin, 1979.
Whybray, Roger N. *The Intellectual Tradition in the Old Testament.* Beihefte zur Zeitschrift für die alttestamentliche Wissenschaft 135. Berlin and New York, 1974.
——. "The Identification and Use of Quotations in Ecclesiastes." Pp. 435–51 in *Congress Volume: Vienna, 1980.* Edited by J. A Emerton. Supplements to Vetus Testamentum 32. Leiden, 1981.
——. *The Composition of the Book of Proverbs*. JSOT Supplement Series 168. Sheffield, 1994.
——. *The Book of Proverbs: A Survey of Modern Study*. History of Biblical Interpretation Series Vol. 1. Leiden, New York, and Cologne, 1995.
Widengren, G., *The Accadian and Hebrew Psalms of Lamentations as Religious Documents*. Stockholm, 1937.
Williams, James G. "Proverbs and Ecclesiastes." Pp. 263–82 in *The Literary Guide to the Bible*. Edited by R. Alter and F. Kermode. Cambridge, MA, 1987.
Wilson, Frederick M. "Sacred and Profane? The Yahwistic Redaction of Proverbs Reconsidered." Pp. 313–34 in *The Listening Heart: Essays in Wisdom and the Psalms in Honor of Roland E. Murphy*. Edited by Kenneth G. Hoglund et al. JSOT Supplement Series 58. Sheffield, 1987.
Wright, C. H. H. *The Book of Koheleth.* London, 1883.
Yadin, Yigal. *The Ben Sira Scroll from Masada*. Jerusalem, 1965.
Yellin, Avinoam. *Sefer Aḥiqar he-Ḥakam*. Jerusalem, 1938.
Zakovitch, Yair. "The Pattern of the Numerical Sequence Three-Four in the Bible." Ph.D. dissertation, The Hebrew University of Jerusalem, 1979 [Hebrew].
Zimmerli, Walther. "Concerning the Structure of Old Testament Wisdom." Pp. 175–207 in *Studies in Ancient Israelite Wisdom*. Edited by J. L. Crenshaw. New York, 1976 [= "Zur Struktur der Alttestamentlichen Weisheit," *Zeitschrift für die alttestamentliche Wissenschaft* 51 (1933), pp. 177–204].
——. "The Place and the Limit of the Wisdom in the Framework of the Old Testament Theology." Pp. 314–28 in *Studies in Ancient Israelite Wisdom.* Edited by J. L. Crenshaw. New York, 1976 [= *Scottish Journal of Theology* 17 (1964), pp. 146–158].

INDEX OF SCRIPTURAL AND OTHER ANCIENT REFERENCES

INDEX OF ANIMALS

INDEX OF SUBJECTS

Observation, empirical, 10–12, 21–22, 28, 31, 34–35, 54, 77–78, 80–81, 102, 104, 106–108, 113,115, 117–120, 122–127, 129, 131, 144–145, 158

Parable, 7–8, 11, 15, 27–28, 91, 103, 106–108, 139–143, 146–147
Parallelismus membrorum, 3, 8, 14, 22, 43
Path (*derek*, *ʾoraḥ*, *maʿgal*), 9, 23, 25–27, 31, 38–39, 84, 94, 97, 100, 103, 105, 110, 123, 126–129, 134, 165–166, 168
Provoker. *See* quarrel monger.
Punishment, corporal, 73–75, 83, 167

Quarrel monger12, 15, 37, 61–62, 65–66, 76–77, 82–83, 89, 99–100, 135. *See also* Drunkard.

Reader. *See* addressee.
Reinterpretation, yahwistic, 14–15, 78, 98
Retribution, divine, 9–10, 26–27, 29, 36, 39, 59, 61–62, 66–67, 69–70, 83, 90, 98, 113, 135, 142, 146, 149, 151, 153–154, 160–161, 164, 168
Reward and punishment. *See* Retribution, divine.

Saying, metaphorical, 13, 18, 79–82, 139, 143
Saying, numerical, 3, 11–13, 21–22, 83, 102, 104, 107–109, 117–118, 121–122, 128–129, 131–132, 134, 139
Saying, numerical-sequence. *See* Graded numerical sequence.
Sheol, 25, 49, 83, 103
Sluggard. *See* Laziness.
Social order, 2, 9, 19, 61–62, 65, 74, 82, 102–104, 106, 108–109, 115–118, 131, 135, 142, 154
Speech, direct, 11, 13, 18–20, 26, 38–40, 90–92, 167
Strange woman. *See* Adulterous woman.
Surety, 13, 40–42, 44, 103

Ṭôb-spruch. *See* "better than" sayings.
Tat-Ergehen Zusammenhang. *See* deed-consequence nexus.
Teacher. *See* Authority, didactic.
"Total interpretation," 9, 139
Transience, human, 32–33, 35, 160–163

Wandering, 8, 15, 52–54, 68–70, 88n, 91, 105
Way. *See* Path.
Wicked. *See* Evildoer.
Wisdom, internalization of, 9, 13, 20, 45–46, 49, 78, 81, 105, 109

Youth. *See* Lad.